# VICTORIAN
# MURDERESSES

'Murderess is a strong word to have attached to you. It has a smell to it, that word – musky and oppressive, like dead flowers in a vase. Sometimes at night I whisper it over to myself: Murderess, Murderess. It rustles, like a taffeta skirt across the floor.'

Margaret Atwood, *Alias Grace*

# VICTORIAN MURDERESSES

## WOMEN WHO KILLED IN NINETEENTH-CENTURY BRITAIN AND AMERICA

DEBBIE BLAKE

PEN & SWORD **HISTORY**

AN IMPRINT OF PEN & SWORD BOOKS LTD.
YORKSHIRE – PHILADELPHIA

First published in Great Britain in 2022 by
**PEN AND SWORD HISTORY**
An imprint of
Pen & Sword Books Ltd
Yorkshire – Philadelphia

ISBN 978 1 39909 451 1

A CIP catalogue record for this book is available from the British Library.

Typeset in Times New Roman 12/16 by
SJmagic DESIGN SERVICES, India.
Printed and bound in the UK by CPI Group (UK) Ltd.

Pen & Sword Books Limited incorporates the imprints of Atlas, Archaeology,
Aviation, Discovery, Family History, Fiction, History, Maritime, Military, Military
Classics, Politics, Select, Transport, True Crime, Air World, Frontline Publishing,
Leo Cooper, Remember When, Seaforth Publishing, The Praetorian Press,
Wharncliffe Local History, Wharncliffe Transport, Wharncliffe True Crime and
White Owl.

*For a complete list of Pen & Sword titles please contact*
PEN & SWORD BOOKS LIMITED
47 Church Street, Barnsley, South Yorkshire, S70 2AS, England
E-mail: enquiries@pen-and-sword.co.uk
Website: www.pen-and-sword.co.uk

Or
PEN AND SWORD BOOKS
1950 Lawrence Rd, Havertown, PA 19083, USA
E-mail: Uspen-and-sword@casematepublishers.com
Website: www.penandswordbooks.com

# Contents

# Chapter 1

# A Temporary Frenzy
## Sarah Drake, London, 1850

The New Poor Law Act introduced in 1834 included a Bastardy Clause, which specified that the responsibility for an illegitimate child lay solely with its mother until it reached the age of 16. In desperation, many unmarried women who were unable to support themselves or their children committed infanticide to avoid the workhouse and destitution.[1] There were many horrifying reports of babies that had been suffocated, strangled, or drowned, found abandoned in the street, parks, and even down the toilet. 'It has been said of the police, with too much truth,' reported Mrs Baines in *The Journal of Social Science* in 1866, 'that they think no more of finding the dead body of a child in the street than of picking up a dead cat or dog.'[2] Prosecutions were high among unmarried domestic servants who had managed to conceal their pregnancies and give birth secretly, sometimes in the home where they worked. Sarah Drake was one of the many women employed in domestic service who tragically found herself not once, but possibly three times in this awful predicament.

Little is known of Sarah's early life, except that she was the eldest of four children, born in August 1813, in the village of North Leverton, Nottinghamshire, to Thomas Drake, a cottage farmer, originally from Upton Lincolnshire, and his wife Mary. After attending the local village school, she was sent out to service where she was employed by Samuel Kay, a butcher and farmer in Sutton-cum-Lound, near East Retford. In December 1832, Kay was robbed and murdered by a young unemployed local lad called William Clayton, and shortly afterwards, Sarah went to live with the family of local landowner,

John Walker Esq. However, it seems that this position was short-lived, as according to the *Morning Chronicle*, 'after having, in order to avoid a prosecution, signed a paper acknowledging herself to be culpable, she was discharged in disgrace.'

Following brief employment with the Rev. John Mickle, vicar of South Leverton, then surgeon, Francis Blagg, Sarah left North Leverton in 1836 and headed to Manchester where she went into service for Mr Hooper and his sister, in Plymouth Grove. But later that year, according to the *Manchester Times*, a purse containing two sovereigns belonging to Miss Hooper was stolen from the parlour table of her father's house. Strongly suspecting the servant, Sarah Drake, whom she also thought was responsible for stealing several silver spoons that were missing, Miss Hooper questioned her, but Sarah denied any knowledge of the purse and swiftly diverted any suspicion to the dressmaker who was also employed in the house.

In a bizarre attempt to back up her story, the next day Sarah told her mistress that 'she had been to a woman who was a "conjuror"'[3] who told her for a fact that the purse had been stolen by the dressmaker. To prove that the old lady was 'thoroughly versed in the "mystic art"', Sarah added that she had foretold that the lost spoons would be found the following morning; one under the grate and the other in the bread basket. 'Under these circumstances,' said the reporter, 'the family felt it imperative upon them, before they made any further inquiry about the matter, to await the result of old Sybil's prediction.' Sure enough, old Sybil's ability to see into the future was confirmed when the next day the spoons were found in the exact places she had predicted.

The Hoopers were so impressed they wanted to meet the conjuror 'who had so kindly afforded her assistance'. However, this request wasn't something Sarah had anticipated, and she had no option but to confess to having stolen the purse and spoons. Her room was searched, where several stolen items of clothing were found in her boxes. She was taken into custody and appeared in court two weeks later where she received a sentence of six months' imprisonment. Afterwards, when she finally returned to North Leverton, Sarah maintained she had been travelling abroad, where she had spent some time in the East and West Indies and on the continent.

By the spring of 1842, Sarah was living in Leytonstone, Essex, where she was employed as a live-in cook for the family of Mr Catley, a magistrate for the county of Surrey. On 15 April, Joseph Timperley, a porter at Knutsford Union Workhouse, in Cheshire, received a box containing the body of a dead baby boy, wrapped in a shawl and a bloodied piece of fine linen, with a note that read, 'You will do your wife a favour by burying this.' Timperley immediately informed the local police, who were able to trace the sender of the box back to the address of Mr Catley, and to his cook, Sarah Drake.

After searching Sarah's room, Constable William Harper found a piece of linen, part of a shawl and paper identical to those found in the box sent to Mr Timperley. When questioned by the constable, Sarah became very distressed and admitted that she had given birth to a baby that had been stillborn and, not knowing what to do with it, had put it in a box and sent it to the country. Afterwards, the surgeon Mr Watson Baird, who had examined the body at the inquest, believed that the baby had been born alive. Having found 'marks of compression' on the infant's neck – a thumb mark on the right side of the baby's neck and finger marks on the left side – he concluded that the death had been caused by 'this violent compression', and that the injuries were inflicted while the child was alive.

The following month, on Tuesday, 10 May, Sarah stood trial at the Central Criminal Court (the Old Bailey), London, charged with concealing the birth of her child. The jury heard from witnesses that on 6 April, Sarah complained of feeling ill and stayed in bed for three days, after which she returned downstairs saying that she felt much better as the tumour in her side that had been troubling her had burst. On 13 April, she borrowed a small deal box from one of the other servants, Mahal Clark, and disappeared to her room for some time before coming back downstairs with the box and some brown paper. She then asked the footman, John Slade, if he would help her wrap and tie up the box, seal it and then take it to the Birmingham Railway Station in London to send to 'Mr Timperley, Knutsford Union Workhouse, Cheshire'. Unaware of what the box contained, the footman did as he was asked.

Ann Williams, the laundry maid, testified that after seeing Sarah's clothes, she suspected that she had given birth, as she had never seen 'clothes in such a state – unless a woman had been recently confined'. She was even more certain when ten days later she saw 'discharges of milk on her under-linen'. Another witness, Mary Chapman, a washerwoman in Leyton who had received Sarah's dirty washing on 12 April, agreed that Sarah's clothing did show signs of having recently given birth.

The jury found Sarah guilty of 'concealment of birth', which carried the maximum sentence of two years' imprisonment, but as Sarah's health had suffered whilst she had been in custody, the court took a lenient view of the case, and she was sentenced to six months' hard labour in prison.

Two years later, on 30 November 1844, Sarah's sister Mary and her husband, Theophilus Burton, a blacksmith in North Leverton, received a box containing the body of a newborn baby boy. At the inquest held on 26 December, Mr Falkland, the coroner, concluded that 'the child had not been born alive, and that from various appearances, he believed its mother had delivered herself'. The jury consequently brought in a general verdict, 'That the child was sent, but it did not appear by whom, and that whether it was alive before, at, or after its birth, to them was unknown.' Although Sarah was suspected of being responsible for the incident, she was never convicted and brought to trial.

The following year, Sarah briefly returned to North Leverton, before leaving to work as a live-in domestic servant for John and Maria Turner Ramsay, of Tusmore House, near Bicester, Oxfordshire.

But by 1847, following a brief liaison with the butler, a Frenchman called Louis Tavern, Sarah had to leave her position as she was once again pregnant. Later that year, on 9 October, she gave birth to a baby boy whom she named Louis Tavern Drake.[4]

In January 1848, when Louis was three months old, Sarah placed him in the care of Mrs Jane Johnson, the wife of a policeman in Peckham, who had been looking for a 'nurse child' – a young child that was brought up in a household of someone other than the parents, usually for money. Miss Harrington, a friend of Mrs Johnson who lived in Chelsea, had recommend Sarah Drake and brought her to meet Mrs Johnson at her home, where it was agreed that Sarah would pay her 6s a week to 'bring up the child as if it was her own'. The payments were to be made once a month through Miss Harrington.

Sarah kept up the payments for the first few months and visited Louis several times. In April, Mrs Johnson received a letter from her saying that she would like to visit and take Louis out. She also said that Louis's father wanted to take him to France, 'a proposal I strongly oppose'. She wrote, 'My hand trembles, I can scarcely write; perhaps you may enter into my feelings.' The letter was signed 'S. Tavern'. But it would be almost a year before Mrs Johnson saw Sarah again, during which time she had fallen into arrears with her payments, and was back living in North Leverton.

In the meantime, Sarah continued to write to Mrs Johnson, at one point asking her to postpone the payments for three months, but the arrears kept mounting up and eventually she owed her £10. In a letter dated 15 January 1849, she wrote:

> In consequence of some property that has just been left me, I shall not be able to see you before 25th January, and on Saturday, the 27th, I shall take my little boy to France, so please be prepared. I only knew this late on Saturday. With trembling hand, I write you this. You will hear from me again in a few days.

The following month, Sarah arrived at Mrs Johnson's house, explaining that she had been unable to come before as her mother had been ill. She paid a small amount of what she owed, then took Louis, saying that she was taking him to an institution in Boulogne, where his father had been brought up. Mrs Johnson went with Sarah to the train station and stayed with her while she bought her ticket and boarded the train to Dover.

However, the next night Sarah returned to Mrs Johnson's house with her little boy, who was very sick. She said that she had been told by the doctor that Louis had water on the brain and did not have long to live. If Mrs Johnson could keep him, she would not take him away again, but go into service to provide for him. Mrs Johnson agreed to lower her fee to 5s a week. Fortunately, Louis soon recovered, but within weeks it was clear that Sarah was still struggling financially: 'I shall not be able to see you at present, as a shilling to me now is a great deal,' she wrote. 'If I could have walked to you, I should have been happy to have done so … I am going almost without food, except a little water and a bit of dry bread.'

Sarah did enclose some of the money she owed in several of the letters that followed, but by the end of the summer the situation had become progressively worse and she was still in debt:

> My Dear Mrs. Johnson,
> I was very glad to hear you had safely received the money. I wish I could pay you the remainder. I am anxious to see you and shall do so as soon as I can. I have been very ill indeed since I last wrote to you. You will be sorry to hear I have been obliged to part with some of my clothes to pay my doctor's bill and my lodging … My greatest anxiety is to get out of your debt … Please kiss my dear baby for me … In hopes both yourself and Mr. Johnson are quite well.
> I remain your sincerely but unhappy Sarah Drake.

Towards the end of the year, matters came to a head, when in November, Mrs Johnson received what would be Sarah's final letter:

My Dear Mrs Johnson,

It is with a trembling hand, and aching heart, I write you this letter. You will be sorry to hear that I have been obliged to sell the greatest and best part of my clothes to pay my expenses. I am better, but I am a poor creature, scarcely able to go about. When walking in the park on Saturday, for the benefits of the air, I accidently met with Mrs Musgrove, a relative to the family I lived with in Manchester. My appearance excited her pity, and she offered to take me with her to Madrid, in Spain, which I have accepted, otherwise I could not have got a place, nor am I able to take one. I hope the sea air may do me good, if I have the strength to bear with sea sickness ... You say I am unkind to the child. I hope and trust you will never be called to encounter with the trouble I have had about him.

I have suffered great privations on his account to pay you the money I have. I do not wish you to get him more things than I am able to pay for, my heart's desire is to pay you. It will take me some time to earn what I already owe you. My wages are but £15 a year. Had I had my health, and stayed my place, my wages would have paid you, and brought him up respectably, but I cannot do impossibilities.

I have not heard from him since I saw you, nor is it in my power to do anything for him but what I can earn. I wish you would let him go to the parish. If I am spared with life to return to my native land, I will then take him, and do all that lays in my power for him. Should I die in going over, I shall request what few things I have left to be sold, and the money sent to you, but you must say it is money I borrowed from you, if it known, my parents will curse me in my grave.

My heart is broken at writing this, but I know not what else to do. If I had not done this, I must have starved to death. If I am spared with life, you will hear from me in a few months. It may be six months, or it may be twelve, before I return to England. If I live, I leave London at six o'clock this evening. Kiss my dear child for me. I hope you are all well. Good night and God bless you.

Yours sincerely,<br>Sarah Drake.

Nov. 26th, 1849. 22, Edward Street.
P.S. I leave here tonight.

Consequently, Mrs Johnson went straight to Edward Street with little Louis in tow, to try and find Sarah. She was redirected to Upper Harley Street, but as she was unsure of the house number, spent the rest of the evening knocking on several doors trying to locate her. Eventually, she gave up and resumed the search the next morning, where she found Sarah at 33 Upper Harley Street, an area associated with high-rolling bankers, brokers, and financiers, as well as members of parliament, lawyers, prominent physicians, and surgeons. Sarah, who came highly recommended by her previous employer, feminist and women's suffrage supporter, Lady Anna Gore Langton, was employed as a cook and housekeeper in the home of Frederick Huth, a merchant banker and founder of Frederick Huth & Co. She had a highly responsible and prestigious position that placed her at the top of the female servants' hierarchy and second in command only to the mistress of the house.

Bestselling author Mrs Beeton wrote that 'the housekeeper must consider herself as the immediate representative of her mistress, and bring, to the management of the household, all those qualities of honesty, industry and vigilance, in the same degree as if she were at the head of her *own* family.'[5] Sarah would have been responsible for all the female staff and required to keep accounts of all the expenses of the house and tradesmen's bills. She would have received a salary of around £30 a year, double the amount she had stated in her letter to Mrs Johnson.[6]

At just after ten o'clock that morning, Mary Ann Wigzell, the kitchen maid, showed Mrs Johnson into the housekeeper's room. When Sarah saw her at the door she said, 'Oh, it is Mrs Johnson. I thought I should see you, by my dream.' Mrs Johnson told her that she was 'a very cruel woman' to cause her 'so much pain and trouble', to which Sarah replied that she could not help it, she could not send her any more money. She also said that she had only found out the night before that she would not be going abroad, as the family had postponed the trip until the following spring. Mrs Johnson looked unconvinced and replied, 'Now don't say so, for you have no intention of going abroad.'

Sarah asked Mrs Johnson not to say to anyone in the house that Louis was her child, then remarked how well her son looked, and was much 'stouter' than when she had last seen him, at which point Mrs Johnson told her that she could not continue to look after Louis and that she would not be taking him back home with her. Sarah begged her to have her child for another week or until she could find someone else to look after him, but Mrs Johnson was adamant; as Sarah had deceived them, her husband had said 'she was to leave the child with her and not bring him back again'. As Mrs Johnson got up to leave, she turned to Sarah and told her that Mr Johnson would be taking out a summons against her for the money she owed. Sarah implored her to get him to change his mind, saying that she would pay the debt as soon as she could, but Mrs Johnson said nothing and took one last look at Louis, who was playing happily with the fire broom, then left. It would be the last time she would see the little boy alive.

The following Friday, Mrs Johnson returned to Upper Harley Street with a parcel containing the rest of Louis's clothes, a note, and a bill. Sarah told her that she had managed to smuggle Louis out of the house to a friend who would lend her the money to pay the debt, and that she had sent Mrs Johnson a letter, by way of explanation. As Mrs Johnson was leaving, she asked Sarah to kiss little Louis for her, to which Sarah replied, 'Yes, I will.' On her return home, she found a letter waiting for her from Sarah, which read:

> Mrs. Johnson,
> I have got a friend who has taken him and will lend me the money to pay you the first week in January; their money is out, and they cannot get it before. I have none of my own till I have earned it, and if you summons me, I cannot pay you now, and I do not know what advantage you will have in depriving me of my place and character, as I shall then be forever prevented from earning my bread, and at that time I will send you the full amount I owe you. Providence so provided for me, that I have kept it from anyone in the house. I hope and trust you will not expose me.
>
> Yours sincerely,
> Sarah Drake

33, Upper Harley Street, Cavendish Square. Nov. 29th, 1849.

After Mrs Johnson had gone, Sarah went back into the housekeeper's room and shut the door. A few minutes later, Sarah Powell, the housemaid, who had received a visit from a friend and wanted to take her into the housekeeper's room to chat, tried the door but found it was locked. Thinking Sarah was inside, she called out, 'Never mind,' then went away. She later said that she heard no reply from Sarah and didn't see her go in or out of her room, but about an hour later saw that the door was open.

Later that morning, Sarah asked Mary Ann Wigzell if she had a small box she could have, as she wanted to send some clothes to her sister's children. Sarah usually dined with the servants, but at half-past one that day, she told the kitchen maid to go to dinner and instructed the housemaid to help with the meal, as she was going upstairs to write a letter.

A few hours later, Sarah came downstairs and told Mary Ann that she had used one of her own boxes she had brought to the house at the start of her employment. Shortly after, Mary Ann went upstairs to the bedroom that she shared with Sarah and saw the box 'wrapped and corded', where it remained until 7.00 the next morning, when Sarah asked her to carry it downstairs to the butler's pantry on the lower floor, to give to Mr Glass, the butler, who she said would send for a boy to take it to the station.

The next day, Sarah's sister Mary and Theophilus Burton received an unsigned letter that said, 'There will be a box at Retford, receive it as soon as possible.' Mary asked her brother William Drake to collect the box from the White Hart Inn, which he did. Sliding a stick through the cord, he carried it over his shoulder back to his sister's house at North Leverton. He took it into the sitting room, where he and Theophilus forced the lock open with a chisel and, to their horror, inside was a body of a small boy. Apart from a white pocket handkerchief around his neck, he was completely naked. Laid next to him were articles of clothing – a frock, a pair of socks, a pair of boots, and a straw hat. Near his face was a white apron that was stained with blood and marked with the name 'S. Drake, 18'.

The next morning, Theophilus took the box to Edward Smith, the local policeman, informing him that his sister-in-law was called Sarah Drake and she worked in Upper Harley Street, London. Smith immediately contacted Superintendent Thomas Kinder of Nottingham police, who, after seeing the contents of the box, subsequently called in Sergeant Jonathan 'Jack' Whicher, to help with the investigation.[7] Both men went directly by train to 33 Upper Harley Street, where, following a thorough search of the housekeeper's room, Whicher found in a cupboard three aprons, all marked with 'S. Drake' in black ink, identical to the one found with Louis's body. Kinder arrested Sarah on suspicion of murdering her son, and she broke down and wept as she was escorted to Marylebone police station.

On Friday 7 December, Sarah appeared before the magistrates at Marylebone Police Court, where she entered a plea of 'not guilty'. She walked with a 'tolerably firm step' as she was led to the dock by Mr Mitchell, the gaoler, but 'on taking her stand at the bar, it was quite evident that she felt most painfully the situation in which she was placed'.[8]

The first witness to give evidence was Superintendent Kinder, who told the court that after making further inquiries, he strongly suspected that the child had been murdered, and 'had every reason to imagine that the prisoner was the murderess'. Subsequently, he and Sergeant Whicher had gone to Upper Harley Street to arrest Sarah Drake:

> I told her that I must apprehend her for having murdered her child, Louis Drake, upon which she looked full at me, and said, 'How do you know that?' I told her that a box had been sent down to North Leverton, containing the dead body of a male child, and that an apron had been found in it marked 'S. Drake.' She sat down and began to cry.

Sergeant Whicher gave corroborating evidence, then the next witness, Mary Ann Wigzell, the kitchen maid, was called to testify. She confirmed that Mrs Johnson came to the house with a child asking for Sarah Drake, at just after 10.00 in the morning on Wednesday 28 November. She saw them together in the housekeeper's room, then Mrs Johnson left the house without the child. Just after midday, Sarah came into the kitchen and told her that Mrs Johnson had caused her a great deal of trouble. She said that she owed her money and now there was a threat of a summons. It was shortly afterwards that Sarah asked her for a small box. Mary Ann was then shown the box and wrapper which she identified as being the one she had taken down to Mr Glass that morning. She remembered it being 'so heavy that she could scarcely carry it down the stairs' and noticed that there was no address on it. She said that Sarah had not wanted any of the other servants to see it, as they might think that she was sending things out of the house. Sarah then gave Mary Ann two letters to post; one was addressed to Mrs Johnson, the other to Mrs Burton, North Leverton, Nottinghamshire.

When Sarah had started her employment at the house two days before on Monday, she had been unwell with a bad cold and 'was not in very good spirits', Mary Ann continued, and during the short time she was employed by Mr Huth, she 'appeared to be remarkably serious and reserved … and rather low spirited'. Whenever she had the opportunity during the day, she would read her Bible and Prayer Book in the housekeeper's room, and again at night in her bedroom, before she said her prayers. The day before Mrs Johnson arrived, Mary Ann witnessed Sarah praying in her bedroom for half an hour or more and after she had left, recalled her saying that Mrs Johnson had 'distracted her' and 'put her out'.

The last witness, Mary Anne Bridge, the searcher employed at the police station, told the court:

> At eleven o'clock last night I searched the prisoner at the station house and found upon her a gold watch and some silver. I asked her what she was charged with, when she at first made me no answer, but presently said to me, 'Are you a married woman?' I told her I was and had a large family, when she said, 'Then you can feel for me, and I will tell you; it is all about a child.' I asked her if it was a new-born baby, and she said it was not; that it was two years old, and she had hung it. I asked her how she came to do such a thing as that, then she said she did not know.
>
> A woman who had had it to nurse and to whom she owed a good deal of money, brought it to her, and she was afraid of losing her place. She did it (the hanging) in a moment, no one else being present. She then packed up the child and sent it into the country to her sister, to get

it buried, and she thought that she (the sister) had made all the noise about it. She further said she supposed she should be hung.

At the end of the hearing, Mr Long, the magistrate, turned to Sarah and asked her if she wished to say anything. Sarah, who had sat very still, with her head bowed throughout the hearing, said between sobs, 'Nothing, sir. Can I have counsel?' Mr Long replied that she would be remanded in custody and brought back to court the following Saturday, when she could have 'any professional assistance' that she 'may think fit'.

By now, newspaper reports of the two previous incidents of 1842 and 1844 had circulated around the country and it had become common knowledge that Sarah had 'murdered no less than three children'. A week later, on Saturday 15 December, *The Standard* newspaper reported that the 'numerous narrow avenues leading to the public entrance of Marylebone Police Court were completely blocked by persons eager to see Sarah Drake'. At the request of her solicitor, Mr Herring, Sarah, who appeared 'wretched to the extreme', was allowed a seat in the dock, as during her time in the House of Detention she had been 'so much indisposed' that she was transferred from the ward to the infirmary.

The following day, a rather unkind description of Sarah appeared in the *Observer:*

> She could not well stand, was nearly bent double and during the whole of the proceedings completely hid her face in her handkerchief. Although stated to have been born in 1813, she looked as if she had been born 13 years earlier. She is a woman of middle height, very thin, almost emaciated, and she could never have possessed even comely attractions. Her forehead is narrow, eyes lack lustre, cheeks lank, face and cheek bones more than ordinarily long, lips and mouth large, nose lengthy, full,

and wide at the bottom. She was dressed in a black figure-striped greyish cotton gown, faded black silk mantle, black bonnet and veil also of black silk, a brown fur boa and cuffs to match.

Opening the proceedings, Mr Phillips, the second clerk, read out the testimonies given by the witnesses at the previous hearing, before Sarah Powell, the housemaid, gave a brief testimony, in which she recalled finding the door to the housekeeper's room locked.

Next, one of the principal witnesses, Mrs Johnson, was called to give evidence. Described by the *Evening Mail* as a 'very mild and delicate looking woman', she told the court that, on Saturday 8 December, she had gone to North Leverton to the inquest held at the Royal Oak Inn, where she was shown a coffin containing the body of a child, whom she identified as Louis Drake. Mrs Johnson confirmed that she had known Sarah for almost two years and that she had looked after her little boy Louis since he was a baby. She gave her account of the events leading up to Louis's death, adding that Sarah had insisted that if she had decided to have the little boy baptised, it must be in a Catholic church, as his father was a Catholic.

In June 1848, Louis fell gravely ill and, following the doctor's advice, Mrs Johnson sent for a Catholic clergyman who came to the house and baptised him. She said she felt Sarah had deceived her by telling her that she was going away, first to the Isle of Man – though in truth she was going to Nottinghamshire – then more recently to Spain. During this period, she had received fourteen letters from Sarah, but very little money, and did not see her again until February the following year.

Mr Long asked Mrs Johnson if she was sure that the child she had identified at the inquest had been Louis, to which she replied that she was certain as she recognised the clothes in the box as belonging to the little boy, some of which he had worn when she had left him with his mother at Upper Harley Street. She started to sob loudly as she began to list them: 'a flannel petticoat, a black petticoat, a pinafore, a pelisse, a cape, a little shirt and a flannel blanket'. The clothes were then produced, and 'the sight of them affected not only the witness, but almost everybody in court', wrote the reporter, while Sarah, 'who was always in a crouching position, crouched lower, and pressed her handkerchief against her face'.

Two of Sarah's letters were then read out in court. As he had not seen all the letters, Mr Herring thought that it would be of no advantage to cross-examine the witness and asked Mr Long if he could adjourn the case until he had the opportunity to read them. Seeing how 'deeply and painfully affected' Mrs Johnson had been, Mr Long agreed and moved on to the next witness, William Hall, the coach driver, who confirmed he had collected the box addressed to Theophilus Burton from the station at Newark and delivered it to the White Hart Hotel at Retford, on Friday, 30 November.

The box was then shown to the next witness, William Drake, who recognised it as the one he had collected from the White Hart at Retford and said that the address label had dropped off along the road on Gringley Hill. He recalled a letter written by Sarah arriving the same day, which his other sister threw into the fire. 'It was a short letter,' he said, 'only a few lines and no name to it. The contents, as near as I recollect were: "Please to fetch as soon as possible the box that will be at East Retford on Thursday."'

Theophilus Burton, Sarah's brother-in-law, verified the contents of the letter but said he had not recognised the handwriting. When the box arrived at about 8.00 that evening, he prised opened the lid and saw the body of the child. He quickly closed it again and went straight back to his work, leaving the box in the sitting room until the next morning, when he handed it over to the policeman, Edward Smith.

Edward Smith confirmed that there was no address on the box he had received from the previous witness on Saturday morning, 1 December. It was first thought that William Drake had destroyed it, but after conferring with him, the policeman later found it 'torn to bits' about a mile and a half from East Retford, at the top of Gringley Hill.

He said that William had since told him that he had torn the address with the hedge stick he used to carry the box on his shoulder. Inside the box, the body of the child was 'quite naked' except for a 'white pocket handkerchief round its neck, the underlap of which was tight, and the two outer laps loose'. There was a 'bruise on the left temple, and one on the left ear. They were round bruises, a little bigger than a halfpenny. They were severe bruises, and quite black, as if inflicted by violent blows … The body of the child was in appearance quite fresh and was not in the least decomposed.'

The next witness, Francis Blagg, the local surgeon who performed the post-mortem examination on the little boy's body, told the court what he had discovered:

> I observed great lividness of the face, particularly of the eyelids, which were swollen. The tongue was compressed between the teeth, the hands clenched, the nails blue. There was a contusion on the left side of the forehead, there was also a bruise on the left ear. I performed a post-mortem examination, and on the scalp, I discovered extensive blows or bruises on the upper portion of the left side of the head, which must have been inflicted by violence with a blunt instrument. On removing the skull, I discovered corresponding marks on the left membrane of the brain. On turning back the outward membrane, I found a considerable quantity of extravasated blood on the left hemisphere of the brain, and the brain was generally congested. On opening the chest, I found the right lung completely collapsed and the left lung was almost in the same state.
>
> In my opinion, the blows I observed on the head were sufficient to have caused death; they were caused by a blunt instrument, or by the child's head being beaten against something, I cannot say which – a blunt instrument would have caused those appearances. A handkerchief

was fastened round the neck; it was passed twice round the neck, the inner fold was tight, the outer loose. I untied the knot of the handkerchief and took it off. I then found a mark round the neck caused by a ligature. There were decide appearances of strangulation about the child.

I think the handkerchief as I found it was not sufficiently tight to prevent respiration, unless it had been held or hung on some substance – the mark of the ligature round the neck indicated a sufficient compression of the throat to cause strangulation. In my opinion, death was caused by strangulation and the blows combined – either would have produced death, but, finding the two, I am led to the opinion that both combined to produce death.

The last witness to be called that day was Sergeant Whicher, who, after searching the prisoner's room a second time, had found a bunch of keys, one of which fitted the lock of the box in which the murdered child's body had been placed. He also found a gold watch, around £1 in silver and numerous items of clothing.

The third and final hearing before the trial was held the following Saturday, 22 December. By 9.00 that morning, a large crowd had gathered outside Marylebone Police Court, hoping to catch sight of Sarah as she was driven by government van to the court from the House of Detention, in Clerkenwell. People rushed towards the van as it approached the private entrance an hour later, but they were held back by the policemen outside. Sarah 'appeared in better spirits' and 'walked with a firm step', looking straight ahead as she entered the crowded court and, as in previous hearings, held a handkerchief up to her face.[9] However, one reporter noted that she did look 'somewhat pale', and during the last week had been confined to the infirmary, where she had been receiving medical treatment. 'Under these circumstances,' he added, 'she was not locked up in either of the cells in the yard but was permitted to sit by the fire.'

Mr Herring stated that since the last hearing he had read all fourteen letters written by the prisoner and as Mr Long had made up his mind to a committal, he would 'not subject Mrs. Johnson, or any other witnesses, to a cross examination'. He agreed to pay Mrs Johnson £4 of the £9 10s debt Sarah owed her, an amount which Mrs Johnson willingly accepted.

Mr Long praised Mrs Johnson's 'conduct' throughout the hearings and assured her that she would receive the remainder of the debt in due course. He asked Sarah if there was anything she wished to say in her defence, she replied in a quiet voice, 'Everything is in the power of my attorney.' Accompanied by Sergeant Whicher, she was then taken to the notorious Newgate prison, to await her trial at the next sessions of the Central Criminal Court, adjacent to the prison.

In the meantime, *The Times* informed its readers:

> The prisoner has behaved herself with great propriety ever since her committal, and we understand that she is frequently visited by Lady Pirie, by whom portions of scripture are read to her, and to which she listens with the most devout attention. She strongly denies having made a confession to the searcher at the station house as to the murder with which she stands charged and is quite confident of being able to satisfy a jury that the searcher has sworn falsely.
>
> None of her relations have called to see her at the prison, but she has received a letter from one of them, in which the writer intimates that it will not be worth her while to do anything for her as she is almost sure to be hanged.
>
> It further appears that the prisoner has for some length of time kept up a correspondence with a highly respectable person, a land steward, and that in one of his letters to her (many of which are in the possession of Mr. Herring), he implores of her not to think of quitting England, as a union between them was essential to his future happiness.

A vast number of applications have been made for 'good seats' by respectable persons, who are looking forward with no small degree of interest to the trial.

On Thursday, 10 January 1850, Sarah Drake sat in the dock at the Old Bailey. She appeared 'dreadfully depressed, and seemed hardly able to stand', said *The Morning Post*. 'A chair was placed in the dock for her, into which she sank almost mechanically, and she remained with her head upon her breast during the whole of the trial.' Messrs. Bodkin and Clarke conducted the prosecution. Mr Collier and John Humphreys Parry, a highly respected and experienced barrister, who appeared for the defence, entered a plea of insanity.

The witnesses repeated the same evidence that had been given before the coroner and police court, then Mr Collier rose to deliver his speech for the defence, in which he urged the jury to consider the situation of the prisoner and her maternal strengths. A summary of the speech was published in the *Observer*:

> As far as the evidence went, she appeared to be a very inoffensive being, injuring none, though herself suffering the deepest injury woman could receive from man, for she appeared to have been the victim of seduction. Was she destitute of a mother's feelings? The evidence showed that she possessed the feelings common to all mothers. So far from being indifferent, she had made many sacrifices in order to maintain her offspring. So far from entertaining designs against its life, she had provided for its welfare. She might have destroyed it before it was three months old; but instead of doing so, she placed it under the care of Mrs. Johnston [sic], and agreed to pay a sum for its maintenance far beyond what her pittance of wages could afford ...
>
> She believed that she had secured a situation which would enable her, out of the savings of her wages, to

discharge her debt to Mrs. Johnston. She believed that there was a chance of recovering herself, and her hopes for the future were raised, when Mrs. Johnston, without any previous warning, came to expose her shame by leaving with her her child, the existence of which she was anxious to conceal. Mrs. Johnston refused to take it back … The prisoner felt that the knowledge of the fact that she had the child would be fatal to her situation. Poverty and destitution stared her in the face. She had no protector, no friend – not a ray of hope – nothing but the prospect of imprisonment, ruin, and infamy. Could the jury, therefore, wonder that these things produced in her mind a state of frenzy?

Dressed 'like a respectable domestic servant' and wearing a 'white cap with plain silk ribands', Sarah sat rocking back and forth, occasionally convulsing. She 'never raised her face from the moment she was placed in the dock, concealing it in her handkerchief'.[10] In summing up the case, the judge told the jury that they must determine whether having the care of her child suddenly left in her hands, and the despair of losing her position and her character, had affected the prisoner's mind and that it was whilst suffering from 'a temporary frenzy' that she committed the crime in which she was charged. He urged them to look carefully at all the circumstances of the case; 'a jury would do very wrong to infer insanity from the mere atrocity of an act that had been committed.'

Sarah was removed from the court while the jury retired. Just fifteen minutes later, they returned to deliver their verdict, followed by Sarah, who was led back to the dock supported by a gaoler and a female attendant. She had uncovered a portion of her face, which the *Observer* noted was 'pale and sickly-looking', and stood completely still, keeping her eyes down towards the ground while the judge read out the verdict: 'Not Guilty, on the ground of temporary insanity.'

'Some slight applause followed the announcement, but the prisoner showed no emotion of joy, and slowly fainted away in the arms of her attendants,' remarked the reporter. Mr Justice Patteson declared that she would be 'confined in gaol during her Majesty's pleasure'.

A few days later, on 13 January, a small piece in the same newspaper read:

> Sarah Drake, the filicide,[11] has been acquitted of the murder of her unfortunate child on the ground of insanity ... and she is now and will be from henceforward the inmate for life of a lunatic asylum. If she be of sane mind at this moment, where there is no reason to doubt, then will this incarceration fall far more heavily upon her than death; but such is the law of this country. Once mad, in such a case, for ever mad.

Sarah was sent to the Royal Hospital of Bethlehem (more commonly known as Bethlem Royal Hospital or Bedlam), where she is recorded in the 1851 national census as a 'criminal lunatic' in residence. But, three years later, on 24 May 1854, records show she was of 'unsound mind' and 'violent', and admitted into the workhouse at Tower Hamlets.

However, according to the 1861 census, Sarah, now aged 46, was living back home in North Leverton, with her parents and younger brother William, aged 39. Having taken over the household duties following her mother's death, Sarah continued to live at home as a 'housekeeper' until she died at the age of 77 in 1891.

# Chapter 2

# The Esher Tragedy
## Mary Ann Brough, Surrey, 1854

When the Prince of Wales was born on 9 November 1841, Queen Victoria insisted that a wet nurse for her newborn son, Bertie, who would later become King Edward VII, must come from the neighbourhood of Esher in Surrey. She frequently stayed at Claremont House, an eighteenth-century Georgian mansion situated on the southern border of Esher and much-loved home of her 'beloved' uncle, Prince Leopold. She had many happy childhood memories spent with 'dear old Louis' on his estate, describing Claremont as 'the brightest epoch of my otherwise rather melancholy childhood'.[1] The Queen suffered from post-natal depression and found it difficult to bond with her baby son. She loathed breastfeeding and claimed that all babies under six months old were 'mere little plants' with 'that terrible frog-like action'.[2] (Though she loved animals, Queen Victoria found the resident frogs at Frogmore Cottage 'quite disgusting'.[3])

Numerous candidates, including several 'ladies of wealth and position',[4] hoping to secure employment as wet nurse to the prince, presented themselves at Buckingham Palace. But the Queen chose Mary Ann Brough, whom she thought a simple countrywoman, who had worked as a housemaid at Claremont House prior to her marriage seven years earlier in 1834, to George Brough, a groundsman on the estate, whose father had also been employed as head coachman at the palace.

Having given birth to her daughter Anne just two months before, Mary Ann would have been lactating, making her a suitable candidate to act as wet nurse to the prince. The Queen, having recognised her from her visits to Claremont, along with four 'medical men', agreed that she was the most 'eligible person that had come before them'.[5] She insisted that Mary Ann brought her own baby with her to Buckingham Palace and both she and Prince Albert 'expressed their anxiety that it should be well taken care of' and that the expense of placing it with a wet nurse would be 'liberally provided for by her Majesty'.[6]

Mary Ann was to be paid the princely sum of £1,000, double the amount received by her predecessor, 'in honour of the birth of an heir to the throne'.[7] The Queen seemed to be delighted with Mary Ann, who was described as 'quiet and temperate in her habits'. She even attended the prince's christening in January the following year. Travelling in the royal procession from Windsor Castle to St George's Chapel, 'the nurse of the Prince of Wales (Mrs. Brough) very considerately held the child up to the windows of the carriage, when the cheers of the crowd burst forth anew with a joy almost frantic,' wrote the *Observer.*

Sadly, in September that year, Mary Ann's baby died. This was a tragic double blow for Mary Ann and her husband George, as only the year before in September 1840, they had lost another daughter, Jane, at just two months old. Shortly after, the newspapers reported that the prince's wet nurse had been dismissed for 'disobedience of orders'. They claimed she had been 'receiving visits from her husband' and had also been 'caught in the act of drinking ardent spirits'.

Nevertheless, Mary Ann insisted that the accusations were false and that the reason for her departure was because the Queen's medical advisers suggested that a change would be beneficial to the royal infant. In her defence, *The Era* condemned the reports as 'malicious' and said that Mrs Brough, who was 'a most sober and respectable woman ... quitted the service of her Majesty, solely because her milk did not agree with the infant, and at the suggestion of the Queen's physicians.' They added that 'as a token of her Majesty's approbation of her conduct', Mrs Brough was presented with a 'piece of plate, of exquisite workmanship, bearing the Prince of Wales arms', with her name engraved on it.

Mary Ann returned to Esher to live with her husband and their remaining daughters, 7-year-old Mary and 4-year-old Susanna, in their cottage at West End. Over the next ten years, the Broughs went on to have six more children, but sadly during this period they would suffer yet another loss, the death of Susanna in 1848, aged 10.

Over the years, George Brough had been employed in various positions at Claremont House and by the summer of 1854, he was working as a house servant, a position where he was required to spend time away from home. It was during this time that George, who had for a while suspected that his wife had been having an affair, received information that she had been frequently travelling by train to London with another man for 'immoral purposes'. He hired a detective called Henry Field to follow her on one of her regular jaunts to the city, where he believed the clandestine meetings took place. Field confirmed George's fears, reporting back that Mary Ann had met a local man from Esher named Woodhatch in a public house, before leaving to go to a 'questionable house' with him, where they remained for some time.

On Tuesday 6 June, George left the family home in a 'very low and dejected state', returning only briefly the next day to retrieve his nightcap and nightgown, which Mary Ann had left in a bundle on the gate. Accompanied by John Birdseye, a friend and landlord of the Wheatsheaf public house where he was staying, he told her that he intended to see a solicitor to start legal proceedings against her and for full custody of the children, a situation that would undoubtedly leave Mary Ann facing admission into the workhouse.

A few days later, on Saturday, 10 June, Henry Woolger, a labourer who worked in the gardens of Claremont House, was walking along the footpath on his way to work when he noticed something odd hanging out over the sill of the upstairs window at the back of the Broughs' cottage. As he drew nearer, he saw to his horror that it was a pillow soaked in blood. Woolger looked anxiously about, but there was no one around and the house was silent. A few minutes later, he heard the back gate click that led from West End common and turned to see Thomas Beasley approaching. He beckoned him over and pointed up at the window, saying, 'Look here, Thomas, here is an awful sight.'

The two men went round to the front of the house where Beasley rang the bell, but no one came, though Woolger was sure he heard someone walking around inside. Presently, a woman dressed in a half mourning shawl appeared at the window and waved a towel, as if to attract their attention. Woolger fetched a ladder from the woodhouse, placed it underneath the window, and climbed up. He peered into the room and saw Mary Ann Brough staggering up the staircase near the window. As she turned towards him, Woolger gasped in horror, hastily slid back down the ladder, and ran to get the doctor.

Meanwhile, John Crockford, a neighbour, who had joined the two men outside the Broughs' cottage, ascended the ladder and clambered into the room, where he faced a horrifying scene. Blood covered the floor and splattered the walls, and in the bed lay a small dead child; its throat had been slit. Crockford walked through to the front bedroom, which was also covered in blood, and found Mary Ann lying on her side on the bed with a deep wound across her throat; two other small children lay dead at the foot of the bed. In another room, three more children lay dead on a blood-soaked bed. All the children's throats had been cut with a razor. The only person alive in the house was Mary Ann, who feebly raised her hand when she saw Crockford.

Dr Mott arrived, followed by PC William Bedser and Chief Superintendent Biddlecombe of the Surrey Constabulary. After Mary Ann's wound had been stitched and dressed, the doctor left Sarah Weller to nurse her during her recovery from her injury. As soon as she recovered enough to be able to speak, Mary Ann told the nurse that her husband had left her without any money and was going to take the children from her. To prevent this from happening, she murdered all six children and then tried, but failed, to take her own life. Only the eldest child survived, nineteen-year-old Mary, who had fortunately left home and was working as a lady's maid for a family in Yorkshire. In the meantime, George Brough had returned from a trip into town and was said to be 'completely paralyzed' after hearing the shocking news.

At the inquest, held on 13 June at the Chequers Tavern, at West End, Henry Woolger, who first climbed the ladder that fateful morning, told William Carter, the coroner, that when he looked through the open window into the room, he saw Mary Ann at the top of the stairs. As she turned towards him, he saw that 'her throat was cut, and her hands and face were covered with blood and her hair hung about her face. She was making a whistling noise, apparently from the wound.'

When Woolger returned to the house after having gone for the doctor, Mary Ann, who was lying on the bed, 'appeared to be waving a towel or a cloth in her hand ... and seemed to desire to obtain some assistance'. He said that he 'recognized her, although she was disfigured. The blood was spurting from her throat. I cannot say whether the whistling sound was caused by her endeavour to speak.' He added that he had often seen Mary Ann with her children and she 'always appeared to be very good and kind to them'.

John Crockford, the second witness to testify, gave his account of the horrendous sight he witnessed after climbing into the bedroom window of the cottage, and confirmed that all the children were lying on the beds and dressed in their 'night clothes'. He added that 'Upon going downstairs, I found the front door half open ... I did not notice any blood on the bolt of the front door.' He also confirmed that 'the prisoner always seemed very kind and attentive to her children'.

PC Bedser gave a similar description, producing a razor that he found at the side of the bed on which Mary Ann lay. It was open and stained with blood which had dried. Superintendent Biddlecombe, who knew the prisoner, arrived at her cottage around 11.00 am. On entering through the back door, he found a pair of women's boots saturated in blood and a pair of bloody stockings under a table. He also found that the bolt on the inside of the door was covered in blood, 'as if it had been drawn back by a bloody hand'. He went upstairs to find 'the dead bodies of three of the children in a small bedroom'. He found Mary Ann alone in another bedroom where Dr Mott was attending to her wound, the dead bodies of the other children having been removed. Biddlecombe left the cottage and returned the next day, where he was told that Mary Ann wanted to see him to 'tell him all about it'.

Before taking a statement, Biddlecombe urged Mary Ann to be careful what she said, as it would be his 'duty to take down everything and produce it as evidence against her'. The superintendent said that he cautioned Mary Ann again, but 'she persisted in making a statement, which I took down in writing'. Biddlecombe returned the next day and carefully read Mary Ann's statement back to her, giving her the opportunity to retract anything she had said the previous day, but she said that it was 'perfectly correct'. He then told her that he would 'lay her statement' before the coroner's jury that afternoon, of which the distressing details were as follows:

> On Friday last I was in bed all day. I wanted to see Mr. Izod. I waited all day, I wanted him to give me some medicine. In the evening I walked about, and I then put the children to bed and tried to go to sleep in the chair downstairs. That was about 9 o'clock. Georgy (Georgina) kept calling for me to come to bed. They kept calling for me to bring them some barley water and continued calling till near 12 o'clock. Then some of them went to sleep. I could not rest. I had one candle lit on the chair. I could not see, and I went and got another candle, but still could not see. There was something like a cloud over my eyes. I thought I would go down, get a knife and cut my own throat. I could not find my way down. I groped

about in master's room for a razor. I could not find one. At last, I found his keys and then I found his razor.

I went to Georgy and cut her first. I did not look at her. I then came to Carry (Caroline) and cut her. Then to Henry. He said, 'Don't mother!' I said, 'I must,' and cut him. Then I went to Bill. He was fast asleep. I turned him over. He never woke. I served him the same. I then nearly tumbled into this room. The two children here, Harriet and George, were awake. They made no resistance at all. Harriet struggled very much after I cut her and gurgled for some time. I then lay down and did myself. I can't tell you what occurred after that, till I seemed weak and found myself on the floor. That nasty great black cloud was gone then.

Then I was thirsty, and I got the water bottle and drank. I fell in a sitting position. I sat a little while, then got up and saw the children and it all came to me again. I wanted to call but could not speak. I did not know what to do. I went to the window and put something out to attract attention. I staggered back to my own bed and lay till I heard the ringing of a bell. They made such a noise. I got up and crawled on my hands and knees to the window but could not make them hear. It was Henry Woolgar [sic]. I went down to unbolt the door. There was only one bolt fastened and that I undid. That is all I know.

Biddlecombe finished by confirming that the statement was signed by 'the miserable woman', adding that he did not believe she had made that statement for the purpose of screening any other person.

Inspector James Martell told the corner that he had arrived at the cottage on the Sunday after the murders. While he sat with Mary Ann, she began crying and said, 'See what I have done.' She then made a similar statement to the one she had made to Biddlecombe, adding, 'If there had been forty children, I should have served them all the same, but what a pity it was that I did not do myself first!' After several hours, the jury returned their verdict that 'the deceased children were wilfully murdered by Mary Ann Brough, their mother'.

A few days later, Mary Ann's eldest daughter Mary, having arrived from Yorkshire, accompanied her father to see her deceased siblings for the last time as they lay in their coffins. 'It was the first time they had seen the unfortunate little creatures since the terrible tragedy, and, as might be supposed, the sight was attended with tenfold horror, especially to the father, who appeared to be completely maniacal,' wrote *The Royal Cornwall Gazette*. 'The rooms in which the horrid tragedy was perpetrated have been undergoing a thorough cleaning, but the flooring is so deeply stained with blood, as to defy all attempts at obliteration.' Afterwards, Mary visited her mother at the cottage, where she had been placed under the surveillance of a policeman, and two nurses, until she recovered enough to be removed to the infirmary at Horsemonger Lane Gaol.

Mary Ann was hysterical and wept bitterly as she described to her daughter the horrific events that unfolded on the Saturday she murdered her children, adding that it was fortunate that Mary had been away in Yorkshire at the time. She told her that she was to sign a document on the Saturday (the day she committed the murders), which she feared would separate her from her children. Their distressing conversation ended with Mary Ann declaring that she had left all her possessions to Mary in her will, which included a silver teapot, a silver basin, and two brooches – one from Queen Victoria and one from the Queen of the Belgians – she had received when she had been wet nurse to the Prince of Wales.

Just before 11.00 in the morning of Friday 23 June, the sombre funeral toll of the church bell rang, as George Brough and his only remaining daughter, Mary, slowly followed the funeral cortege consisting of the coffins carrying the bodies of Georgina, aged 11, Caroline (Carry), aged 9, William, 6, twins Henry and Harriet,

2½, and lastly, the smallest coffin of little George, aged 21 months, to their final resting place in the local churchyard at Esher. Police from Surrey constabulary were present to maintain order as crowds of people from the surrounding villages descended outside the Brough's cottage and lined the road to the church.

Several women were sobbing as the funeral procession reached the church, and a few fainted and were taken into nearby houses. Even the elderly rector, the Rev. Mr Harton, had to be replaced by his curate, the Rev. Mr Williams, as he was too distraught to conduct the burial service. Inside the church, the congregation wept throughout the service, while George Brough sat with his face buried in his hands, his body convulsing with grief. He struggled to walk across the graveyard and had to be held up while the coffins were lowered into the graves. When the service finished and the clergyman, who appeared to be deeply affected by the distressing scene, started to walk away, both George and his daughter Mary became so overwhelmed with grief that they fainted and had to be carried out of the churchyard.

Afterwards, a small crowd congregated outside the Broughs' cottage, hoping to see the rooms where the murders had taken place. One 'respectably dressed' gentleman approached the police officer on duty and informed him that if he could 'succeed in getting him possession of the premises, he would give £200 for them, and make the officer a present of £50', as he intended to 'make a public exhibition of the property at a certain sum per visitor'.[8] Evidently the officer refused.

On Thursday, 29 June, accompanied by Superintendent Biddlecombe and Inspector Martell, Mary Ann was driven to Esher and brought before the county magistrates' court held at the Bear posting house, opposite Esher Green. 'She alighted from the vehicle with a firm step, looked at several of the persons standing in front of the doorway whom she knew, and then passed hurriedly into the premises,' said *The Guardian*. Described as 'about 42 or 43 years old, about 5 feet 6 inches high' and having 'something rather peculiar in her walk', Mary Ann, dressed in black and carrying a small wicker basket, was taken into a private room, where she sat chatting freely to her attendant, remarking on the fine weather that morning, and asked first for a glass of wine, then a glass of brandy. She 'did not seem to care in the least for what she had done', while her husband George, who was seated in the private bar, appeared 'dreadfully cut up'.

At the end of the hearing, Mary Ann approached George, took off her wedding ring and offered it back to him. When he refused, she remarked that he must want her to wear it, so she put it back on her finger. She was then taken back to Horsemonger Lane Gaol, to await her trial. In the meantime, her married lover Woodhatch sold his business and, in the dead of the night, fled the village to escape retribution and death threats from his neighbours, leaving behind his wife, who was seriously ill in bed, and family.

At just after nine o'clock on the morning of 10 August, Mary Ann, dressed in a deep mourning gown, stood before a crowded court at the summer assizes in Guildford, charged with murdering her six children. As the circumstantial evidence combined with Mary Ann's statement was sufficient to prove she had murdered her children, the issue at the trial was not if she had committed the crime, but to determine if she was legally responsible for her actions. She appeared unmoved as she pleaded 'not guilty' to all the indictments. The first and only indictment to be heard was the charge of the murder of 2-year-old Harriet.

William Bodkin, conducting the prosecution, said Mary Ann was charged with murdering a 'child of her own body', and that there was no doubt that she was alone in the cottage with her six children that night. Although she was a married woman, due to circumstances that had recently occurred between her and her husband, he had felt 'justified' in leaving her. Bodkin then told the court that to confirm his suspicions of her alleged affair, Mr Brough had had his wife followed. He apologised for referring to 'these matters, affecting the moral character of the prisoner', but did so in order that the jury 'might understand the case'. He went on to say that on the day of the 'fatal occurrence', Mary Ann was seen by several people going about her affairs in an ordinary manner.

In Mary Ann's statement to Sarah Waller, the nurse who attended to her following her failed suicide attempt, she said her husband had left her with no money and that she intended to stop him taking the children away from her. Bodkin, recounting this, did not believe there would be the slightest doubt that it was by the hand of the prisoner that the lives of the six children were sacrificed, and the only question raised was whether, at the time, the prisoner was in such a state of mind as rendered her responsible for her actions.

The counsel for the defence, Mr Edwin James, who addressed the jury in a speech of 'great eloquence and power', entered a plea of insanity. He pointed out the significant fact that, prior to the murders, Mary Ann had been a kind and devoted mother to her children.

'All the circumstances of the case showed that the act was committed under the influence of some sudden frenzy,' he said, 'and being relieved by the quantity of blood that escaped from the wound she had inflicted upon herself, the "dark cloud," as she expressed it, passed away and she then, for the first time, became aware of what she had done.' He added that Mary Ann had made no attempt to escape, but instead had sought assistance and had promptly made a statement. He could see no adequate motive for the crime, and the only reason for her actions was that 'her mind had suddenly broken down, and she was not conscious of the act she was committing'.

Several medical witnesses were then called to give evidence in support of the insanity defence. Dr Izod, a surgeon at Esher, who had attended Mary Ann for several years, testified that in 1852, Mary Ann had suffered from 'severe bleeding at the nose' and had complained of 'great pain in her head' for which he had to administer 'powerful medicines and to blister her'. Then, in September 1854, eight days after she gave birth to her youngest child, George, she was 'attacked by paralysis' (a stroke). She completely lost the use of her left side, her face was 'distorted', and her speech was so affected that at times she was unable to speak at all.

Although she improved, Mary Ann never fully recovered and Dr Izod, who believed her symptoms were that of a 'disordered brain', advised her to 'avoid excitement of every description', warning her that any 'sudden excitement would be dangerous to her'. He said he had seen Mary Ann on the Wednesday before the murders, and though he felt the need to 'caution her strongly not to excite herself', he did not think it necessary to administer any medicine that day because 'there were not any new symptoms'.

The next witness, Dr Forbes Benignus Winslow, a prominent psychologist, who had for a number of years studied diseases of the brain, had spoken at length with Mary Ann in Horsemonger Lane Gaol the previous day. He told the court that it was his opinion that the attack of paralysis suffered by her was the result of a diseased brain. 'Paralysis may exist in some cases without actual insanity,' he said, 'but it is always symptomatic of a disease of the brain. Bleeding at the nose is a symptom of congested brain, and it is considered as an effort of the brain to relieve itself.' Though he did not observe any symptoms of insanity during his interview with Mary Ann, cases of temporary insanity resulting in a desire to commit murder or suicide were common. 'I have known many instances where the patient had made an attack upon some near relative with whom he had previously been on the most affectionate terms, and it frequently occurs with mothers and children. In such cases the patient suddenly suffers under a strong homicidal impulse which he cannot control.'

Winslow went on to explain, 'In cases of transient insanity it was very common for patients to say that they experienced the sensation of a dark cloud passing before their eyes and during this paroxysm would not be able to distinguish between right and wrong.' Winslow agreed with Dr Izod that 'the condition of the prisoner's brain rendered her peculiarly liable to suffer from excitement; and he had no doubt that her brain had been in a disordered state ever since the attack of paralysis.' The other witnesses, Dr Daniel and Dr Ingledew, who were then examined, both agreed with Dr Winslow.

It took the jury two hours to deliver a verdict of 'not guilty' on the grounds of insanity. Mary Ann, who showed no emotion throughout the proceedings, was ordered to be detained 'in safe custody during her Majesty's pleasure'. She was escorted back to Horsemonger Lane Gaol where she remained incarcerated until 25 August, when she was admitted to Bethlem Hospital to be detained indefinitely.

According to Dr William Charles Hood, Bethlem's Resident Physician, a few days after Mary Ann was admitted, she showed 'peculiar symptoms of mental derangement', then, in November 1856, she had a 'paralytic attack' that affected her left side, and another in December 1858, affecting her mouth and tongue. She suffered a third attack the following year in September, when she almost lost the use of her legs, and another in January 1861 that left her so weak she was unable to sit up and was provided with a waterbed.

Two months later, on 18 March, Mary Ann lost consciousness and died. At the inquest held in the hospital two days after her death, Dr Hood confirmed that the cause of death was 'Paralysis, resulting from apoplexy' and the jury returned a verdict of 'natural death'. When William Payne, the coroner, asked the doctor if insanity had anything to do with her death, he replied, 'Yes it had, and although there was considerable doubt expressed as to the propriety of the verdict, for when she was tried there was not much evidence to prove her insanity, yet I have no doubt that even then the brain was diseased, and that she committed that act while under the influence of insanity.'

Just over a year after the murders, on 27 August 1855, Mary Brough, George and Mary Ann's eldest and only surviving child, married Benjamin Sorby, an agricultural labourer, at St Mary's Church in Ecclesfield, Yorkshire, and they went on to have five children together. Mary remained in Yorkshire until her death in 1891.

After the funeral of his children, many people expected George Brough to move away from the village, and according to several newspapers, it was the 'intention of the Crown to propose pensioning him off, and thus allow him to leave the scene of an occurrence which must forever remain forever uppermost in his mind.' However, according to the 1861 national census, George Brough was still living in West End with William Beauchamp and his family, his occupation recorded as a 'yeoman farmer'. Ten years later, in 1871, he was still lodging with the Beauchamps, but is down as a 'domestic pensioner to the late king of Belgium' (King Leopold, who died in 1865). George died of 'senile decay' on 27 April 1874.

# Chapter 3

# The Wretched Woman
## Mary Ann Cotton, County Durham, 1872

During the mid-nineteenth century, the number of women convicted of poisoning their husbands increased considerably. Money was often the motive and as arsenic was inexpensive, easy to obtain, and largely undetectable, it was frequently used by women to bump off their spouses and even their children, in order to claim the cash from insurance policies that had been taken out in their names. Mary Ann Cotton, who is believed to have murdered as many as twenty-one people, including members of her own family, repeatedly received money in this way for a number of years, without arousing any suspicions whatsoever.

She was born Mary Ann Robson in 1832, in Low Moorsley, a small mining village in County Durham, where her father worked as a miner in the local coal mine. The eldest of three children, she had a younger sister, Margaret, who died in infancy, and a brother, Robert. She was said to have been an exceptionally pretty child – a neighbour many years later still remembered her 'fine dark eyes'[1] – and appears to have been very happy, later recalling her childhood as 'days of joy'.[2]

Soon after her birth, the family moved a few miles away to East Rainton, where her father worked as a 'pitman' in the Hazard colliery. Raised a strict Methodist by her father, Mary Ann regularly attended Sunday school and as a teenager went on to teach at Wesleyan Sunday school. It was while the family were living in East Rainton that Mary Ann allegedly pushed a boyfriend to his death down a mineshaft.

As the colliery contracts were often short, usually no longer than a year, it was not unusual for families to move to other areas and so by 1841 the Robsons had moved again to Murton. The miners' wages were dependent on how much coal they produced, so they worked at backbreaking speed in extremely cramped and dangerous conditions. There was a constant threat of an accident or death from falling stones, gas explosions, suffocation, drowning, and men falling down the mineshaft.

At home, it was a hard life for the miner's wife too. She would work from early in the morning until late at night, running a household that revolved around the routine of the pit and the needs of the miners. In addition to her husband, she may have had several sons working down the mines, who probably worked different shifts, so they arrived home at different times smothered in coal dust. As well as having a meal ready, she would carry buckets of water from the water-barrel outside or the standpipe in the street and heat it in a pot on the fire for the tin bath that was expected to be ready in front of the fire for each of the workers when they returned home. She would then scrub the grime and coal dust from their backs, before emptying the bath and cleaning the kitchen. Coal dust was also trodden into the home from the filthy streets outside, so it was an endless task for the miner's wife to keep both her family and house clean. Nevertheless, she would constantly wash, scrub, and polish her home until it was spotless.

A year after the Robsons' move to Murton, Michael Robson was repairing a pulley wheel when he slipped and fell nearly 200 feet down the mine shaft to his death. His broken body was brought home in a sack carried in a wheelbarrow marked 'PROPERTY OF THE SOUTH HETTON COAL COMPANY', a sight which must have been extremely traumatic for the young Mary Ann. A year later, Margaret Robson, now widowed with two children to support, soon married her second husband, George Stott, who was also a miner and fellow Methodist.

Mary Ann despised her new stepfather and, as soon as she turned 16 in 1848, she left home to work as a nursemaid for the colliery manager, Edward Potter, his wife, and their twelve children, in the nearby village of South Hetton. She would have worked extremely long, relentless hours, starting from early in the morning, usually at dawn, until very late in the evening. In addition to feeding, bathing, dressing, and nursing the children when they were ill, she would also light the fires, wash the children's clothes, and clean their rooms. Though the work was laborious and unrewarding, Mary Ann did gain an insight into how the middle class lived, which may have ignited her yearning to escape the prospect of a life as a miner's wife, surrounded by dirt, grime, hardship, and the constant threat of death, a life which seemed inevitable for a young woman living in an area dominated by collieries.

It is believed that Mary Ann continued working for the Potters for three years, during which time a Methodist minister is thought to have fallen for her, but it appears that their courtship was not to last as, on 18 July 1852, Mary Ann married a miner called William Mowbray. She was pregnant when the marriage took place twenty miles away in Newcastle Register Office. Perhaps to avoid the gossip back in their neighbourhood, the newlyweds immediately left north-east England and travelled to the other end of the country to Cornwall, where William Mowbray secured work with a railway contractor. If Mary Ann hoped for a better life in the south-west of England, she must have been bitterly disappointed, as the railway workers or 'navvies' and their families lived in dreadful conditions in the railway shanty towns that consisted of temporary timber and turf huts with poor sanitation, constructed alongside the railways, bridges, and tunnels that were being built to form Britain's new railway network.

Mary Ann and William stayed in Cornwall for over four years, during which time they had four, possibly five children, but only one survived. The children may have succumbed to disease, given the appalling conditions in which the Mowbrays lived, but, as there are no death certificates, the question remains as to whether Mary Ann was responsible for her children's deaths, though there is no evidence to support this.

In 1857, following a visit from Mary Ann's mother, the Mowbrays and their only surviving child, Margaret Jane, moved back to South Hetton in County Durham. Coal was in huge demand during the Industrial Revolution in the nineteenth century and the rapid expansion of the coal-mining industry in the north of England drastically increased the population, as workers and their families from across Britain flocked to the small towns and villages. Housing was in short supply and large families were forced to live in very cramped and often damp conditions with inadequate sanitation. William Mowbray soon found work in the local coal mine and Mary Ann once again found herself back in the life that she so desperately wanted to escape.

By 1858, the Mowbrays were living in a public house owned by Mary Ann's stepfather, George Stott, and in September that year, she gave birth to another baby girl, Isabella Jane. Two years later, on 22 June 1860, 4-year-old Margaret Jane died of scarlet fever. The following year, in October, Mary Ann had another baby girl whom she also called Margaret Jane, then two years later, in November 1863, her first known son, John Robert, was born. During this time, the family relocated to Hendon, Sunderland, where William Mowbray left the mines and secured a job as a stoker on a steam ship.

Mary Ann was well aware, due to the death of her own father, of the perils of working down the mines, and had previously urged William to take out an insurance policy. Within a year of his birth, little John Robert Mowbray died of diarrhoea and then shortly afterwards in 1865, his father William Mowbray, who had been at home on leave with an injured foot, also died following a violent attack of diarrhoea. Although diarrhoea was a common cause of death at the time, it was also a symptom of arsenic poisoning. Initially, Mary Ann appeared to be distraught over the death of her husband; even the doctor present was affected by her distress. However, it seems that her grief may have been short-lived, as the doctor claimed that shortly afterwards, as he was passing Mary Ann's house, he heard singing and through the window saw the 'new widow pirouetting before a mirror as she sang a popular song'.[3]

After her husband's death, Mary Ann received £35 insurance money from the British Prudential Insurance Company. She left Sunderland and went about five miles away to the coal port of Seaham Harbour with her two daughters, where she took a room in a house in North Terrace, overlooking the sea. It was here that Mary Ann met Joseph Nattrass, who, despite being engaged to a local girl, became Mary Ann's lover. Nattrass did marry his fiancée, however, and moved to Shildon, near Bishop Auckland, to work in the colliery.

Mary Ann had only been in Seaham Harbour a few weeks when her youngest daughter, 4-year-old Margaret Jane, fell seriously ill and within a few days died of gastric fever. Shortly afterwards, Mary Ann sent her remaining child, 6-year-old Isabella, to live with her mother, Margaret Stott, who was now living nearby at New Seaham. Mary Ann was now alone for the first time, giving her the opportunity to start a new and different life.

She soon found employment as an untrained fever nurse in the Sunderland Infirmary Fever House, where she impressed the doctors with her hard work and apparent sympathy towards the patients. She befriended a patient named George Ward, an engineer and a single man of 32, the same age as Mary Ann. Their friendship blossomed into a romance and following George's discharge from the hospital, they married on 28 August the same year, at St Peter's Church, Monkwearmouth.

George, who was normally a strong and stocky man, found it difficult to find work after his illness and the couple's only income was four shillings a week from the local parish relief. Mary Ann, having left her job at the infirmary, found herself once again impoverished and at home tending to her husband's needs. Within the year, George fell ill with a mysterious illness that baffled the doctors. He suffered for many months and became very weak, until finally, in October the following year, he succumbed to what the doctors believed was typhoid fever.

In November 1866, James Robinson, a shipwright who was recently widowed with five children, advertised for a housekeeper. Mary Ann applied for the position, was successful, and moved into the household in the Sunderland suburb of Pallion shortly afterwards. Within a week, the youngest child, 10-month-old John Robinson, fell ill and died twenty-four hours later following a succession of convulsions. The doctor certified gastric fever as the cause of death.

The following March, Mary Ann, who was pregnant by James Robinson, was summoned to New Seaham to nurse her mother, who was ill. Nine days later, her mother suddenly died. A few days before, Mary Ann had expressed her fear of her mother's impending death to the neighbours, who had listened in disbelief as they expected Mrs Stott to make a full recovery. Following a disagreement with her stepfather, George Stott, Mary Ann returned to James Robinson at Pallion with her daughter Isabella Mowbray. Thereafter, a succession of deaths took place in the Robinson household.

In April, 6-year-old James Robinson and 8-year-old Elizabeth fell ill and died of gastric fever. Mary Ann voiced her concerns to the neighbours of Isabella contracting the illness, which inevitably she did and died on 2 May. The cause of death given for all three children was gastric fever. The infant mortality rate was extremely high in the nineteenth century, mainly due to poor sanitation, and it was not uncommon for a series of deaths to occur in one household from gastric fever and other infectious diseases, particularly in the overcrowded mining communities of Northeast England, where the death rates were often higher than the national average. Nevertheless, James Robinson's three sisters, who disliked Mary Ann, strongly suspected that she had poisoned the children, as did Superintendent Henderson, who requested that their bodies be exhumed, though it appears this never happened. However, James Robinson staunchly defended Mary Ann against the accusations and, much to his sisters' surprise, married her a few months later, on 11 August at Bishopwearmouth Church.

As Mary Ann was five months pregnant at the time, she must have felt quite confident that the marriage would take place, despite the opposition from her future sisters-in-law. In November, she gave birth to a baby girl whom she named Margaret Isabella Robinson, but just three months later, in February 1868, little Margaret died of gastric fever. She would be the fifth and last child to die whilst Mary Ann was living with James Robinson. Mary Ann was already pregnant again with a baby boy, George Robinson, who was born four months later, but fortunately, a change of events instigated by his mother's criminal actions would eventually dissolve the marriage and ensure the survival of little George, his father James, and his two remaining siblings.

Mary Ann had tried on previous occasions to persuade James Robinson to take out an insurance policy for himself and his children, but when he refused, she still tried to insure him herself without his knowledge. Fortunately, Robinson received a tip-off from his neighbour regarding his wife's intentions, and went to the insurance company's office in Sunderland, where he found Mary Ann filling out a form to insure both him and the children.[4]

James Robinson had two building society accounts in which he regularly deposited money, which had accumulated to a considerable amount. But early in 1869, he discovered that Mary Ann, who had charge of his passbook, had been forging his account by entering additional sums of money she had never deposited, eventually amounting to £50. He also found that she had used the names of his brother-in-law and uncle as guarantors for a loan for £60 and had been secretly sending his son to pawn some of his clothes and household goods. Robinson was not only left with very little money, but he was also in debt. The damage to their marriage was irreparable and Mary Ann left the house with her son George, whilst her husband, who was facing financial ruin, went to live with his sister in Coronation Street, Sunderland.

Later that year, Mary Ann and baby George visited a friend in Johnson Street, Sunderland. She left George with her friend while she went to post a letter, but never returned, so fortunately for him, he was reunited with his father, James Robinson. In the meantime, Mary Ann had found work as a laundry supervisor in Smyrna House Home for Fallen Women, owned by Quaker and retired banker Edward Backhouse. Despite having been married three times and now living an independent life with no children, Mary Ann was soon in search of a new husband. By the spring of 1870, she had found a potential partner in recently widowed Frederick Cotton, who was the brother of an old friend, Margaret Cotton. Frederick Cotton was a coal miner, who had lived with his wife Adelaide and their four children in the small mining village of North Walbottle, Northumberland. His wife and one of his children had died during the winter of 1868, then in January 1870 he lost his 9-year-old daughter, Adelaide Jane, to typhus fever.

Mary Ann had stayed with the Cotton family several times during that period and although it's certain that she had nothing to do with the first deaths as she was still in Sunderland at the time, she had been staying with the family for a short time in January when Adelaide Jane had died. At some stage, Mary Ann learnt that Margaret Cotton had almost £60 saved in her bank account. She visited the Cottons again at the beginning of March that year and stayed for several weeks; then, on 25 March, Margaret Cotton died of severe stomach pains.

By this time, Mary Ann and Frederick had become lovers and by April she was pregnant. But instead of moving in permanently with Frederick Cotton, Mary Ann went about twenty miles away to Spennymoor in County Durham, where she worked as a housekeeper for a German doctor for a few months until June, when she returned to Frederick Cotton in North Walbottle. They bigamously married on 17 September 1870, at St Andrew's Church, Newcastle, where Mary Ann gave her surname as Mowbray and her 'condition' as widow, even though James Robinson was still alive. Within weeks, Mary Ann had managed to persuade Frederick Cotton, who was already insured, to take out life insurance policies on both his sons, Frederick and Charles.

Mary Ann's baby, Robert Robson Cotton, was born in January 1871 and by the summer, the Cottons had moved to the mining village of West Auckland, where Frederick Cotton worked in the colliery. It may have been Mary Ann's intention, or just a coincidence, but the family moved into Johnson Terrace (now called Darlington Road), the same street where her former lover Joseph Nattrass lived, and they rekindled their relationship.

In September, just a year and two days after their marriage, Frederick Cotton fell ill at work and died suddenly of what the doctor believed was gastric fever. Mary Ann waited a seemly three months before moving Joseph Nattrass, now a widower, into her home as a lodger and within a few weeks there were rumours of marriage. In the meantime, Mary Ann had taken a job at the local hospital, where she was asked by a patient, John Quick-Manning, who had contracted smallpox, to nurse him during his recovery.

John Quick-Manning was a bachelor who lived further down the street in a large house called Brookfield Cottage and earned a good salary working as an excise officer at the brewery in West Auckland. His wealth and status appealed to Mary Ann and her attentions were quickly diverted from Joseph Nattrass. Nevertheless, she knew that it was unlikely that an eligible bachelor like Quick-Manning would ever consider marrying her with three children in tow.

In the spring of 1872, in the space of just three weeks, a series of deaths occurred in Mary Ann's home which aroused suspicion and ultimately led to her downfall. On 10 March, young Frederick Cotton Jr. died from what the doctors believed was gastric fever, then two weeks later, on 28 March, Robert Robson Cotton died of teething and convulsions. Within a few days, on 1 April, Joseph Nattrass was also dead, allegedly from gastric fever. Both Frederick Jr. and baby Robert were insured, and Joseph Nattrass had signed a will leaving Mary Ann his watch, clothes, and savings of around £10 and 15s.

By mid-April, Mary Ann was pregnant with Quick-Manning's child, but despite rumours that they would marry, in May she took her last surviving child, 7-year-old Charles Edward Cotton, and moved into 13 Font Street, West Auckland. Perhaps Mary Ann felt that Charles Cotton prevented her from marrying Quick-Manning or that he was just simply in the way of any other plans she may have had, but it was obvious she didn't want the little boy. The neighbours later claimed that he was often beaten, starved, and left alone in the house for days, or locked outside in all weathers.

On 6 July, Mary Ann received a visit from Thomas Riley, the local parish relief overseer who lived across the street. He asked her if she would nurse another smallpox patient, but she told him that she had to refuse any work on account of having to look after Charles Cotton, a duty she clearly resented. She said that she had tried to pass the little boy on to his uncle in Ipswich, but he had refused to take him, and asked Riley for an order to admit Charles into the workhouse, but Riley told her that he could only be allowed if she went with him. Mary Ann refused and complained that it was difficult supporting Charles, especially as he was not her own. Not only did he prevent her from 'making many a pound',[5] he also prevented her from taking in a lodger. Riley laughingly asked her if the lodger would be Mr Quick-Manning, adding that he had heard that they might marry, to which she replied, 'It might be so. But the boy is in the way. Perhaps it won't matter, as I won't be troubled long. He'll go like all the rest of the Cotton family.'[6] Riley thought that Mary Ann was implying that the little boy was sickly and was surprised at her remark, as he thought Charles Cotton looked a 'fine healthy boy'.[7] Yet six days later, Charles Edward Cotton fell ill and died, allegedly from natural causes.

The rapid succession of deaths occurring in the Cottons' house and the subsequent demand for parish coffins had aroused suspicions with Thomas Riley. He was also troubled by the remark Mary Ann had made regarding Charles Cotton and expressed his concerns to Dr Kilburn, who, having seen the little boy only the day before and thought him healthy enough, refused to write a death certificate.

Consequently, Mary Ann was unable to collect the £4 10s. insurance money from the Prudential.

The next day, a post-mortem examination was carried out on a table in Mary Ann's house at Font Street. After a hasty examination, the doctor arrived at the inquest held an hour later at the Rose and Crown public house next door, a little uncertain of the cause of death. He suggested that it might have been gastroenteritis, so after an hour's deliberation, the jury returned a verdict of death by natural causes. Thereupon, a death certificate was issued to Mary Ann, and she was free to collect the insurance money. Even though she had received considerable sums of insurance money and a regular supply of coal from the colliery, who also allowed her to live rent free for some time, Mary Ann always maintained she was penniless (yet she would sometimes pay someone to clean her house), so Charles Cotton, along with the other members of the family, was buried in a pauper's grave at the expense of the parish.

Dr Kilburn, who had not been completely satisfied with the hastily conducted post-mortem, had kept the fluid contents of Charles Cotton's stomach in a jar for further analysis. A few days after the inquest, he decided to test it for arsenic poisoning, using the Reinsch test, a procedure discovered thirty years previously by a German Chemist called Hugo Reinsch, to detect the presence of various metals including arsenic in blood, urine, or stomach contents. Copper wire or foil was placed with the sample in a nitric acid solution, then heated with hydrochloric acid. Once the solution had cooled, if the copper darkened, deposits of arsenic were present. Samples were sent to Dr Thomas Scattergood, a lecturer in forensic medicine and toxicology at Leeds School of Medicine, who confirmed that arsenic was indeed present and most definitely the cause of death.

The following day, Mary Ann was arrested and charged with the murder of Charles Edward Cotton and taken to Durham Gaol to await her trial. In the meantime, the Home Office had granted permission to exhume the remains of the little boy, where during his analysis Dr Scattergood found a considerable amount of arsenic in his stomach, bowels, liver, lungs, heart, kidneys, and faeces.

In addition to being used to control vermin, arsenic was widely used in many Victorian homes as a cleaning product, where it was added to soft soap and rubbed into the bedstead to kill bedbugs and lice. It was also found in medicine, cosmetics, and wallpaper, giving it the green hue that was so popular at the time and was inexpensive and readily available in a variety of shops, including chemists and grocery stores.

Odourless and tasteless, depending on the amount given, the deadly effects of arsenic could be relatively quick or if given over a period of time in small quantities, the result would be a gradual deterioration in health, eventually resulting in death. The symptoms of severe stomach cramps, vomiting, and diarrhoea, associated with arsenic poisoning, mimicked those of other common illnesses of that period, such as cholera and gastric fever, which would have enabled Mary Ann to poison her victims without arousing suspicion. However, deaths caused by inhaling arsenic particles that had flaked or brushed off the wallpaper in people's homes were also common during the nineteenth century.

After the first magistrates' hearing, held in August 1872, an investigation was carried out into the other deaths that had occurred in Mary Ann's house and the bodies of Joseph Nattrass, Frederick Cotton Jr., and Robert Robson Cotton were exhumed. After examining the viscera, Dr Scattergood confirmed that they all contained a large amount of white arsenic, which he had no doubt was the cause of death. Frederick Cotton's remains, however, could not be found as the graves were 'as thick and close as furrows in a lea field'.

As Mary Ann was heavily pregnant, her trial was postponed until the following Spring Assizes in Durham, but on 21 February 1873, she was brought by train from Durham Gaol to Bishop Auckland, to appear before the magistrates a second time on three additional charges of the wilful murder of Joseph Nattrass, Frederick Cotton

Jr., and Robert Robson Cotton. Despite the enormity of the charges made against her, the crowd waiting at the station for her arrival were surprisingly calm when Mary Ann appeared accompanied by the gaoler and the matron. According to *The Northern Echo*, 'She was very pale, and appeared weak, and was obliged to take hold of the matron's arm for assistance' as she boarded the bus that took them to the magistrates' court.

But by the time the party reached the magistrates' court, Mary Ann had regained her composure and appeared much calmer as she sat nursing her baby daughter, Margaret Edith Quick-Manning Cotton, who had been born in Durham Gaol in January. Throughout the hearing, the baby remained quiet and content, while she was dutifully breastfed by her mother. Mary Ann's solicitor, George Smith, who seemed more intent on spending her money than offering any legal representation, failed to appear at any of the court proceedings. One sympathetic reporter wrote, 'Everyone must regret that she is undefended. She sat alone and friendless ... without anyone to cross-examine the witnesses, or to say a single word on her behalf.' In a letter to a neighbour, Mary Ann wrote of her frustrations at George Smith's incompetence and his advice to her to remain silent in court. 'Smith has led me rong. He told me not to speake a single word if I was asked.'

Among the witnesses called to give evidence were several neighbours including Phoebe Robson, a frequent visitor to Mary Ann's home, who told the court she had noticed that Mary Ann had tended to Joseph Nattrass 'particularly closely' during his illness, not allowing anyone else to intervene. 'I many a time said to [her] that [he] would be better if he had some support.' She described how Mary Ann held him down on the bed while he 'scringed his hands, grinded his teeth, turned up the whites of his eyes, drew his legs up and stiffened his body' during one of the several 'fits' that became more frequent towards his death.[8]

Sarah Smith, who lived six doors down from Mary Ann, had noticed that Frederick Cotton Jr. was laid out in a coffin in the same room, and asked Mary Ann when she intended to bury him, to which she replied that she did not think Joseph Nattrass would live long, so she would wait and have them buried together. His clothes were ready but her main concern was if the linen would be washed in time to lay out his body.

Jane Headley, who lived further down the street, said that Mary Ann used soft soap and arsenic to clean her house, which she kept in a pot on the top shelf of her pantry. She saw her use 'about a knife pointful' to put on the walls to kill the bugs. Another neighbour, Mary Ann Dodds, confirmed that when she helped Mary Ann clean her house, they had rubbed the mixture into the bedsteads to kill the bugs.

Next to give evidence was Dr Kilburn's assistant, Archibald Charlesworth, who had visited Frederick Cotton Jr. during the last week of his life. He found him to be 'sick, purged and complaining of a pain over the stomach and bowels', and had prescribed him medicine for gastric fever. 'If it had been gastric fever the medicines prescribed should have relieved it, but they had no effect whatsoever,' he told the court.

James Young, the agent for the Prudential Insurance Society, and last witness called for the prosecution, confirmed that all members of the Cotton family were insured including Charles Edward Cotton and Robert Robson, and a sum of money had been paid to Mary Ann shortly after their deaths.

Mary Ann's trial for the murder of Charles Edward Cotton began on 5 March and ended on Friday 7 March 1873. As public interest in the trial had greatly increased, mostly amongst women, tickets were issued for entry into the courthouse. Recently knighted Sir Thomas Dickson Archibald, a Canadian-born judge, presided over the court proceedings and Charles Russell was appointed to lead the prosecution.

At just before ten o'clock, Mary Ann was brought in by two female warders and placed in the dock. She looked 'care-worn, depressed and pale' and appeared to have aged since her first appearance in court in Bishop Auckland. Her lips quivered as Charles Russell summed up the case for the prosecution. He told the court how Mary Ann had complained that Charles Cotton was an extra expense and had prevented her from working and that he was 'a tie she would willingly get rid of and a tie of which she had already tried to rid herself and failed'. He also pointed out that Mary Ann had insured Charles with the Prudential Assurance company for the sum of £4 10s.

Russell argued that as the poison had been found in various organs, it must have been administered over a period of several days, therefore it could not have been given accidentally. Referring to the other three deaths, he asked the court if they believed that there were four accidental poisonings. 'The evidence had shown that she alone had the means, the motive, and the opportunity, and they were irresistibly driven to the conclusion that all the circumstances of the case were consistent with and pointed to the guilt of the prisoner.'

Thomas Campbell Foster, who had been assigned by the judge for the defence, argued that the prosecution had failed to make a case against the prisoner and by including the deaths of Frederick Cotton, Robert Robson Cotton, and Joseph Nattrass, had only shown the weakness of the case. 'The deaths by poison were accountable in several ways – by poison falling from the green paper on the walls, or arsenic falling from the mixture put on the bedstead to kill vermin and being taken up by the child in play or when taking its food,' he said.

But despite the circumstantial evidence, after an hour, the jury found Mary Ann guilty of the murder of Charles Edward Cotton. She stood trembling violently as the judge passed the sentence of death, before she collapsed back down on the seat, and had to be carried from the dock.

The press had a field day, calling Mary Ann 'a monster in human shape', who had 'killed for gain with fiendish relish'. Some reports said that during his illness, Joseph Nattrass had suspected 'all was not right', and had remarked to one visitor at his bedside, 'If I was only better, I will be out of this.' He had told another that he had 'no more fever than the doctor had', and 'refused to take any more of the medicine prescribed to him shortly before his death'.

Mary Ann continued to protest her innocence right to the end of her life, declaring, 'I never gave that boy, Charles Edward Cotton any poison wilfully. It was the arrowroot, and we all got it. I am going to die for a crime I am not guilty of.' She wrote numerous letters to various people asking for a petition to be set up to save her life and a plea of clemency to the Home Secretary, but all were rejected. She even wrote a letter to James Robinson:

> Will you be as good as to go to the bank (meaning the Wear), on the other side of the bridge, and try what you can do by getting up a petition for getting my life saved. I should like to see the three children; bring them with you and see me along with my aunt. I would like to be tried on the other three charges, for you know that I am innocent of the lies that have been told about me. You have been the cause of all my trouble, that when I left you and came back, I could not get back, but had to wander about the streets with my baby.[9]

James Robinson refused to see Mary Ann, but those who did visit her in Durham Gaol, expecting to find her in a dismal cell, found her in the women's warders' retiring room where 'everything was as clean as a new pin' and where she seemed to 'have every comfort this earth could afford'. Well lit, with a south facing window and a fire 'blazing brightly' in the grate, it had 'pretty paper' on the walls, books to read, three chairs, one table, a bed, and a cradle for her baby. She 'had been sleeping lightly but her appetite was good … At times she is taciturn, and scarcely deigns to look or even speak to those about her, while at others she converses freely,' reported one journalist.

Around fifty applications were made to adopt Mary Ann's baby, including many 'in a good position in society'. But, to many people's surprise, including the press, Mary Ann's former neighbours from Johnson Terrace, William and Sarah Edwards, a childless couple 'in humble circumstances', came to collect little Margaret Edith Quick-Manning five days before the execution. The wardens who had watched Mary Ann nurse and bounce the baby on her knee were tearful as she clung desperately to her child when she was taken from her.

On the morning of the execution, Rev. J. M. Mountford, hoping for a confession, visited Mary Ann. She admitted administering poison to all the deceased victims, but still insisted that she had not done so intentionally, claiming that the arsenic had been mixed with the arrowroot she had bought from a grocer in West Auckland for Charles Cotton when he was ill. At 7.55 am, William Calcraft, the public executioner, and his assistant, Robert Evans, entered Mary Ann's cell, quickly grabbed her and held her arms to her sides while a broad leather belt was strapped around her arms and chest, then she was led from her cell to the execution gallows in the prison yard. Sobbing and shaking uncontrollably, she was placed on the trap door on the platform, where Calcraft swiftly strapped her ankles together, pulled a white cap over her head, drew the noose around her neck, and pulled the handle.

A man in his early seventies, Calcraft was notorious for his cruel, incompetent, and botched hangings. He would often displace the noose around the prisoner's neck and favoured the 'short-drop' method of execution, where the prisoner only fell three feet, enduring a more lingering, painful death by strangulation, rather than instantly breaking their neck. He was often forced to pull the victim's legs or climb onto their shoulders to speed up the process. Several decades earlier, Charles Dickens, after having witnessed William Calcraft's maladroit executions, had written a letter to *The Times*, imploring that Calcraft be 'restrained in his unseemly briskness, vulgar humour, lurid language and brandy!'

It took an agonising three minutes for Mary Ann to die; her chest heaved as she swayed, writhing and twitching in pain. Calcraft grabbed her shoulders to steady her, but when he let go, she continued to sway from side to side. The sight was so distressing that the Under Sheriff, Richard Bowser, almost fainted and had to be supported by two wardens. According to witnesses, Mary Ann was 'strangled like a rabid dog, with no dignity even in death'. The *Newcastle Daily Chronicle* said that she was 'terribly slow to yield the last sign of life' and that there was 'an age of horror between the first convulsive spasm of the whole body and the last final shudder of the pinioned arms'.

An hour later, her body was taken down and lowered on to the wooden planks of the gallows. The blood-stained white cap was removed, revealing her bloated and contorted face. Her mouth was open, her lips were swollen, and one eye was slightly protruding from its socket. She was then laid in a black painted coffin and placed in the prison chapel, where afterwards the jurors questioned the whereabouts of the rope used for her execution, insisting that it should be buried in the coffin with her and not be exhibited for money. But Calcraft had already taken it back with him to London, where it was later sold. A cast was taken of Mary Ann's head for further scientific research by the West Hartlepool Phrenological Society, where a report from an amateur phrenologist read; 'Veneration small; no love for children; destructiveness very large: secretiveness very large; calculation good; language deficient.'[10]

Shortly after Mary Ann's death, a 'great moral drama – The Life and Death of Mary Ann Cotton' was staged at the New Gaiety Theatres of Varieties in West Hartlepool and a few local penny-shows followed. Her notoriety continues in the children's skipping rhyme that is still chanted in County Durham today:

Mary Ann Cotton
She's dead and she's rotten
She lies in her bed
With her eyes wide open.

Sing, sing, what can I sing?
Mary Ann Cotton is tied up with string.
Where, where?
Up in the air,
Selling black puddings, a penny a pair.

Mary Ann's daughter, Margaret Quick-Manning, went on to live a long but sad life. In 1890, she married a pitman, Joseph Fletcher, and two years later gave birth to their daughter, Clara. Within the year, they emigrated to the United States, where their son William was born. But sadly, during her pregnancy with their third child, her husband was knocked down by a wagon and tragically killed. Margaret returned home to County Durham and lived with her adoptive parents in their pub, the Garden House Hotel in Low Spennymoor, where her second son John Joseph Fletcher was born in 1895.

A few years later, the family moved to Ferryhill, where they ran the Greyhound Inn. Margaret met and married Robinson Kell, a miner at the Dean and Chapter Colliery and in 1902 their son, Robinson Kell, was born. Margaret had been suffering from cataracts in both eyes and by now was completely blind. Both William and John Joseph fought in the First World War, but sadly neither returned home. Margaret died in County Durham in 1954, at the grand age of 81.

# Chapter 4

# The Bender Slaughter Pen
## Kate Bender, Kansas, 1873

On 9 March 1873, Dr William York left his brother's house at Fort Scott, Kansas, and started the long journey on horseback along the lonely Osage Trail to his home in Independence. He had intended to go straight home, but after an overnight stay at Osage Mission, he told some friends he had met along the road the next day that he would stop at the Benders Inn for some lunch and feed his horse. At around noon that day, a member of the Bender household opened the door to the well-dressed doctor, who wore an expensive watch, carried a large amount of money, and wanted feed for his very fine and valuable horse. Neither the doctor nor his horse were ever seen again. He would join the long succession of missing persons in that area and become the Bloody Benders' final murder victim.

Just over a decade earlier, during the American Civil War, on 20 May 1862, President Abraham Lincoln signed the first Homestead Act. The Act encouraged western migration and allowed any US citizen over the age of 21, including immigrants, women, and freed slaves, to live on and improve an area of unoccupied public land up to 160 acres. After five years, for a small registration fee, they could claim the ownership of the land. John Bender, a German immigrant, had joined the many people who had headed west, taking advantage of the opportunity presented by the Act and had arrived with his family in the north-west part of Labette County, Kansas, in October 1870. He claimed 160 acres of land close to the Osage Trail, the only main road that ran across the prairie heading west at the time.

Little is known about the background of the Benders. They were believed to have been a married couple with a son and daughter, but there was much speculation as to whether they were related at all. John Bender Sr., the head of the family, was a bearded, stocky man in his early sixties who spoke very little English. When he did speak, his brusque manner, combined with his strong German accent, often made him incoherent. His alleged wife, Mrs (Kate) Bender, was an aloof, sturdy woman about 50 years old, who rarely engaged in conversation with anyone outside the household. She spoke in German, as her English seemed to be very limited, but later it became evident that she could in fact speak English very fluently. In contrast, young John Bender Jr., who was in his mid to late twenties, was more sociable and talkative and spoke fluent English, but with a strong German accent.

Kate Bender Jr., allegedly the daughter, also spoke fluent English with very little trace of a German accent. She and young John Bender were rumoured to have been Mrs Bender's children from a previous marriage and some people suspected they were involved in an incestuous relationship. Thought to be in her early twenties, Kate was outgoing and friendly, and often flirted with her many male companions who admired her stunning looks, her tall slender figure, dark rich auburn hair, and fair complexion. But Kate was strong-willed, ruthlessly ambitious and determined to gain wealth and status by whatever means she could, however extreme.

Although she was the youngest of the family, according to defence attorney, John T. James, Kate was the most dominant and malevolent. He later wrote: 'Her will was indomitable and all of the family feared her, dreaded her, obeyed her, and did the "devilish" work that she required of each of them. She was the ruler of the household and directed the notions of each one, whether that was for good or for evil – most usually for evil.'[1]

The two men of the household built a small cabin on their land, measuring about 16 x 24 ft, which consisted of two rooms divided by a long heavy canvas curtain, which hung loosely to the floor. The smaller front room was used mainly as the living, dining, and cooking area, whilst the rear room was their bedroom. There was also a circular cellar of about six feet in diameter and six feet in depth, which was accessed from the inside of the house through a trap door on the floor of the rear room near the curtain. A narrow passage, just wide enough for a man's frame to fit through, connected the cellar to the outside at the rear of the cabin, into a garden area where there was a small orchard and a stable.

The cabin faced the Osage Trail, which was frequently used by travellers between Fort Scott and Independence, Kansas. Although isolated, the Benders saw the opportunity in the passing trade and opened a small grocery store in the front room of the cabin, where they kept a stock of canned and preserved foods, coffee, and tobacco. The rear room, which consisted of a stove, table, and two benches, provided weary travellers with a meal and accommodation for the night, where, along with the Benders, they slept on pallets on the floor. The remoteness of the cabin also gave the Benders the chance to prey on visitors that were unknown in the area, as they were less likely to be missed. Years later, one visitor to the Benders Inn told *The Topeka State Journal* that he was convinced that his life had only been spared when he informed the Benders that he had recently moved to the area.

The Benders soon settled into their new life in the country, appearing to be no different to any other new settlers on the prairie, displaying no unusual behaviour that would arouse any suspicions from their neighbours. Kate and John Jr. gave the impression that they were very pious, regularly attending church, and John would often be seen sitting outside the Benders' cabin all day reading a Bible.

However, neighbours later recalled that Kate in particular had been quite impertinent on more than one occasion and at times her behaviour had been somewhat odd. She believed in spiritualism and claimed to be a medium, who could locate missing persons and lost objects. Neighbours would attend her séances in the darkened front room of the cabin, where she would go into a trance and mumble nonsensically, as she contacted the spirits of departed loved ones.

Kate also maintained she was a healer and would concoct remedies of herbs and roots, which she and her mother would administer to the sick in the neighbourhood, claiming they had 'charms and spells'[2] that would cure ailments and diseases. In 1872, she distributed the following handbill advertising her services:

> Prof. Miss KATIE BENDER
> Can heal all sorts of Diseases; can cure Blindness, Fits,
> Deafness, and all such diseases, also Deaf and Dumbness.
> Residence, 14 miles East of Independence, on the road
> from Independence to Osage Mission, one and one-half
> miles South East of Norahead Station.

Though most visitors received a warm and welcome reception at the Benders Inn, a few sensed an uneasy atmosphere in the company of their hosts and accounts of strange and disturbing experiences soon circulated amongst the neighbourhood. But Kate's God-fearing facade quelled any mistrust towards the family so the stories were ignored, and people remained oblivious to the horrendous criminal acts being carried out behind the closed doors of the Benders Inn.

In May 1871, the dead body of a man named Jones was discovered in Drum Creek, a stream near to the Benders' cabin. It was clear he had received severe blows to his head, crushing his skull, and his throat had been cut from ear to ear. The owner of the Drum Creek claim was suspected of having committed the murder, but no action was taken. Then, in February 1872, a further two unidentified male bodies were found with the same fatal injuries. In the months that followed, people were disappearing at an alarming rate in the area and concerned relatives were increasingly reporting men who had vanished without a trace. Many of the men intending to settle in southeast Kansas carried large amounts of money to buy stock such as machinery, cattle, and horses, or to purchase a claim. As the area was so sparse and communication between communities were unreliable and intermittent, it was easy for travellers to go missing.

A significant number of people who vanished during 1872 had allegedly visited the Benders Inn whilst travelling along the Osage Trail. In autumn of that year, Johnny Boyle, a well-dressed man, carrying over $1,500 in cash, intended to stop at the Benders Inn for a few days while he looked for some land to buy. He never purchased any land and never returned to his home. Shortly after, a succession of people mysteriously disappeared. They were usually male and either carried a significant amount of money or had valuable horses with them.

Among those who went missing was George Loncher, who, following the recent death of his wife, travelled with his young daughter along the Osage Trail heading to Iowa, to visit his dead wife's family. They also failed to arrive at their destination. Soon, slanderous rumours directing suspicion towards the residents of the town spread from the surrounding neighbourhood, so travellers began to avoid the Osage Trail.

By April 1873, the townsfolk had had enough, and a meeting was held at the Harmony Grove school house, about two miles from the Benders Inn, to try to resolve the problem. John Bender Jr. shamelessly joined the seventy-five people or so who attended the meeting and any further meetings that were held to try and solve the previous mysterious disappearance of the eminent Dr York.

In the meantime, Dr York's brother, Colonel Alexander York, after hearing from his sister-in-law that his brother had not returned home, had organised a search party, where they retraced Dr York's final journey, painstakingly scouring the area for any hint of him or his horse's whereabouts. They stopped at of all the houses within several miles of the route, to make enquiries, but the search was fruitless. By this time, rumours of the disturbing events experienced by some of the visitors to the Benders' house were rife and, as it was the last place that Dr York was last seen alive, Colonel York, accompanied by twelve other men, decided to pay them a visit.

As they rode up to the cabin, Mrs Bender saw them and stood in the doorway saying in German that it was 'too bad a peaceable family must be disturbed by such a crowd of men'.[3] Kate, however, was less hostile than her mother and verified that Dr York had indeed dined there but had continued with his journey shortly afterwards. John Bender Jr. told them that one evening, whilst riding past an isolated spot near Drum Creek, he had been shot at by bandits and suggested that they could be responsible for the doctor's disappearance.

John Bender Sr. and John Jr. accompanied Colonel York and his men to Drum Creek to show them where the alleged attack on John Jr. had taken place. To convince them of his story, John Jr. showed them a tree peppered with bullet holes. The two men offered to help search for the doctor and, along with the rest of the party, spent the day dragging the creek, but nothing was found. Having heard about Kate's so-called psychic powers, the colonel returned to the cabin and, in desperation, offered Kate $500 if she could reveal his brother's whereabouts or locate his body. Kate agreed, but no sooner had she gone into a trance she claimed that 'the spirits refused to answer her, because there were several unbelievers present'.[4] She told Colonel York that if he returned alone in five days, she was certain she would have more information for him.

Fortunately, Colonel York did not follow up Kate's offer, but returned to the Benders Inn about a week later, accompanied by around thirty men, intending to investigate the matter further. They arrived to find several neighbours searching the cabin, including Silas Toles, who had been passing the Benders' house the previous morning, and heard the bawl of a hungry calf in its pen, while its mother, her full udders clearly causing her pain and distress, stood helplessly outside. Silas was concerned and at first thought that there must be an illness in the family, so he knocked on the front door to offer his help. When no one answered, he peered in the window and saw the room in disarray; the cabin looked like it had been abandoned. After reuniting the cow with its calf, he set off to alert the neighbours.

Silas returned the next day with two other men and forced open the front door. Once inside, the men found the cabin in chaos with clothes and other items strewn across the floor. The curtain separating the two rooms had been pulled down and was lying in a bundle on the floor. It was clear the Benders had fled in haste. Colonel York joined Silas and the rest of the men as they scrupulously searched every corner of the Benders' abandoned home and garden.

A strong foul stench wafted through the cabin, which the men discovered came from the cellar. Armed with a long sharp iron rod and lamps, Colonel York and one of the men opened the trap door and descended into the darkness. 'Here and there little damp places could be seen as if water had come up from the bottom or been poured down from above,' wrote a reporter from the *Weekly Kansas Chief.* 'They groped about over these splotches and held up a handful to the light. The ooze smeared itself over their palms and dribbled through their fingers. It was blood – thick, foetid, clammy, sticking blood – that they had found groping there in the void.' The men continued to poke and probe with their rods into the ground of the cellar, but it was empty, so they made their way through the narrow passage that led outside to the garden.

Outside, the men had been prodding the ground with their rods for over an hour when Colonel York suddenly cried, 'Boys, I see graves yonder in the orchard!'[5] He beckoned them over to where the surface of the ground had recently been ploughed and harrowed and pointed to several long depressions in the disturbed soil that resembled graves. After a frantic search around the yard for shovels, the men dug down to a depth of about five feet, where they discovered the body of a virtually naked man buried face down, with just a torn and discoloured shirt covering him. They gently lifted the dead man to the surface and laid him on his back, where they could see it was Dr York.

'Upon the back of his head and to the left and obliquely from his right ear, a terrible blow had been given with a hammer,' continued the reporter. 'The skull had been driven into the brain, and from the battered and broken crevices a dull stream of blood had oozed, plastering his hair with a kind of clammy paste, and running down upon his shoulders.' Colonel York, he said, was 'utterly overwhelmed' and 'could not be comforted'.

The men continued to probe and dig the soil in the orchard until by the evening a total of eleven bodies had been exhumed. Nine of them were men, one a young woman in her early twenties, and the other a little girl aged about 18 months old, found lying underneath the body of her father, George Loncher. 'Men wept aloud when the body of that little girl was by gentle hands tenderly lifted up from its grave,' wrote John T. James. 'From the horribly distorted appearance of the features, limbs and body of that little girl, many of those present insisted that it was clearly evident that she had been put into that hole while she was yet alive.' *The Weekly Kansas Chief* also concluded that the little girl had been 'thrown into her grave alive' as her 'body showed no marks of violence'.

Several bodies were in the last stages of decomposition, and except for the little girl, had been virtually stripped of their clothing and bludgeoned by a hammer or similar blunt implement, crushing their skull. Some were badly mutilated, and their throats had been cut from ear to ear. Apart from the young woman and one man, the victims who could be identified were Benjamin M. Brown, William F. McCrotty, Henry McKenzie, Johnny Boyle, George Loncher and his daughter, Dr William York, John Greary, and George Brown.

Afterwards it was ascertained that the Benders had acquired around $5,000 or more from their victims, along with their horses and wagons. Although it was evident that the purpose of the murders was mostly for financial gain, it was known that at least two of the men had carried very little money, one as little as 25 cents, so their murders had most likely been committed purely for sadistic satisfaction.

As the search expanded further afield, various body parts were discovered, but they did not belong to any of the victims that had been found. Other human remains and skeletons were unearthed on the Benders' land and nearby in Drum Creek, so it is highly probable that there were many other victims whose bodies were never found. According to one report, 'One corpse was so horribly mutilated as to make the sex even a matter of doubt.'

The body of a little girl, aged about eight years old, who was also found amongst the disinterred remains, was described as having 'long sunny hair, and some traces of beauty on a countenance that was not yet entirely disfigured by decay'. Her horrific injuries were detailed in the report: 'One arm was broken, and the breastbone had been driven in. The right knee had been wrenched from its socket and the leg doubled up under the body.'

Rudolph Brockman, who owned a claim adjoining the Benders' homestead, had joined the men, along with other neighbours, in their search that morning. Also German, he had been quite friendly with the Benders and had often visited their store and they had visited him in his home. One of the men in the search party insinuated that Brockman must know more about the crimes than he was letting on and may even have been an accomplice of the Benders, but Brockman fiercely denied any accusations.

Nevertheless, having sworn vengeance on anyone involved in the murders, several men seized Brockman, while another shouted, 'Get a rope!' A rope was found, and a noose was made on one end and put around Brockman's neck, while the other end was thrown over a beam. Two of the men pulled on the rope and hoisted the terrified man up into the air. He was held there while the men shouted, 'Confess! Confess!' But when they lowered him down to admit his guilt, he still denied any wrongdoing, so they raised him again and repeated the procedure several times until eventually he was 'more dead than alive', so he was released to 'stagger away in the darkness as one who was drunken or deranged'.

Following the swift and mysterious departure of the Benders, several people who had visited their inn came forward to describe their experience at what the press now dubbed 'The Bender Slaughter Pen'. One incident reported in *The Kansas Chief* described how a woman who had been travelling by foot along the main road to Independence stopped at the Benders Inn for some supper and a bed for the night. Exhausted, she welcomed Mrs Bender's offer to rest on the bed in the back room while her supper was being prepared.

> Almost immediately, the woman dozed off but was soon awakened by the touch of the old hag of the den, who pointing to an array of pistols and double-edged knives, of various sizes, lying on the table, said in the spirit of hellish malignity; 'There, your supper is ready.' Mrs. Bender then picked up the knives one by one, and drew her finger along the blades, whilst glancing menacingly at the terrified woman.

After a while, the guest somehow managed to contain her fear and appear outwardly calm, as she made an excuse to go outside. She went towards the darkened stable and, once she was hidden from view, ran in the direction of the nearest house, repeatedly looking behind to see if she was being pursued. But all she saw was the light from the open doorway, 'as though the devils inside were awaiting her return'.

There were also reports of a local woman who was suffering from ill health, heard of Kate Bender's so-called medicinal skills, and approached her hoping for a cure for her illness. Kate prescribed a remedy but said that she only required payment if it turned out to be beneficial to the woman. Nevertheless, the neighbour insisted that she leave her side-saddle as proof of her intention to pay Kate. Within a few days, however, having felt no improvement in her health, she returned to the Benders to retrieve her side-saddle.

Shortly after she arrived, the whole family gathered in the front room, closed the doors, and seated themselves around the table, where they proceeded to summon the presence of the spirits, followed by a 'series of incantations, something after the fashion of those supposed to have been indulged in by the breeders of witchcraft'. They each held a large butcher's knife, which they drew across their throats and used to display other 'significant motions ... with a uniformity that indicated that they had been thoroughly drilled in this spiritualistic manual of arms'.

During the performance, the woman, although petrified, concealed her fear and casually stepped outside, leaving her bonnet to give the impression that she would be returning. Once outside, she ran towards the fields, but hadn't gone far before she heard footsteps behind her, so she hid in the long grass until her pursuer had passed, then crawled on her hands and knees until she was far enough away to run to safety. When she told her neighbours of her terrifying experience, they just dismissed it as her overreacting to one of the Benders' séances.

On another occasion, a man named Corlew narrowly escaped his demise when, on route to Independence, he stopped at the Benders' store to buy a can of oysters for his lunch. He heard a moaning and what seemed like a struggle under the house. When he inquired what it was, Kate told him that a hog had got into the cellar. Corlew offered to help to get it out, but John Bender Sr. aggressively told him to mind his own business and 'move on'. Kate, however, invited Corlew to stay and eat his lunch at their table, but he declined her offer and left – a decision which undoubtedly saved his life.

Visitors who ate a meal or stayed at the Benders Inn and survived said that they were deliberately seated on a bench at the table with their back close to the curtain partition, while Kate entertained them with food, drink, and conversation. It was speculated that one of the male Benders would be standing behind the curtain holding a hammer, waiting for the right moment to strike a blow to the head of the unaware diner. The curtain was then silently slid by the assailant's foot towards the back of the person seated, until the outline of their body clearly showed through the light-coloured cloth, at which time the hammer was raised and a single blow was struck to the back of the victim's head, crushing their skull. The stunned victim was then dragged to the nearby trap door, which was swiftly lifted, to hang the victim's head over the edge to the cellar below. It was then thought that one of the women, allegedly Kate, would slit the victim's throat with a large knife; the body would then be pushed and dropped down into the cellar, along with any evidence of the crime, and the trap door hastily shut.

The whole execution was believed to be completed so quickly and systemically that the Benders were back in the front of the house, ready to welcome the next visitor in no time, as if nothing had happened. It was supposed that later in the evening, after dark, the body would be stripped of clothing, money, and any valuables, then dragged out through the narrow passage leading to the garden, where it was buried. The noises that Corlew had heard coming from the cellar were later thought to have been from the latest victim who had succumbed to the evil deeds of the Benders.

Kate Bender used her striking good looks and charm to lure any unsuspecting male callers into her home and into her evil clutches. One man who was fascinated by Kate and willingly accepted her invitation to spend an evening in her company was known as 'Happy Jack' Reed. He also agreed to stay the night but was one of the few who lived to tell the tale. He claimed that during the night he heard a wagon drive up to the house and John Bender Sr. lead the driver and horses to the stable. He heard what he thought sounded like a 'heavy blow followed by a scream. Then there was a rain of blows in rapid succession.' Kate Bender came over to Reed's bed and stood over him, but he pretended to be asleep, and she walked away. When Kate inquired the next morning if he had slept well, he told her that he had slept all night. Afterwards, he divulged his story to his friends, who disbelieved and mocked him for being cowardly, so he dropped the subject.

News of the brutal atrocities carried out by the Benders spread rapidly around the shocked community and beyond. Before long, thousands of people gathered at the burial site, including newspaper reporters from as far as New York and Chicago. On 22 May 1873, *The Wichita City Eagle* gave an account of the scene:

> On last Sunday there were about one thousand men, women, and children at the Benders grounds, gazing with mingled emotions of horror and curiosity. The graves even yet sent forth a sickening stench, and women held their noses as they peered down into the now tenantless holes. Two special trains were run, one from Independence, and one from Coffeyville, to a point on the railway line about two miles from the house and teams were busy running to and from the cars to the grounds, while the greater portion of the crowds were prepared to walk. These trains brought about 300 persons. There were about six or seven hundred persons there from all parts of the surrounding country, in wagons, carriages and on horseback.

According to the report, many of the visitors were mostly interested in collecting macabre mementoes from the Benders' homestead: 'The blood-stained bedstead was smashed to pieces and divided in the crowd, all the shrubbery and young trees were broken or torn up and carried away, and pieces of the house borne off by the curious.' The search for evidence continued until eventually very little remained of the Benders Inn; the wallboards and shingles had been stripped from the cabin and even stones were pulled out of the cellar wall. The house was removed from where it stood in order to search underneath it, but nothing more was found.

However, during the search, a man called Leroy F. Dick retrieved some evidence in the form of three hammers, a knife, a clock, and an old German Bible left behind by the Benders. A short note written on the family record page, translated by a German resident, read, 'big slaughter day, Jan, eighth (8)' and another, 'hell departed'. A Catholic prayer book was also found and had the following inscription, 'Johanna Bender, born July 30th, 1848. John Gerbardt came to America July 1st, 18_,' which revealed John Bender Jr.'s true identity. It also transpired later that John Bender Sr. was John Flickinger, and it was widely believed that Mrs Bender was really Almira Meik Griffith, and Kate Bender, whose real name was Eliza Griffith, was her daughter.

The wide coverage in the newspapers, telegrams circulated with descriptions of the Benders, Colonel York offering $1,000 and the State of Kansas offering a substantial reward of $2,000 all assured the townsfolk of a prompt recapture of the Benders, but, as time progressed, it began to look more and more unlikely. It was as if they had vanished into thin air. Initially, it was thought that they must have had accomplices living nearby, to help dispose of their victims' clothing and horses so efficiently, so several arrests were made in the neighbourhood, but due to insufficient evidence they were discharged.

Meanwhile, a posse of armed men who had set out in pursuit of the Benders had found their abandoned wagon with a starving team of horses near Thayer, twelve miles from the Benders Inn. At the train station, the ticket clerk confirmed that tickets had been sold to four people travelling to Humboldt, matching the Benders' descriptions. It was then thought that Kate and John Jr. had boarded a train travelling south from Humboldt, while the two elder Benders took another train to St Louis. But although detectives followed their trail and any further reported sightings of the Benders, their search was futile.

The newspapers reported numerous possible sightings of the Benders as the search extended overseas to Europe. On 17 July 1873, a small piece in the *Weekly Kansas Chief* read:

> An agent of the Special Detective Agency of New York is now in Paris in pursuit of the Bender family ... Detectives from the same agency have been sent to London and all the leading European cities ... She [Kate] was seen on a steamer which left New York for Havre, and it is supposed that the whole family are at present concealed in the French capital or the environs ... If they are really in France, now that the police are on their tracks, it will be impossible for them to escape detection.

Many suspects were detained all over the country and some were brought back to Kansas for identification, but they bore very little or no resemblance to the Benders. In October 1889, two known criminals, Mrs Almira Griffith and Mrs Sara Eliza Davis, believed to have been Mrs Bender and Kate Bender, were arrested in Michigan and brought to Oswego, Kansas, to stand trial for the murder of Dr York. Although numerous witnesses confirmed their identity, others disputed it, and as the evidence against them was very weak, they were acquitted.

Numerous stories of the Benders being captured by vigilantes and even of their deaths continued to circulate for many years after they had fled their home. There were reports that John Bender Sr. had committed suicide in Lake Michigan in 1884 and one account published five years later read:

> The posse overtaking the fugitives in the groves west of the Verdigris River, where a desperate fight took place, in which both the women were accidently killed ... It is safe to say that the Bender family 'ceased to breathe' soon

after their fight, and their carcasses rotted beneath the soil
of the state so scandalized by their crimes.

Many years later, the press published several accounts of so-called
close encounters with the Benders. One that gained much publicity
was that of Frank Ayers, a cattle rancher from Colorado, who in the
summer of 1901 claimed that he had been married to Kate Bender
for fourteen months when she had tried to poison him. He maintained
that 'the woman gave him "knock out drops" in hopes of killing him
and to avoid suspicion he was carried in an unconscious condition
to a nearby railroad track and left on the rails to be killed by passing
trains.' Luckily, he was found by some friends who rescued him.

Frank's suspicions regarding his wife were further fuelled when
a travelling family, passing through the area where he lived, claimed
to have known the Benders and supposedly recognised his wife as
Kate Bender. Subsequently, Frank Ayers was said to have been so
scared of his wife that he insisted on carrying his rifle whenever she
was around him. The situation reached a climax when he donned
women's clothes, so his wife wouldn't recognise him and 'track him
down', and headed to Kansas City, where he conveyed his story to the
authorities. Mrs Ayers strongly denied the accusations and, following
an investigation by the officers which proved to be fruitless, the
charges were dropped, along with Frank Ayers' claim to the reward.

On 5 May 1910, the *Topeka State Journal* published an article
informing the public that Kate Bender, otherwise known as Mrs Gavin,
then later Mrs Peters, had been found dead in her home in Rio Vista,
California. Jack Collins, a local resident and friend of Kate Bender,
told the newspaper that she had 'died a week or ten days before from
natural causes. She had been conducting a resort for several years and
lately had been living alone.'

Apparently, she had 'revealed her identity to him a number of
years ago, while critically ill and believing that she was at the point
of death'. Collins claimed that 'the woman gave him a detailed

account of many murders which she and her brothers committed in the Bender home at Cherryvale, Kansas in the seventies'. Evidently, he was threatened by Kate not to say anything until after her death. As no one else identified the deceased as actually being Kate Bender, Jack Collins's account was largely overlooked.

Despite the countless stories and assumptions regarding the Benders, it has never been fully proven what really happened to them and to this day their fate remains a mystery. However, the intrigue surrounding them continued way into the twentieth century. In 1961, the Bender Museum in Cherryvale, Kansas, was built in the form of an exact replica of the Benders' cabin, attracting more than 2,000 visitors within three days of opening its doors. A few years later, in 1967, the son of LeRoy Dick donated the hammers that his father had found during the search of the Benders' cabin back in 1873.

The museum continued to be a popular tourist attraction until it closed in 1978, when the site was acquired for a fire station. There was much controversy surrounding the relocation of the building, as although many people were in favour, the locals objected to Cherryvale being known for the Bender murders. Eventually, the hammers were placed in the Cherryvale Museum, where they are still displayed today. A knife bearing reddish-brown stains allegedly found by Colonel York, seemingly hidden in a mantel clock in the Benders' cabin, was donated by his wife and has been in the state's possession since 1923. It is now housed in the Kansas Museum of History, where it can be seen upon request.

# Chapter 5

# An Inhuman Monster
## Kate Webster, Surrey, 1879

Just before 11.00 in the morning of Wednesday, 5 March 1879, Henry
Wheatley, a coal porter, and his companion, Mr Kennison, were
driving a cart along the banks of the River Thames, when they spotted
a wooden box bobbing up and down, half-submerged in the shallow
water below Barnes Bridge. Wheatley got down from his cart and
dragged the box onto the bank. Curious to see what was inside, he cut
the cord that was tied around it with his knife, then kicked the side of
the box, where it collapsed into pieces, revealing, much to his horror,
'a mass of flesh'. At first, Wheatley thought it was cooked animal
meat, but after a second glance, he realised that it was something
much more sinister and rushed to the police station, leaving Kennison
to mind the box.

Presently, he returned to the riverbank with Sergeant Thomas
Childs. The sergeant immediately called for Dr James Adams, a local
doctor, who confirmed that they were portions of a human body. The
box and its gruesome contents were then taken to the mortuary at
Barnes, where, after an examination, Dr Adams believed the body
parts belonged to a young woman, about 5ft 3 or 4 ins tall, probably
between 18 and 30 years old. The police immediately started an
investigation into the disappearance of a young girl, possibly a
German girl who had left her position a week earlier with a similar
box to that found by Wheatley.

The grisly murder was dubbed the 'Barnes Mystery' by the
newspapers, who speculated that the body in the box had been a
'ghastly hoax' perpetrated by some medical students, but as it soon

became apparent that the mutilation of the body had been conducted by an amateur with no anatomical skills, this theory was soon dismissed. It was also suggested that the story was a hoax instigated by a journalist intending to make a profit.

Less than two months earlier, Kate Webster, a tall, strongly built woman, started employment as a live-in domestic servant for 54-year-old former schoolteacher, Julia Martha Thomas, at 2 Vine Cottages, Park Road, Richmond, Surrey. Mrs Thomas had been widowed twice, her second husband having died in 1873, and had no children. She lived alone in the grey stone semi-detached two-storey villa, which she rented from her landlady, Elizabeth Ives, who lived in the adjoining house, 1 Vine Cottages, with her mother, Mrs Jane Ives.

Mrs Thomas was a 'small, well-dressed lady',[1] whose late husband, having worked for many years at Eyre and Spottiswoode's printers in London, had left her in 'comfortable circumstances'. Regarded by her neighbours as a woman of 'decidedly eccentric habits', Mrs Thomas frequently moved from one residence to another, without informing her friends and relatives, who often for months at a time would have no idea of her whereabouts. She was also known to have an 'excitable temperament', and often became agitated for no apparent reason.

Mrs Thomas liked to give the impression that she was a 'lady of means' and often claimed to be better off than she actually was, dressing in smart, expensive clothes and jewellery and employing a domestic servant. However, as she had a reputation for being difficult, she had trouble finding and keeping servants and there was only ever one maid who stayed with her for any length of time. Prior to moving into 2 Vine Cottages, Mrs Thomas had placed the following advertisement in the local newspaper:

A lady wishes to meet with an elderly or widow lady to join in taking a house at once in Richmond. Companionship desired. Willing to let rooms not required. Could furnish in part. References exchanged. – J. Thomas

74

But there was little response and Mrs Thomas's request for a companion was unsuccessful.

A few months later, she mentioned to her friend, Lucy Loder, who lived nearby, that she would like a servant. Lucy said that she knew of a woman called Kate Webster, who had been lodging with her little boy at her friend Sarah Crease's house and had also done the odd day 'charring' for her. She did admit, though, that she only knew the woman by sight and knew nothing about her background. Despite having no recommendation of her character, it seems that on this occasion Mrs Thomas was willing to forgo any references and took Kate into her home regardless. If she had delved a little more into her employee's background, she would have discovered more about Kate's unscrupulous past, as by the time she had arrived to start work at 2 Vine Cottages, she was already well known to the police, with a string of convictions for theft and fraud behind her, dating as far back as her teenage years.

Little is known about Kate's early life, but according to her own statement, she was born Catherine Lawler in Killane, near Enniscorthy, Co. Wexford, Ireland, around 1849, and was brought up a Roman Catholic. She claimed that while she was in her teens, she married a sea-captain called Webster with whom she had four children. All her children died in infancy, followed soon after by her husband. She said it was then that she turned to crime, to make ends meet. But, as Kate later proved to be a persistent liar, it is debatable how much or if any of the story is true.

In 1864, following a conviction for larceny, Kate was imprisoned for a short term and, on her release, she left Ireland and travelled to Liverpool, where she continued her life of crime, robbing various lodging houses. A few years later, after being convicted again for larceny, Kate found herself serving four years' penal servitude. She served her sentence, then made her way to London, where she claimed she fully intended to make an honest living, taking several positions as a domestic servant. However, it was while she was working as a cook and housemaid at a house in Norland Crescent, Notting Hill, that she met a man named Strong, allegedly the father of her child, and whom she later blamed for her subsequent downfall. 'I was induced by him to go to live with him at his house, and he seduced me while there, and I became in the family way of my little boy...'

Kate lived with Strong in Acre Road, Kingston, until he deserted her shortly after her son's birth, leaving her to pay the rent and fend for herself and her child. 'I became very impoverished, forsaken by him, and committed crimes for the purpose of supporting myself and child,' she said, 'I could not get a place to leave the child and was open to all kinds of temptations.' Subsequently, at the Surrey Sessions on 4 May 1875, Kate was convicted of thirty-six charges of larceny, all committed in and around the Kingston area, and sentenced to eighteen months' imprisonment at Wandsworth Prison.

As she became more known to the police, Kate frequently changed her address and adopted the surnames Webb, Webster, Gibbs, Gibbons, and her maiden name, Lawler. Nonetheless, they soon caught up with her, and on 6 February 1877, she was again convicted for larceny and imprisoned for twelve months. Despite her felonious lifestyle, Kate was devoted to her little boy and always made sure that in her absence he was well cared for, often leaving him with Sarah Crease, who presumed that her absent friend was in service.

On 29 January 1879, leaving her little boy in the safe hands of Mrs Crease, Kate moved into 2 Vine Cottages to start work as Mrs Thomas's live-in domestic servant. But she had only been employed for a few weeks when she was given notice to leave. Mrs Thomas was fanatical about cleanliness and would often criticise Kate's work; she became increasingly irritated and resentful towards her employer, which led to frequent, heated arguments. Soon the situation became so difficult that Mrs Thomas, who had become nervous and fearful of her servant, persuaded another woman and her daughter to lodge with her temporarily, so as not to be alone with her. Having other company in the house may have reassured Mrs Thomas, as she summoned the courage to give Kate her notice; the last entry in her diary read: 'Gave Katherine warning to leave.' It was agreed that she would go on 28 February, but when that day arrived, Kate asked Mrs Thomas if she could stay on for a few more days and whether through fear or kind-heartedness or both, as by now her two lodgers had left, Mrs Thomas relented.

On Sunday, 2 March, after having spent her afternoon off drinking in the public house, Kate returned home that evening, as she later admitted, having 'had quite enough'.[2] Mrs Thomas, who was a deeply religious woman, had been waiting for Kate to return home, before she left to attend the evening service held at the new Richmond Presbyterian Church on Richmond Green. A fierce argument ensued and, according to Kate, Mrs Thomas 'became very agitated and left the house to go to church in that state'.

The service had already started when Mrs Thomas arrived at the church. According to one witness, Julia Nicholls, who spoke to her in the lobby, she appeared to be in 'a state of great excitement' and 'seemed vexed at something'. Her voice was shaking, her face was flushed, and her bonnet had slipped off her head. She told her that the cause of her delay was 'the neglect of her servant to return home at the proper time' and added that 'when reproved for her fault Kate flew into a terrible passion'. Instead of taking her usual seat near the pulpit, Mrs Thomas sat in a seat behind the door and left the service about ten minutes early, which was unusual for her.

Shortly after Mrs Thomas returned home that evening, at around 9.00, her neighbour Mrs Jane Ives heard a noise next door that sounded like a heavy chair falling to the floor. At just before 6.00 the following morning, Miss Elizabeth Ives, who had gone outside to turn on the water tap, noticed a light on in one of the back bedrooms of Mrs Thomas's house. An hour later, she heard the poking of the copper fire and the sound of brushing coming from the scullery. As they were familiar sounds associated with the process of washing, which often began in many households early on a Monday morning, she thought no more of it. At around 11.00 am, she noticed several items of clothing and linen hanging on the washing line in Mrs Thomas's back garden, where they remained until Wednesday. All that morning, both Mrs Jane Ives and her daughter Elizabeth noticed a strange and unpleasant smell, which they initially thought was a gas leak in their house, but after checking they found that it was coming from next door.

Kate continued to be busy with her usual duties throughout the day. Several people called at the house, including William Thomas Deane, a coal merchant, who came regarding a settlement on Mrs Thomas's account. According to Deane, Kate answered the door but only opened it slightly. When he enquired after her mistress, she was very abrupt, telling him that she was not at home and did not know when she would return, before slamming the door shut.

At around 6.00 that evening, Emma Roberts, a friend of Mrs Thomas, also called at the house. No one answered when she knocked at the door; the house was very quiet and there was no sign of Mrs Thomas, though she noticed a light in the hall, the basement, and the drawing room.

The following morning, on Tuesday 4 March, Elizabeth Ives sent her young apprentice, Mary Roberts, next door to inform Mrs Thomas that she would be sending some workmen round to fix the roof. Kate opened the bedroom window above the front door and explained that there was no need as it was only snow that had caused the leak, which had now disappeared, and the roof was dry. Kate, who had her sleeves rolled up, informed Mary that she was cleaning the house as she was expecting visitors that evening.

Later that day, dressed in Mrs Thomas's black silk dress and wearing her gold watch and chain, plus several of her gold rings, Kate went to visit her old friends, Henry Porter and his wife Ann, in Hammersmith, West London. Kate had lived next door to the Porters, but apart from an occasional visit, had not seen them since she had left the area six years before. When she knocked on the door at 10 Brentwood Cottages, Rose Gardens, late that afternoon, Ann Porter failed to recognise the smartly dressed woman, wearing expensive gold jewellery, standing on her doorstep. It was not until Kate said cheerfully, 'How are you, Mother?' that Mrs Porter realised who she was. 'Kate, how are you? I…' Mrs Porter started to say as Kate swept past her and went into the back living room. She sat down, carefully placing the large black cloth bag she was carrying underneath the table and pulled a small bottle of whisky out of her pocket, offering some to Mrs Porter. As they drank, the two women chatted and caught up with each other's news.

A few hours later, when there was very little whisky left, Kate sent the young girl who was living with the Porters out to get half a pint of gin. At around 6.00 pm, Henry Porter came in from work and joined them. Kate seemed pleased to see him, but like his wife before, Henry did not recognise her either until she spoke to him. 'Father, how are you getting on?' she said. 'I have been longing to see you.' Henry thought it odd that Kate would call him 'Father' as she generally liked to call him 'Harry'.

By now, Ann Porter was feeling a little worse for wear and left her husband with their guest while she went upstairs to lie on the bed. Curious to know how his old neighbour had come to do so well for herself, Henry pulled up a chair and joined Kate with a glass of gin. Kate told him that she had been married and had a little boy called Johnny, and that her name was now Mrs Thomas, but sadly her husband had since died, and she was now a widow. But she had been fortunate, as her aunt had recently died and left her a nice, comfortable home in Richmond, along with all her belongings.

At around 7.30 pm, as Kate got up to leave, she asked Henry if he would carry her bag and accompany her to the railway station. Henry was only too happy to oblige and they set off towards the station, joined by Henry's 15-year-old son, Robert, who picked up the bag from under the table. As he lifted the bag, both he and his father noticed that there was what appeared to be a package wrapped in brown paper inside.

As they walked along the road, Kate chatted to Henry about her home in Richmond. She told him that she needed to sell the house as she had been unlucky retaining her lodgers and she feared that her father, who had become very frail, was on his 'last legs', so she needed to go back home to Ireland to care for him. She asked Henry if he could find her a respectable broker to dispose of her home. Henry wondered why she would not find a local broker in Richmond as it would be more convenient, but Kate said that she would rather he dealt with it, as she was not acquainted with anyone there.

Meanwhile, Robert was lagging quite far behind them. Henry thought he was looking in the shop windows, but when they stopped outside the Angel public house and waited for him to catch up, he said that the bag was too heavy and asked his father to carry it, which he did. Henry later estimated that the bag, which was 'about 18 or 20 inches long, and nearly 12 inches in depth' must have weighed about 20 or 25 lb. Little did he know that the reason the bag was so heavy was that it contained some recently dismembered body parts and the decapitated head of Mrs Julia Martha Thomas.

Henry Porter's 22-year-old son William, who worked in a baker's shop near the Angel pub, was standing outside and after chatting with him for about ten minutes, Kate, Henry, and Robert joined him inside for a glass of ale. After they left the Angel, Kate said she wanted to go and see a friend who lived in Barnes, on the other side of the river, so the three of them walked along Hammersmith Bridge Road, where on the way, they called in at the Oxford and Cambridge public house, close to Hammersmith Bridge. When she finished her glass of ale, Kate got up from her seat and, as she reached for the bag, said, 'I want to get over to see my friend at Barnes. I don't want to make it too late before I get home. I want to get back to Richmond.' Henry offered to go with her to carry her bag, but she declined, telling him to wait for her as she would not be long. Robert followed Kate outside and watched her disappear into the darkness towards the bridge.

Twenty minutes later, Kate returned without the bag, but neither Henry nor Robert paid any attention to the fact that it was missing. 'I have seen my friend,' she said to Henry, 'but I would not stay long, as I would not keep you waiting.' While they drank another pint of ale, Kate brought out a small case from her pocket which contained five gold rings in wadding and showed them to Henry. She said that they had belonged to her sister who had recently died and had been sent over to her from Ireland as a keepsake, then she produced a photograph of her deceased sister and another of a man with a long beard, whom she said was her father.

After they had finished their drinks, the three of them walked to the railway station in Hammersmith. On the way, when Kate pressed Henry again to find her a broker, he assured her that he would and said that he knew of a very respectable man, Mr Brooks, in Hammersmith. When they reached the station, Kate asked Henry if Robert could escort her back home. He agreed on the condition that she would send him back to Hammersmith that night as he was due to be at work at half-past five the next morning. Kate promised she would, and Henry waited until they had boarded the train to Richmond.

When they reached Vine Cottages, Kate unlocked the side door, as she said that the front door lock was broken. Once inside, she found some matches on the table and lit the gas lamps. Robert followed her into the front room, where she poured them both a glass of rum. Clearly delighted to have inherited such an elegantly furnished home, as she chatted, Kate nonchalantly ran her fingers over the keys of the piano belonging to Mrs Thomas, remarking that it was a fine instrument. Keen to impress her guest further, she went to the cupboard and took out two £5 notes, a Post Office Savings Book, and a Monarch Building Society Book, that she said had been left to her by her aunt. She showed them to Robert, asking him tally up the amount. Presently she said, 'I want you to help me carry a box to Richmond Bridge, because I have to meet a friend there.' She left the room and came back a few minutes later, dragging a wooden box, tied with cord. The box, which was about a foot square, had been used by Mrs Thomas to store two of her bonnets.

It was nearly 11.00 pm before Kate took hold of one side of the cord, which was tied round twice, and Robert took the other and together they carried the heavy box along the road towards Richmond Bridge, where they crossed over to the other side and placed it in the farthest recess on the ground. Kate told Robert to go on ahead to the station and she would catch him up, when she had seen her friend. The young lad did as he was told and started to walk slowly back the way he came. As he got to the other side of the bridge, he heard a splash in the water below. A tall dark gentleman walking a short distance in front of him, who also heard it, briefly stopped and turned, then carried on walking. Kate reappeared a few minutes later, 'Come on, Bobby. I've seen my friend,' she said, as she walked briskly along the road, steering him towards the station. By now, Robert had missed the last train home to Hammersmith, so Kate insisted that he went back with her to Vine Cottage, where he spent the rest of the night, sleeping on the floor of her bedroom.

The next morning, after Robert had left to catch the train back to Hammersmith, Kate arrived back at the Porters' at Rose Gardens, where she spent the day. In the evening, Kate seemed reluctant to go back to Richmond, so she stayed the night, sleeping downstairs on the sofa in the front parlour. She was still at the Porters' the following evening when Henry came in from work. As soon as he walked in the door, Kate asked him if he had found her a respectable broker as he had promised. Henry replied that he had and, later that evening, they went round to Mr Brooks, who owned a shop nearby, but it was closed. Kate was again unwilling to go back to the house in Richmond, and asked Henry to go with her, so she could show him her 'comfortable home that she wanted to dispose of'. Henry declined, but promised he would go on Saturday, as he finished work early that day.

When Ann Porter went downstairs the next morning, she noticed that Kate had left her purse on the table from the night before.

Inside were five small rings, a postage stamp, and the keys to 2 Vine Cottages. She decided that she would take them over to Richmond, as it would also be an opportunity to see the grand house Kate had inherited that she had heard so much about. An hour later, Ann arrived at Vine Cottages and knocked on the door, but there was no answer. She waited a while, deciding whether to leave, when she saw Kate hurrying up the road. 'Oh Mother, I have been to Hammersmith looking for you,' she said as she reached the front door.

Once inside, Kate made some breakfast and, while they ate, she spoke about what she intended to do with the contents of the house. A paper boy walked past the house, calling out a newspaper headline: 'Supposed murder; shocking discovery of human remains in a box found in the Thames!' Unflinching, Kate went to the door and said, 'Well, let's have a paper, but I suppose it's only a catchpenny,' then beckoned the boy over and bought a copy.[3] As Kate was proudly showing Mrs Porter around the house, she told her that she would take the best items back to Ireland, but promised to give her all the kitchen utensils, the rest she wanted to sell privately. However, Mrs Porter later complained that she only received 'a portion of the things' that Kate had promised her, including some old chairs, which were 'not up to much … they were old rotten chairs – cane-bottomed chairs with no bottoms in.' Furthermore, her husband Henry Porter 'had to pay four shillings for bringing them home'.

The following morning, Kate visited Mrs Crease and told her that she would collect her little boy on 12 March, as she was sending him to some relatives in Glasgow. That afternoon, Henry Porter arrived at Vine Cottages to view the furniture Kate wanted to sell. After giving him a tour of the house, Kate asked Henry what he thought of it; he told her that it was a very 'comfortable' and 'respectable' home. She told him that apart from the best bed and bedroom furniture, which she would keep for her own use, she wanted to dispose of the rest of the contents by means of a respectable broker, as she was not permitted to hold an auction sale on the premises. Three hours later,

Kate joined Henry on his trip back to Hammersmith, and again spent the night on the sofa in the Porters' cottage.

The following day, Sunday, 9 March, Henry took Kate to see John Church and his wife Maria, landlords of the Rising Sun public house, a few doors down the road. Henry introduced Kate as 'Mrs Thomas' and said that she had some furniture to sell. Kate appeared to know Church, but he claimed he had never seen her before. She insisted they had known one another when she lived next door to the Porters, but Church was adamant that they had never met. Henry described the items to Church, who said that he would go to Richmond to see them for himself, which he did two days later, on Tuesday, 11 March.

Described by the newspapers as 'non-conspicuous' in appearance, Church was about 41 years old, had 'a sandy beard and moustache, a rather bold forehead, small eyes and lank hair, brushed up in a heap on top'. He liked to wear a light tweed suit and deerstalker hat, which gave him the appearance of a 'well-to-do tradesman'. Church was an ex-soldier who had been bought out of the army by his brother James in 1866. He worked as a coachman for a couple of years, before buying the Rising Sun public house, which he had gradually improved and built up over the years to be a respectable and prosperous business.

Clearly enjoying her new role as mistress of the house, Kate led Church into each room, proudly showing him her fine furniture and possessions. She drew his attention to a portrait that hung over the mantlepiece in the sitting room, telling him it was her late husband, Mr Thomas, and showed him a photograph in a frame, which she said was of her father, who was a solicitor in Scotland. Sadly, he was unwell, she said, so she was going to Scotland to look after him. Later that evening, Kate walked with Church, who still hadn't examined the furniture, to the Railway Tavern, where they had a few glasses of ale, then Church caught the train back to Hammersmith and Kate returned home.

Church returned to Vine Cottages the following day and continued to visit every day for the rest of the week, where he spent several hours alone in Kate's company, smoking and drinking. Kate later hinted that they had become intimate, which Church strongly denied. In between entertaining Church, Kate collected her little boy on 12 March from Mrs Crease as arranged, but instead of taking him to Glasgow, took him to Annie Porter in Hammersmith, and she agreed to look after him.

In the meantime, the inquest had been held on Monday, 10 March, at the Red Lion Inn in Barnes, where Dr Adams was called to give evidence. He told the coroner that after examining the remains of the box discovered at the shore of the River Thames, he found them to consist of the trunk and other portions of the body of a woman:

> The heart was in the cavity of the chest. I found a portion of the right lung, but the left lung was absent. Attached to the trunk was the right shoulder. The upper part of the left arm had been detached, and I found it to be perfect down to the elbow. A portion of the thigh of the right leg and the remainder of the leg down to the ankle was also among the remains. A part of the pelvis was present, as also a small portion of the spine – the rectum was divided. The head was absent. The woman had been dead about a week, while the remains might have been in the water about two days.
>
> From what I can see, I should say that the remains must have been those of a woman between 18 and 30, and she may have borne children. Her height may have been about five feet three or four inches, judging from the measurement of the parts that were found and making allowance for those that were absent. I think she must have been a dark-haired woman.

In my opinion, all the fractures to the bones, must
have been made after death, and had been made very
unskilfully and with very bad instruments. The mutilation
must have been a work of time. The bones must have been
smashed with a blunt instrument. I could see no marks on
the remains which could have been inflicted before death
or could have caused it.

As no other evidence had been found, the court was adjourned,
pending further investigations.

That morning, George Court, who had been working at the
allotment ground at Twickenham, was spreading dung from the dung
heap over the garden, when he discovered a human foot and ankle,
which appeared to have been recently severed from a leg. He took
them to the police station, where they were then taken to the mortuary
at Twickenham, before being moved to the mortuary in Barnes, and
placed with the other remains.

Two days later, on 12 March, Dr Bond, a renowned surgeon and
lecturer on forensic medicine at Westminster Hospital, also examined
the human remains. He confirmed that the severed foot and ankle
found by George Court in the dung heap belonged to the body parts
found in the box under the bridge at Barnes and that he was sure they
had been boiled. He agreed with Dr Adams that the deceased had
been dead a week or perhaps a fortnight, but no decomposition had
taken place, due to the very cold weather. However, he did not agree
with the estimated age of the deceased, as he was sure that it was an
older woman over 50 years of age.

Back at Vine Cottages, having made a list of the furniture that
Kate wanted to sell, Church offered her £50, but Kate thought that
figure was too low and eventually agreed to £68. She told Church that
she needed to pay some bills and asked him if he would pay some of
the money in advance, so he gave her £18 as a deposit. Kate gave him
a plate and a few other items as security.

On Sunday, 16 March, Kate joined Church, his wife and daughter, William Porter, and a friend on a boating trip and on the Monday, Church went with Kate to pick up a watch that had belonged to Mr Thomas from the jewellers in Richmond, where he bought Kate a pair of earrings for the princely sum of £1. Afterwards, they went back to Vine Cottages, where they spent the rest of the afternoon and evening drinking brandy.

The next day, just before 7.00 in the evening, Henry Weston, a greengrocer in Hammersmith, who also moved furniture as a sideline, arrived at 2 Vine Cottages with three other men and two vans. John Church supervised the men, instructing Weston to take some of the items to his house. Porter helped the men load the van while another man, John Maryon, a wheelwright who lived in Rose Gardens, dismantled the bedsteads and packed the crockery. Weston later recalled that Church and Kate appeared to be on 'very friendly terms'. She called him 'Jack' and Church referred to her as 'Kate', certainly not Mrs Thomas or as the lady of the house. Yet, not only did Church continue to deny having known Kate prior to being introduced to her by Porter in the Rising Sun on 9 March, he later testified in court that he 'knew her by no other name than as Mrs Thomas'.

Elizabeth Ives, the landlady who lived at 1 Vine Cottages, had been observing the goings-on next door for the last two weeks. She had seen a cabdriver go to the house several times and different men coming and going at odd hours and, on one occasion, had heard a man singing in the kitchen, in between what sounded like the sound of filing, which continued all evening. Elizabeth Ives knew Mrs Thomas's servant Kate was there as she had seen her through the window in the dining room and saw her leave the house several times, but there had been no sign of Mrs Thomas for over a fortnight, not since Saturday, 1 March, when she had seen her in the afternoon, planting flowers in her garden. It all seemed very strange.

During the evening of 18 March, Elizabeth looked out of the window and was astonished to see two men carrying Mrs Thomas's furniture down the path and loading it into a van. She thought it odd that Mrs Thomas had not mentioned to her that she intended to move out, so she hurried next door, where she met Henry Weston in the front garden and asked him where he was taking the furniture. He told her that 'Mrs Thomas' had requested they take it to Hammersmith.

Shortly after, Kate went next door to speak to Elizabeth Ives. 'Mrs Thomas has sold her furniture. A man here can show the receipts,' she told her. 'Mr Weston is going to take them to Hammersmith.' Miss Ives demanded to know the whereabouts of Mrs Thomas. 'I don't know,' Kate replied, rather lamely, then as she turned to hasten back down the path, Elizabeth retorted that she would inquire further and slammed the front door. She noticed that Kate seemed very agitated, 'her face was quite convulsed, and she could hardly speak to me', she later testified. Back inside the house, Kate remarked to Porter, 'What's she got to do with it? I can manage my own business. I don't want her interference.' She told him to follow her upstairs, where she showed him two dresses and a fur jacket she wanted taken down from the pegs, as she wanted them to 'go to Hammersmith in the van'.

Ten minutes later, carrying a hat box, her coat and bonnet over one arm, and several dresses over the other, Kate ran down the path of 2 Vine Cottages. She threw the dresses into one of the vans, hesitated, then hastily snatched back a black silk dress and ran down the road towards Richmond station. John Church came out to the van a few minutes later, muttering something about having been 'led astray'. He said aloud to the men, 'There's something wrong. Bring the things back. I'll have nothing to do with it.' After he had agreed to pay Weston £3 for his trouble, the men carried the furniture back inside the house.

Meanwhile, Kate had hailed a cab at Richmond railway station and was on her way to the Porters' house in Hammersmith. She told Frederick Bolton, the cabdriver, to wait at the corner of Rose Gardens, as she would only be a few minutes. Kate ran down the road to the Rising Sun, where she borrowed a sovereign from Maria Church, before dashing into the Porters' house.

A quarter of an hour later, she came back carrying another hat box, and a small bundle. Having woken her little boy, who had been asleep in bed, she quickly dressed him in his knickerbocker suit and a pea-jacket and asked Robert Porter to carry him to the top of the street to the waiting cab. Bolton drove her and her little boy to Hammersmith railway station, where she asked him to follow her with her hat box and bundle, while she carried her little boy onto the platform. She paid the cabdriver, then boarded the train to King's Cross, where she caught another train to Liverpool. From there, she travelled to Ireland on a coal steamer, which, for a few shillings, carried passengers to the coal quay in Dublin. Kate then made her way down to New Ross in County Wexford, where she caught a cab to her uncle's farm in Killane, near Enniscorthy.

In the meantime, Church was left feeling very disgruntled, especially as he had been swindled out of £18. He presumed that rent arrears had instigated Kate's sudden departure, so the next day, he and Henry Porter decided to call round to Mrs Thomas's landlady, who they thought might know the whereabouts of her tenant. But when Miss Ives opened the door to them, she looked at the two men suspiciously and said, 'I know nothing about Mrs Thomas,' and slammed the door shut.

The previous evening, when Church had arrived back home with Weston, he had handed Mrs Church a hat box containing the dresses that Kate had left in the van. Mrs Church had taken the dresses upstairs and put them on the club room table, where they remained untouched until a few days later, when she decided to have a look at them. As she turned them over, she felt in the apron pocket of a blue dress and found several items belonging to Mrs Thomas, including two pocket-handkerchiefs and a letter from Mrs E. Menhennick, of 24 Ambler Road, Finsbury Park. Mrs Church took the items downstairs to show her husband, who decided to visit Mrs Menhennick that evening.

Charles Menhennick and his wife were friends of Mrs Thomas and had known her for over a decade. Their 13-year-old daughter Edith had often stayed with her, sometimes for several months at a time. Mr Menhennick was puzzled as to why two strangers were enquiring after Mrs Thomas at Richmond, but when Church explained the purpose of their visit and showed him the letter, Mr Menhennick asked Church to describe the woman they referred to as Mrs Thomas. Church said that she was a 'big, tall woman, who spoke with a strong Irish accent'. Mr Menhennick shook his head and replied that was not like the Mrs Thomas he knew. He wondered why Church had not given the plate and other items to the police. Church said that he presumed 'Mrs Thomas' would come back to collect them, and he would get his money back. Slowly it dawned on the men that for the past fortnight Kate had been masquerading as Mrs Thomas.

Mr Menhennick, who was now most concerned about the welfare of the real Mrs Thomas, contacted her solicitor Mr Hughes, early the next morning. Mr Hughes was unwell, so he sent his brother, William Henry Hughes, who had known Mrs Thomas for thirty years, to see John Church at the Rising Sun in Hammersmith. After answering several questions about Mrs Thomas, Church showed Hughes the purse that his wife had found in the pocket of one of the dresses, which contained five rings wrapped in wool. Hughes sent for Porter and the three of them went to Richmond police station. Early that evening, after Church had made a statement, all three men accompanied Inspector John Pearman to 2 Vine Cottages, where he conducted a cursory search of the house.

Holding a candle in one hand, the inspector made his way through the house, where he found 'everything to be in a state of great confusion'. In the dim light, he could see that the furniture had been packed up, the beds had been pulled out and left in the middle of the room, all the carpets had been taken up and there were three large boxes full of bed linen ready to be taken away. As the men entered the drawing room downstairs, Church went straight to the cupboard, opened the door, and said, 'Here's Mrs Thomas's watch and chain we left behind.' He turned around and showed them a gold watch and chain. As Inspector Pearman and Mr Hughes had only casually looked at Church when he opened the cupboard, they could not be sure if he had found the watch and chain in the cupboard or taken it out of his pocket. Church then made some remark about a large photograph that 'Mrs Thomas' had told him was of her father, which Mr Hughes recognised as a photograph of his own father. An hour later, as it was getting dark, Inspector Pearman decided to finish the search as nothing more of any significance was found.

The following afternoon, the inspector interviewed Church at his house in Hammersmith. Church told him that Mr Porter's son Robert had helped Kate carry a box down to Richmond Bridge. The inspector sent for Robert Porter, who, accompanied by his father, made a statement of his version of events. Later that day, Robert was taken to Barnes police station to identify the box which had contained the human remains, where he 'declared emphatically' that it was the one that he had helped Kate Webster carry across Richmond Bridge. Inspector Pearman then instructed a police constable to watch Mrs Thomas's house.

A telegram was sent to Mrs Thomas's older brother, Mr Batterbee, who lived in Shoreham, near Brighton, urging him to proceed to his sister's house immediately. He arrived in London that evening, where the police informed him of his sister's disappearance and requested that he send telegrams to as many of her friends as he could think of, inquiring if she was staying with them or if they knew of her whereabouts. But no one had seen her. Mr Batterbee was shown the box that had contained the dismembered body parts, but he could not be sure that it belonged to his sister. He knew she had a distinctive birthmark on her left leg, but that had been destroyed during the mutilation of the body. As he was unable to assist the police any further, Mr Batterbee returned to Brighton the following evening.

On Monday, 24 March, the inspector resumed his search of 2 Vine Cottages. On entering the property, he noted that both the front and back door locks worked perfectly, and he was able to unlock them both with ease. He searched the ashes under the kitchen grate, and found a quantity of charred bones, dress buttons, and two pieces of house flannel. In the coal cellar in the basement, he found a chopper, and in a room next to the scullery, he found a razor and a torn nightdress, which appeared to be burned. He put all the items in a carpet bag he had found in the back room that contained some under-linen and took them back to the police station, where he gave them to Inspector Shaw.

Three days later, during a more thorough search of the property, the inspector discovered blood splashed on the wallpaper at the bottom of the staircase leading from the hall to the kitchen, and blood smeared on the wainscot in the back bedroom upstairs. He chipped off the bloodied wood of the wainscot and cut out a piece of the blood-stained wallpaper. There were stains of blood on the wall of the pantry and on the jamb of the door, which appeared to have been 'rubbed over with something', in an attempt to conceal it. Further inspection of the copper grate not only revealed more charred bones, but the inspector also saw that the brickwork on the outside of the copper was 'well whitened over and clean'. He found the whitening in a dish on the dresser. He took out the copper from the brickwork and about halfway down he found a 'fatty substance', which he 'scraped off and placed in a small earthen pot'.

In the dining room, the inspector found a small diary and under the sink in the scullery, he found a handle of a box, which, he found afterwards, fitted the box found on the shore of the Thames. There was also some cord which was the same as that used to tie the box. On the landing, he found a piece of brown paper stained with blood. The next day, the inspector took all the evidence he had collected from Vine Cottage, along with a bonnet he had received from John Church two days before, to Dr Bond for analysis.

The police now had sufficient evidence to arrest Kate for the murder of Julia Martha Thomas and distributed the following description of the female suspect who had absconded from Richmond:

> Wanted for stealing plate, &c, and the supposed murder of her mistress, Kate—, aged about 32, 5ft 5in. or 6 in. high: complexion sallow, slightly freckled: teeth rather good, prominent. Usually dressed in dark dress, jacket rather long and trimmed with dark fur round pockets. Light brown satin bonnet. Speaks with an Irish accent, and was accompanied by a boy, aged five, complexion rather dark, dark hair. Was last seen in Hammersmith.

Reports soon followed that a woman of that description had been seen travelling by third class on the midnight train from St Pancras Station to Liverpool. After being shown a photograph of Kate, a stewardess on board the steamer confirmed she had been a passenger.

Kate may have fled to Ireland, but her criminal record made it easier for the police to track her down. Telegrams were sent to all the Irish police stations and on Friday, 28 March, after reading the description, Head Constable Callaghan of Wexford constabulary thought it resembled a prisoner who had previously been convicted for larceny at Gorey Quarter sessions in December 1864. By checking the conviction books, he was able to trace Kate at her uncle's farm in Killane, where she was apprehended and taken to Enniscorthy jail.

The following day, Scotland Yard police officers, inspectors Henry Jones and John Dowdell, who had arrived from England, charged Kate with the murder of Julia Martha Thomas and a further charge of stealing her furniture and other property belonging to her. Kate calmly listened to the charge but made no reply, showing 'hardly a trace of emotion'. The next morning, the two officers escorted Kate back to London. As the train pulled out of the station at Enniscorthy, Kate asked: 'Is there any person in custody for the murder? If there's not there ought to be. It is very hard the innocent should suffer for the guilty.'

When the party arrived in Dublin, Kate was taken to the police station in Chancery Lane, situated behind Dublin Castle, then discreetly brought to Westland Row Station (now Dublin Pearse railway station) where they boarded the express train to Kingstown (Dún Laoghaire). The officers had purposely chosen the quietest route and in doing so managed to complete the long trip to the port and get Kate on the steamboat to Holyhead, Wales, virtually unnoticed.

During the crossing, Kate, though feeling rather seasick, made a long statement in which she insisted the officers had arrested the wrong person, and blamed John Church, landlord of the Rising Sun public house, for the murder of Mrs Thomas.

During the rough voyage across the Irish Sea, Inspector Dowdell had not taken Kate's allegation 'down as she said it', so when they finally reached the police station at Richmond, it was repeated in a formal written statement. A summary of Kate's version of events reads as follows:

I have known John Church for nearly seven years. I first got acquainted when I was living two or three doors from him at Porter's. He used to take me out to London and to various public houses. I met him again some months ago, and he came to my mistress's house one night the worse for drink. After remaining there for some time, I told him he would have to go, as I expected my mistress home from church. My mistress came home, and knocked at the door, and I let her in. He [Church] had previously told me to say that he was my brother.

A few days after, he came again into the house, and during conversation I had told him the mistress had no money in the house. He said, 'Could we not put the old woman out of the way?'

I said, 'What do you mean?'

He said, 'Oh, poison her!'

I said, 'You must do that yourself; I'll have nothing to do with that.'

He said, 'We could have her things and go off to America together and enjoy it, as I'm getting tired of my old woman.'

He left late in the evening. He came again on Monday night, 3rd of March, and had tea with Mrs. Thomas. I waited upon them. After tea I asked Mrs. Thomas if I could go and see my little boy, and she said, 'Yes Kate, and you need not hurry back.'

When I returned late that evening, I noticed the light was turned down. I knocked three times at the door. At the third knock Church opened the front door. I saw Mrs. Thomas lying on the mats in the passage, struggling and groaning. I drew back on the step, frightened to go in. At this time, there was a policeman standing on the opposite side of the road, a tall, dark man. Church seized me by the arm, pulled me in, and closed the door.

I said, 'Whatever have you done?'

He said, 'Never you mind, I have done it for her, and if you say a word about it, I'll put this knife into you up to the handle.' It was a carving knife belonging to Mrs. Thomas. I felt very faint.

I said, 'No, John, don't. I won't tell.' He offered me what I thought was a glass of water, but I said, 'No, I am better now,' thinking it was poison, and that he was going to serve me the same as Mrs. Thomas. Shortly after we left the house together, leaving Mrs. Thomas there, and took a cab. I had told him I would not stay in the house by myself. We drove to near Church's house. He saw me into Mrs. Porter's and I remained there for the night.

I got up early the next morning and went into Church's house. Church was there and beckoned me to go up the street. I went up and he joined me shortly afterwards, and said, 'I can't get over to your house before one o'clock, as I got into a row with the old woman last night for being out so late again, and I must stay at home this morning to make it up with her.' I said I should not go back to the house by myself. He told me to meet him at the Richmond Hotel, over the bridge. I took the boy [Robert Porter] with me, and as I passed the hotel, I saw Church inside, and asked the boy to go a short distance and wait. I went into the hotel and spoke to Church. He gave me the keys of the house and said I was to go there and take the boy with me, and he added that I should find a box in the back room, which he had packed up tied with cord. The boy was to assist me to bring it away. I carried the box to the bridge. The boy went away, and Church appeared.

I said, 'What are you going to do with the box?'

Church said, 'That is my business.' Then he said, 'Follow the boy.' I left and heard a splash in the water.

I joined the boy Porter at the foot of the bridge. We went to the railway station and found that the last train had gone. I said, 'You shall come home and sleep with me.' We both slept in one room. On going downstairs into the kitchen, I found the carpeting rolled up, and the table with a leaf let down put up against the cupboard, and the boards wet, as if they had been washed, a large fire in the kitchen and a large saucepan on the fire full of water. About two days after, when I was cleaning up the scullery, I saw some blood on the carving knife. There was usually a meat saw hanging up over the fireside, but on that day, I found it in a box in the scullery quite clean.

Kate added that since Mrs Thomas had disappeared, Church, Mr Porter, and his son had been frequent visitors to the house. Church had told her to order food for the house, as if it were for Mrs Thomas, which had been taken to both his and Porter's house, where it had been cooked and eaten. He had also told her not to pay Porter for his valuation of the furniture, nor to pay any bills, but to pay Elizabeth Ives, the landlady, 'to keep her quiet'.

> I went to pay her when they were removing the goods, and she said 'No.' She refused to take the money and thought there was something wrong. I went back into the house and told Church. He said, 'I'll go out to Porter, and say I think there is something wrong about this; don't move the things.' He came back and said, 'You will have to clear out and go to your friends,' and I left soon after. He knew where I was going; he gave me a card with his address and said I was to write to him, and he would 'stop at home and brazen it out.'
>
> This was on Tuesday, the 19th, and I reached my uncle's house on the following Friday night. I wrote to Church to his address in Hammersmith, telling him I had arrived home safely. Before leaving it was partly arranged that I should remain at home for about three weeks, that he would send me money to come back with, and then we were to go to America. I never laid a hand on Mrs. Thomas, and had nothing to do with murdering her, but I knew Church had done it.
>
> All the money left in the house belonging to Mrs. Thomas was a £5 note and 30s. This note I changed at a fishmonger's in Richmond. Church and Porter were with me at the time. I intend to tell the whole truth, as I don't see why I should be blamed for what Church has done. I wouldn't accuse my greatest enemy of anything wrong, let alone a friend, which Church has been to me up till now.

John Church was immediately called in and asked to identify the prisoner, whom he said was Mrs Thomas. When Kate's statement was read to him, he laughed, as though the allegation was absurd, and said, 'The lying woman, how can she say that about me? I know nothing of her … I was not in Richmond at the time. Porter and his son can prove I was not there, so can the baker next door. Mr Porter will tell you what day he took me down there.' Despite his protests, Church was searched and found to have in his possession one gold watch and chain, £39 in gold, and some other items.

The previous day, Inspectors Pearman and Jones had searched Church's house, the Rising Sun, in Hammersmith, where they recovered several items belonging to Mrs Thomas, including the purse that contained the five rings, which consisted of two plain gold wedding rings, one keeper, one set with pearls, one mourning ring set with hair, with the inscription 'J. Thomas died June 28th, 1873', and an address card, six postage stamps, and the letter from Mrs Menhennick. They had also taken away a bonnet in a box, a pair of men's trousers and two vests that appeared to be stained with blood spots, which were sent to Mr Bond for analysis. Mrs Church, who was present during the search, explained to the officers that shortly before the murder of Mrs Thomas, her husband had intervened in a drunken fight between two men, during which there had been a great deal of blood drawn. Nonetheless, Church was arrested and charged with the murder of Mrs Julia Martha Thomas and stealing her property in conjunction with Kate Webster. Both he and Kate were taken into custody to spend the night in the police cells in Richmond, before appearing at the magistrates' court the next day.

The news of Kate's arrest and her arrival back in Richmond spread rapidly and throughout the following morning people loitered outside the police station, hoping to find out more information and to catch a glimpse of the 'inhuman monster' who was responsible for what was now dubbed the 'Richmond Murder'. But the police, in preparation, had quietly escorted Kate to the magistrates' court an hour earlier than expected. However, when Church was brought to the court later, hardly anyone took any notice. According to *The Standard* newspaper, Kate apparently 'passed a tolerably comfortable night' having been 'supplied with refreshments' during the evening, and had jokingly asked the officer 'how her sweetheart was', meaning John Church.

At 2.00 pm, the doors of the courthouse were thrown open and the crowd of people flocked in until it was full. Amongst them was Mr Batterbee, Mrs Thomas's brother, and several friends and relatives of the family. Twenty minutes later, Church was brought into the court, followed by Kate, who was described by one newspaper as 'above medium height, strongly, though not stoutly, built, dark complexioned, with sharp darkish eyes, and a palish-sallow face ... the features being tolerably regular, neither showing refinement not absolute coarseness.' Her attire, according to the reporter, was 'in itself a contrast'. She wore a 'gay-looking light grey bonnet, trimmed with brown velvet and feather. Her jacket of black cloth, trimmed with sable, looked shabby, as did her dress of a puce hue; while around her neck was an old fashioned, well-worn brown fur boa, and on her arm a dark waterproof cloak.'

Kate appeared 'calm and indifferent' and gave a 'long-drawn sigh' as she was placed before the magistrates. Throughout the proceedings, which lasted an hour and a half, she stood very still, 'never so much as moving a finger', and kept the cloak draped over her arm, 'like one just about to go on a journey', remarked a reporter. As her statement was read out, Church, 'a fresh-coloured, sandy-whiskered man, attired in a light suit', stood next to Kate, and cast her several glances of 'indignant surprise'. Both prisoners were charged with the murder of Mrs Julia Martha Thomas, on 3 March 1879, and stealing property belonging to her. Police officer Claydon's request for bail for John Church was denied and he and Kate were remanded in custody until the next hearing, on Wednesday, 9 April.

Mr Poland, conducting the prosecution on behalf of the Crown, declared that the statement made by Kate Webster 'left no question in the minds of the officers that Church ought to be charged as participating in the dreadful tragedy'. Accompanied by Inspectors Jones and Dowdell, Kate and Church were taken by cab to the House of Detention in Clerkenwell. Despite his efforts to talk to Kate in the waiting rooms, in the court and in the cab, she refused to engage in any conversation with Church nor answer any of his questions, so they travelled in silence for the duration of the journey.

When the proceedings resumed three days later, a large and rowdy crowd had gathered outside the court; many were women, who had been standing by the doors for more than an hour, hoping to secure a good seat inside. Inside the court, it had become so crowded and hot that one woman fainted during the proceedings and had to be carried out. Although the strain of the last two weeks had started to tell on Church, who 'had the look of a worn and anxious man', he was again refused bail and the court was adjourned. The police struggled to keep the crowds back as Kate left the building and, as she was driven away, an angry mob ran after the cab, threatening to break the windows.

Over the following weeks, Kate was brought before the Richmond magistrates several times, as various witnesses were examined. After examining the trousers taken from Church's home, it was concluded that they were stained with beer, not blood. Church continued to deny ever having known Kate before Porter introduced her on 9 March and insisted that his purpose in visiting 2 Vine Cottages was purely business. Kate's defence lawyer, Warner Sleigh, argued that Church and Kate had indeed been intimate, and he had been the instigator in carrying out the murder, while Kate had merely been 'a tool in Church's hand'. But Church was able to produce a watertight alibi for 3 March, allegedly the date Mrs Thomas was murdered. He was at a Slate Club meeting held that evening in his home, the Rising Sun, which was confirmed by various members of the club, and by entries in the club books on that date signed by Church.[4]

In desperation, Kate made another statement on 10 April, in which she attempted to incriminate Henry Porter, as well as Church.

She claimed that Porter was at the house with Church that evening and changed the date of the murder of Mrs Thomas from Monday to the previous day, Sunday, 2 March. But witnesses verified that both Porter and Church were at the Rising Sun that day, where during the afternoon and evening Church served behind the bar. Following a brief consultation amongst the bench at the magistrates' hearing on 17 April, Church was acquitted of murder and ordered to appear as a witness for the prosecution. The court broke out in cheers and applauded as Church left the dock and sat down beside his wife. Tears ran down his cheeks as several of his friends and relatives 'heartily congratulated' him. The news that he had been released spread rapidly and Church returned home to find a large crowd waiting outside the Rising Sun to congratulate him.

At the final hearing on 16 May, Kate Webster was committed to stand trial for the murder of Julia Martha Thomas on Wednesday, 2 July, at the Old Bailey. At just before 10.00 that morning, Kate entered the court accompanied by a female warder and was placed in the dock before Mr Justice Denman. According to the *Daily News*:

> She wore a black cloth jacket, trimmed with fur at the collar and sleeves, a black dress, and an open-worked white woollen kerchief round her neck ... The character of her face is somewhat hard and masculine, and her complexion is distinguished for its total absence of colour. She appeared to be quite unaffected by the impressive surroundings of her situation, but nevertheless maintained an attentive and respectful attitude throughout the whole of the long day's proceedings.

The prosecution was led by the Solicitor General, Sir Hardinge Giffard KC, Mr Harry Poland, and Mr. A. L. Smith, and the counsel for the defence was Mr Warner Sleigh and Mr Keith Frith. Mr Brindley watched the case on behalf of John Church, now a prosecution witness.

The Solicitor General opened the proceedings by summarising the details of the case. He told the court that from the month of January, when the prisoner went into service at 2 Vine Cottages, until 2 March, the alleged date of the murder, Kate Webster and Mrs Thomas were the only occupants of the house.

Although Mrs Thomas had not been seen since that fateful evening, orders were still being given to tradesmen who called to the house as usual, but nothing was mentioned about her absence. After briefly relaying the events leading up to the mysterious disappearance of the black bag, the disposal of the box at Richmond Bridge, and its subsequent discovery a few days later, he then drew the jury's attention to the contradictory statements made by Kate, in which she admitted that a murder had been committed but had accused both Church and Porter of being the perpetrators. The Solicitor General concluded his speech by proposing that on hearing the evidence the jury would have no doubt in concluding that the prisoner standing at the bar was fully responsible for the death of Mrs Thomas. He then proceeded to call the witnesses.

Among the first witnesses to take the stand was Julia Nicholls. She confirmed that she had last seen Mrs Thomas alive at the Presbyterian service in the Lecture Hall on 2 March and that the bonnet produced in court was the one worn by Mrs Thomas at church that fateful evening. She had also seen her wearing it on previous occasions.

Mary Roberts, a young woman employed by Elizabeth Ives, testified that on Monday 3 March, she had seen a card in Mrs Thomas's window advertising 'Apartments to let', but the following day, when Miss Ives had sent her next door with the message about the repairs to the roof, she noticed it had gone. Later that evening, at around eight o'clock, she heard people next door, the fire being poked, and someone banging on the keys of the piano. She knew it could not be Mrs Thomas as she could play the piano quite well. She also recalled, the following week, seeing Kate Webster at the top of the road, walking towards the house, arm in arm with a dark-haired man, who was wearing an Ulster coat.

The landlady, Elizabeth Ives, was next to enter the witness box. She confirmed that she had heard the familiar sound of washing taking place next door early in the morning on Monday, 3 March, but she noticed that the clothes had been hung out on the line by 8.00 am, which was unusually early. That afternoon, she was in her garden and saw through the window of next door that the breakfast things were still on the dining room table, and they were still there the following day.

On Tuesday, 4 March, Elizabeth Ives heard the voices of men and women in Mrs Thomas's house and, on Wednesday evening, she heard sounds of filing and, at the same time, a man with a child singing in the kitchen, which continued at regular intervals throughout the evening. On 11 or 12 March, at around 11.00 pm, she saw two women, two or three men, and a small child leave the house in a cab. She was almost certain that one of the women was Kate. 'During the ten days or fortnight, people were continually coming to the house at all sorts of odd hours, and taking away things in cabs, and we thought it strange.'

The next witness called to give evidence was Robert Porter, who was also recalled the following day, where he was cross-examined by the defence counsel, Mr Warner Sleigh. Robert told the court that it was on 6 March when he first heard that a box containing the body parts of a woman had been found in the river at Barnes, but he did not think it was the same box that he had helped Kate carry to the bridge. He said that he hadn't mentioned the box to anyone, not even his parents, until he told Inspector Jones about it on Sunday 23 March.

However, according to his father, Henry Porter, who was next called to the witness box, it was on Sunday 9 March, after having read about the Barnes Mystery in *Lloyd's Newspaper*, that Robert first mentioned to him that he had helped Kate Webster carry a similar box to the bridge. Mr Justice Denman asked him why, having known this, did he wait so long to inform the police, and did he not have suspicions regarding the accused? 'I had a suspicion after my son told me that it was like the box, but I did not give information, because I did not suspect the accused in the least,' Porter replied, adding that if he had, he would have been 'the first to make a complaint'.

Although he could not be sure of the date, Porter recalled that during one of his visits to 2 Vine Cottages, Kate showed him a gold plate with two artificial teeth, which she said had belonged to her late aunt. She asked him to take it to a jeweller's shop in Hammersmith, which he did, where he sold it for 6s. When he paid Kate the money, she gave him 1s. back for his trouble.

During her son's testimony, Ann Porter could be heard muttering from the back of the court and was duly chastised by the judge, who became more exasperated when she was called to the witness box. She 'laughed, cried, muttered, shook her head inexplicably, and repeatedly spoke in such a low tone', so that only the jury could hear what she was saying. After a while, the judge ordered her to come and stand beside him to give evidence. Mrs Porter stated that she had also known on 9 March that her son had carried the box to the bridge, but she could give no reason why she kept it to herself and not said anything sooner.

Before she left the stand, Mr Justice Denman addressed Mrs Porter's drinking habit: 'You have been examined a good deal about this whiskey drinking. I am afraid you are too much given to it.' Mrs Porter laughed. 'Don't laugh,' retorted the judge. 'It is a horrible thing for a wife and the mother of a family. You stink with drink today, as I am afraid the jury must have found out. It is a miserable habit and makes you a terrible spectacle.'

On the third day of the trial, Mr Sleigh questioned John Church about his relationship with Kate Webster. Church was adamant that he only knew the prisoner as Mrs Thomas and that their acquaintance was purely business, insisting, 'She was no more friendly to me than a customer or any person I had transactions with.' Mr Sleigh then proposed that it seemed strange to spend so many hours alone with the prisoner, whom he had stated was a stranger to him, at the house in Richmond. Church said that he did not think it was strange, as he was there to look at the furniture and ascertain its value. 'You appear to have gone to Richmond with the prisoner a great many times,' Mr Sleigh persisted. 'What were you doing so many times?' Church replied firmly, 'I was looking at the furniture.'

Mr Sleigh then asked Church if he had called the prisoner Kate and if she had called him Jack. 'I might have called the accused Kate,' he said, 'because I have heard Porter call her Kate. I will not swear whether she called me Jack or not. She might have called me Jack.' When Church was asked if he had bought the earrings for Kate as a present, he said that he had merely paid for them on the pretext that she would pay him back when she received the money for the furniture. At this point, Kate burst into tears and buried her face in her hands.

Church was very evasive when he was asked about his earlier life. Several times, he was asked how he earnt his living prior to his enlistment into the army, and each time he said that he could not remember. 'Were you a barman before you went into the army?' suggested Mr Sleigh. Church replied that he had no recollection of his occupation at that time. 'It is extraordinary you do not remember certain things about yourself,' remarked the judge.

Maria Church followed her husband into the witness box. After confirming that Church was at home all day on 2 March, she immediately said, before being asked, that he was also at home on Monday, 3 March, which caused some amusement in the court. She had also believed the prisoner was Mrs Thomas and though she knew her husband had gone to Richmond on several occasions to look at furniture, she had no idea he had spent so much time alone with the prisoner drinking brandy and smoking cigars, nor did she know that he had bought her a pair of earrings.

Mrs Lucy Loder was next to take the stand. She confirmed that she had known Kate by sight when she had lived with her friend Sarah Crease and had recommended her to Mrs Thomas. When she had called round to see Mrs Thomas on Saturday, 8 March, Kate had told her that she had gone out. She also said that she had told Mrs Thomas she was going to live with her aunt who was 'very well-to-do' in Glasgow, and her mistress was out looking for a replacement for her. Mrs Loder said that Kate appeared to be a 'very obliging girl, and did her work well', and as far as she could see, 'there was no animosity between her and Mrs. Thomas'.

The next witness, Mrs Sarah Crease, confirmed that Kate had been staying with her before she had left to work for Mrs Thomas on 29 January. She had known the prisoner for three and a half years and had always found her to be a good, kind-hearted girl:

> My husband had an illness for four months, during which time she nursed him and waited on him all day and did all she could for him. She was then in a situation at Mr. Mitchell's and came backwards and forwards simply for the purpose of being kind to my husband ... She was fond of him and very fond of her child. I never heard her say or do anything unkind to anybody. She came to my house every Sunday night but one to see her child ... She was never away two Sundays running.

Mrs Crease finished by saying that Kate had always referred to Mrs Thomas as 'a very nice lady, very kind and good hearted' and 'appeared very fond of her as a mistress'.

Harry George Penny, manager of Mr Niblett's jewellers, in Hammersmith, confirmed that a man had brought a gold plate with two teeth on each side of it into the shop on Friday 7 March, for which he paid him 6s, though he could not be sure that it was Henry Porter.

George Henry Rudd, a surgeon dentist in Richmond, told the court in his brief testimony that Mrs Thomas had first attended his surgery on 22 February, where he found it had been necessary to make a cast of her mouth for the fitting of gold plate on her lower jaw. He became aware that Mrs Thomas had been murdered when the bill he had forwarded for his work had been returned through the dead letter office, which in turn had brought him in contact with the police.

Over the next few days, further witnesses gave evidence, including Inspectors John Dowdell and Henry Jones, the officers from Scotland Yard who had escorted Kate back from Ireland. Inspector Dowdell said that during the voyage, Kate was very calm, 'except when she was sick', and 'appeared an amiable, pleasant sort of woman', who 'gave no trouble and came back quite quietly and calmly'. Inspector Jones noticed that the prisoner was wearing three rings; one was a wedding ring, which he took off her finger.

Mary Ann Kent, a relative with whom Mrs Thomas had lodged for a year, recalled seeing her wear a wedding ring and two keepers and recognised the deal box produced in court as belonging to Mrs Thomas. 'She had it while she lodged with me and used to keep her bonnets and hats in it. I tried to pack her family bible in it when going to Devonshire, and the handle would always slip out.' Mrs Kent was then shown the bonnet, which she confirmed also belonged to Mrs Thomas, 'I remember her purchasing it,' she said, 'and she and I had part of the same ribbon … I recognised all the articles shown me by Pearman and Jones, as Mrs Thomas's.'

Mrs Emily Hoare, who used to do needlework for Mrs Thomas, identified the coloured skirt that Kate wore when she was apprehended as a garment she had made for Mrs Thomas the previous year.

But the most important and incriminating evidence came from Mary Durden, a straw bonnet and hat maker from Kingston, who testified that Kate had visited her at her house on Shrove Tuesday, 25 February, a week before the murder. She told the court that Kate had been in an 'excited state of mind' and had laughed a lot during their conversation which lasted over an hour:

> She told me she was going to Birmingham to see about
> some property which her aunt had left her. She told me

she had had a letter from her aunt telling her where to find her gold watch and her chain and her jewels; and everything her aunt had was to come to her. She told me that she was going to sell the furniture and said her aunt's will and jewels were in a drawer.

Kate also spoke about her little boy and said that Mr Strong had sent him to school.

Having heard Mary Durden's testimony, the prosecution implied that Kate had premeditated the murder of Julia Martha Thomas. Mr Sleigh, however, suggested during cross-examination that there was animosity between the witness and the accused, as there had been rumours that the two women had quarrelled after Kate had been seen fraternising with Mary Durden's husband in the Three Tons public house. Though Mrs Durden admitted that on occasion she may have gone to the Three Tons to find her husband, she 'never found him drinking there with the accused, or in any other public house' and denied ever having quarrelled with the prisoner. 'I was always on good terms with her,' she said. 'I never had any angry words with her on any occasion.'

Dr Thomas Bond, who was next to take the stand, gave a detailed account of his examination of the human remains found in the box and the charred bones and other items contained in the carpet bag brought to him by Inspector Pearman. He was certain the victim was a woman of over 50 years of age and was around 5 ft 2 ins in height, but he could not ascertain the cause of death, whether she had met a violent end or died of natural causes.

Shortly before her disappearance, Mrs Thomas's face was flushed and she had been agitated: 'Were these the symptoms that preceded the bursting of a blood vessel?' Mr Sleigh asked the doctor. 'Yes, I think so,' replied Dr Bond. 'Intense nervous excitement, a tremulousness of the voice, and flushing of the face are symptoms which would naturally precede a person attacked with a fit. If I had heard of a woman being intensely excited, or that her bonnet fell off, and her hands trembled, and her face flushed, I should consider these preliminary symptoms.'

The next witness, Dr James Adams, who first examined the human remains at the side of the river, and initially thought that the victim was younger, now agreed with Dr Bond that the victim had been an older woman over 50 years of age.

Several more witnesses were recalled, including John Church who, during further cross-examination by Mr Sleigh, still seemed to have trouble remembering his occupation before enlisting in the army. When asked several times if he had ever worked as a barman, each time he answered, 'I might have been,' until eventually the judge snapped, 'Don't say that anymore. Now, upon your oath, were you a barman or not?' Church replied that he had worked in a public house before he went into service.

'Have you ever been in prison before this case?' Mr Sleigh continued.

'Not to my knowledge,' answered Church.

'Not to your knowledge?' exclaimed the judge. 'Have you or have you not, been in prison before you were arrested on this charge?'

'No,' replied Church. 'I suppose I spoke too rapidly.'

After the Clerk of Arraigns read the three statements made previously by Kate Webster, Sleigh gave a lengthy speech for the defence. He argued that the evidence for the prosecution was circumstantial. There was no conclusive proof that Mrs Thomas had met a violent death or that the remains found in the box at Barnes were those of the deceased. 'Assuming that Mrs Thomas died on 2 March, was there any evidence that she did not die from natural causes? Was there any evidence to show that she did not die from heart disease, apoplexy, or the bursting of a blood vessel?' he asked. 'On the contrary, there was something in the evidence to indicate that she did.'

Sleigh pointed out that Mrs Thomas had been prone to fits and asked the jury to recall the evidence of Miss Nicholls and Dr Bond, regarding the 'state of excitement' in which Mrs Thomas appeared before going into the church that evening. Her symptoms – 'flushed face, intense excitement, forgetfulness of self to the extent of allowing her bonnet to drop off' – were, as Dr Bond stated, premonitory symptoms which ultimately could have led to her having a fatal fit when she returned home. The prisoner had said in her statement that on the night Mrs Thomas had disappeared, she had returned to 2 Vine Cottages and found her mistress 'lying on the mat in the passage, struggling and groaning', which was 'quite consistent with the supposition that Mrs Thomas might have died from natural causes'.

Referring to Kate Webster's character, Sleigh stressed the fondness she had for her little boy, describing her as a 'woman of motherly and womanly instincts'. Mrs Crease, whose husband Kate cared for when he was ill in bed, had also confirmed the prisoner's love for her child and described her as a 'kind good-hearted woman', as did several other witnesses. She always respected and spoke kindly of her mistress, Mr Sleigh continued: 'Were not these things worth considering before the jury sent a woman to the gallows?'

Sleigh then accused Church and Porter of giving false evidence and trying 'to throw dust in the eyes of the jury'. Mrs Porter had read in the newspaper about the box being found in the river on 9 March, yet neither Porter nor Church had informed the police about the box being carried to Richmond Bridge on the night of 4 March. 'There had been much talk about the "Barnes Mystery" – it had been plastered all over the newspapers – why had young Robert Porter kept it from his father until 23 March?' Sleigh asked the jury. Kate had been accused of lying, when she claimed that she and Church had been intimate, but as Sleigh reminded the jury, Church had spent time alone with the prisoner, and on at least one occasion, had been in her house for five or six hours, drinking brandy.

'The case was surrounded with mystery from beginning to end,' concluded Sleigh, addressing the jury.

They were asked to take a leap in the dark and it might be afterwards they would think they acted upon moral belief, and not upon legal belief. They might say to themselves afterwards, 'Church was such an unmitigated scoundrel, and the whole transaction with regards to Rose Gardens, was so tainted with nefariousness from beginning to end, that it really was not safe to act upon such testimony.'

For almost a week, the court had been packed with people, who had listened intently to evidence given by more than fifty witnesses, until finally, on 8 July, the sixth and last day of the trial, after having retired from court for an hour and a quarter, the jury found Kate Webster guilty of the wilful murder of Julia Martha Thomas. The clerk of court asked the prisoner if she had anything to say. Kate struggled to keep her composure as she replied:

I am not guilty, my lord, of the murder. I have never done it, my lord. When I was taken into custody I was in a hurry, and I made a statement against Church and Porter. I am very sorry for doing so, and I want to clear them out of it. And another thing. I was led to this my lord. The man who is guilty of all this is not in the case at all, not never was. Therefore, I do not see why I should suffer for what other people have done. There was a child put in my hands in 1874. I had to thieve for that child, and go to prison for it, which can be brought to your lordship. Anybody can tell it round Kingston or Richmond too. Therefore, the father of that child is the ruin of me since 1873 up to this moment, and he is the instigation of this; he was never taken into custody. I have cherished him up to this minute, but I do not see why I should suffer for a scoundrel who has left me after what he has done.

Mr Justice Denman, having donned the black cap, said:

> You tell us now for the first time, that you were instigated
> to that crime by someone who is not in custody, and whose
> name is not before us, and you have made some reparation
> at this moment by exonerating from all charges two
> persons, who might have been sent to the scaffold upon
> the statements that you made against them. Though you
> put it to me that you ought not to suffer because another
> instigated you to this crime, that is a consideration which
> will not warrant me one moment from hesitating to pass
> upon you the sentence of the law.

He then passed the sentence of death, to which Kate repeated, 'I am not guilty, sir.'

The Clerk of Arraigns asked whether the prisoner had anything to say in stay of execution, to which Kate replied that she was pregnant. Thirza Belcher, the matron of Newgate prison, said that she had examined the prisoner only a few days before and she had not been pregnant. A jury of matrons, selected from twelve married women attending the court, were immediately empanelled to determine whether Kate was telling the truth. Accompanied by two women warders, Dr Bond, and the jury of matrons, Kate was taken to the jury room to be examined, where after a few minutes, it was confirmed by the twelve women and Dr Bond that she was not 'quick with child', and in the doctor's opinion, there was nothing 'in the prisoner's condition to justify any delay in carrying out the sentence'. After hearing the matrons' evidence, Kate swooned, then when Dr Bond entered the witness box and gave his evidence, she fainted again. She was taken from the dock in a 'half lifeless condition' and escorted back to her cell in Newgate prison, before being transferred to Wandsworth Prison the following morning to await execution.[5]

During her incarceration at Newgate prison, Kate was known to be 'most violent in temper and addicted to the most frightful language'.[6] However, there seems to be a marked improvement in Kate's conduct at Wandsworth, as the prison doctor, Captain Colville, found her to be 'remarkably submissive and docile'. Kate continued to maintain her innocence and wrote two further statements, one in which she implicated Strong, the father of her child.

A memorial requesting a commutation of the sentence was sent to the Home Secretary on Kate's behalf, but on 26 July, the appeal was rejected, and the date for the execution was set for Tuesday, 29 July 1879, at 9.00 am. On hearing the news, Kate 'frantically clasped her hands and burst into a flood of tears', and cried, 'What shall I do? Oh! What shall I do?'[7] Knowing that there was no possibility of a last-minute reprieve, on the night before her execution, Kate finally made the following confession to her spiritual adviser and prison chaplain, Father McEnery:

> I made a statement in the presence of the warders to Mr. O'Brien, my solicitor, on the 10th July, and a second statement on the 17th July, both in reference to the Richmond murder. These statements were untrue in many ways, especially that portion of them which referred to the murder of Mrs. Thomas and the man Strong, whom I named in the last one, and I am now informed by Mr. O'Brien, my solicitor, that the memorial presented on my behalf has not been successful, and I will be executed at 9 o'clock on Tuesday, 29th July. I see, therefore, that there is no visible hope for a respite of my sentence, and I am advised by him, and feel that I am bound in the sight of Almighty God to clear every one of suspicion, and especially those whose names were mentioned in my said statements, before I die, which I am now happy in doing. In the first place, I heartily beg God's forgiveness and

mercy for numerous falsehoods I have told throughout this unfortunate case, especially because they affected the character and reputation of persons whose names are mentioned, and secondly, because of the injury they have done to myself in the sight of Almighty God, whose mercy and forgiveness I have no doubt of having obtained.

Since I was arrested, I was always in dread of the consequences of the crime, and although I had all the assistance of my solicitor, who exercise every possible means, both before and after my trial, to rescue me from my untimely end, yet I had my doubts that I should escape the penalty which I must now pay to the law. I was inwardly unhappy throughout, but bore up under such a terrible trial with the greatest fortitude and courage I possibly could; but when I was approaching the day of my execution, and fearing that nothing could be done to save me, I immediately requested the governor to send for Mr. O'Brien, my solicitor, that I might open my mind and reveal all things to him immediately, without the slightest hesitation or reserve, which I now proceed to do, knowing well that I have no hope of mercy in this world.

With respect to the death of Mrs. Thomas, the circumstances surrounding the murder of that lady are as follows:

I entered the lady's service in the month of January. At first, I thought her a nice old lady, and imagined I could be comfortable and happy with her; but I found her very trying. She used to do many things to annoy me. When I had finished my work in the rooms, she used to go over it and point out places where she said I did not clean, thus showing evidence of a nasty spirit towards me. This sort of conduct made me have an ill-feeling towards her, but I had no intention of killing her, at least not then. One day

I had an altercation with her, and we mutually arranged I should leave her service, and she made an entrance to that effect in her memorandum book.

On the Sunday evening, 2nd March last, Mrs. Thomas and I were alone in the house. We had some argument at which she and myself were enraged, and she became very agitated and left the house to go to church in that state, leaving me at home. Upon her return from church, before her usual hour, she came in and went upstairs. I went up after her, and we had an argument which ripened into a quarrel, and in the height of my anger and rage, I threw her from the top of the stairs to the ground floor. She had a heavy fall. I felt that she was seriously injured, and I became agitated at what had occurred, lost all control of myself, and, to prevent her screaming or getting me into trouble, I caught her by the throat, and in the struggle, she was choked. I threw her on the floor. I then became entirely lost and without any control over myself, and looking on what had happened, and the fear of being discovered, I determined to do away with the body as best I could. I chopped the head from the body with the assistance of a razor, which I used to cut through the flesh afterwards. I also used the meat saw and the carving knife to cut the body up with. I prepared the copper with water to boil the body to prevent identity; and as soon as I had succeeded in cutting it up, I placed it in the copper and boiled it. I opened the stomach with the carving knife and burned up as much of the parts as I could.

During the whole of this time there was nobody in the house but myself. When I looked upon the scene before me and saw the blood around my feet, the horror and dread I felt was inconceivable. I was bewildered, acted as if I was mad, and did everything I possibly could to conceal the occurrence, keep it quiet, and everything regular, fearing the neighbours might suspect something had happened. I was greatly overcome, both from the horrible sight before me and the smell, and I failed several times in my strength and determination but was helped on by the devil in this vile purpose. I remained in the house all night endeavouring to clear up the place and clean away traces of the murder.

I burned one part of the body after chopping it up and boiled the other. I think I boiled one of the feet. I emptied the copper, throwing the water away after having washed and cleaned the outside. I then put parts of the body into the little wooden box which was produced in court, and tied it up with cord, and determined to deposit it in the Thames, which was afterwards done (in the manner already described) with the help of young Porter.

I remember the coalman, Mr. Deane, coming to the house and knocking at the door. I was greatly frightened, but in dread of creating suspicion I opened the door to answer him, and spoke to him, as he stated in his evidence. When he called, I was engaged in regulating the place, and was in a dreadful state of mind.

I put the head of Mrs. Thomas into the black bag and being weary and afraid to remain in the house, I carried it to the Porters, and had some tea there. I placed the bag with the head in it under the tea table, and afterwards took it away from the house and disposed of it in the way and in the place I have described to my solicitor, Mr. O'Brien.

The deposition of this black bag gave me great uneasiness, as I feared it might be discovered, and the identity of Mrs. Thomas thereby proven, and when I heard that a black bag had been found I was greatly troubled. I pretended to Mr. O'Brien that the bag contained nothing of the kind. The foot found in the dunghill at Kingston was placed there by me, for when I came to realise the true state of things and the great danger stood in, I resolved to do everything in my power to keep everything secret and prevent being discovered.

When I placed the box in the river and disposed of the head and other parts of the body as best I could, and cleared up the place, so that a person coming in might not suspect or see anything irregular, it was suggested to my mind to sell all that there was in the house and go away; and with that view I went and saw Porter, and introduced the sale of the things to him. I gave the chairs to Porter as a gift, and also kept ordering things for the house from tradespeople in order to evade suspicion.

At the time of the murder, I took possession of Mrs. Thomas's gold watch and chain, and also of all the money in the house, which was only seven or eight pounds. I accompanied Church to the watchmaker's and asked for Mrs. Thomas's watch. Church only paid me £13, not £18, as stated … I threw the dresses and bonnet of Mrs. Thomas into the van which was brought to fetch the furniture, and they were taken to Church's … I determined to proceed to Ireland at once, to avoid being discovered, but I was not surprised at being arrested.

I did not murder Mrs. Thomas from any premeditation. I was enraged and in a passion, and I cannot now recollect why I did it; something seemed to seize me at the time. I threw her downstairs in the heat of passion and strong impulse … I never had a hatred or what may be termed as a bad feeling towards anybody in my lifetime, certainly not such as would ever have induced me to do them bodily injury; and I cannot account for the awful feelings that came over me from the time Mrs. Thomas came home from church until the murder was completed. It is true I went by the name of Mrs. Thomas and that I wore her gold watch; and with regard to the false teeth, I took them from Mrs. Thomas and gave them to Porter to sell, the proceeds of which he gave me, except one shilling which I gave him.

I have now relieved my mind by making a full and sincere confession that myself, without help or assistance of any person whatever, committed the murder ... I heartily exonerate every one from having any hand or part in it. When I got into trouble in Liverpool, it was owing in a great measure to poverty and evil associations, which led me step by step into badness. When I got over that trouble, I formed an intimate acquaintance with one who should have protected me and, being led away by evil associates and bad companions. I became, as it were, forlorn, and forsook everything that might have kept me in the path of rectitude and prevented my unhappy end.

I was afraid to make known the real state of things to my solicitor, lest he might have abandoned my case and taken no interest in it. I therefore concealed the truth from him until I sent for him, when he told me of the reply to the memorial sent up for me. I then fully and candidly confessed to him at the last moment the whole of the facts, in order that everything might be cleared up, and that I alone should be blamed. I am perfectly resigned to my fate and am full of confidence in a happy eternity. If I had a choice, I would almost sooner die than return to a life full of misery, deception, and wickedness.

I die with great fortitude and confidence in my faith, and in our blessed God, whom I beseech to have mercy on my soul.

Afterwards, having resigned herself to her fate, Kate told Father McEnery that she 'felt greatly relieved at having unburdened her conscience' and that she 'would sleep more calmly on her last night on earth, than she had done since her condemnation'. After having slept 'fairly well', Kate rose the following morning shortly after 5.00 am. Captain Colville, the governor of the prison, visited her soon after, followed by Father McEnery and the prison surgeon. William Marwood, the public executioner, having slept on the premises the night before, had risen early and was making the final preparations to the rope and scaffold to carry out the execution.

Just before 9.00 am, as the prison bell tolled, Kate left her cell and, leaning on the arm of Father McEnery, made her way down the steps towards the scaffold. She remained calm while her arms were pinioned, then walked 'firmly' to the scaffold, where her legs were strapped and Marwood placed the noose around her neck, while Father McEnery read the Roman Catholic service. As he read the words, 'Jesus, Good Shepherd, come,' Kate said in a loud voice, 'Lord, have mercy upon me,' and the bolt was drawn.[8]

Marwood's development of the 'long drop' method of hanging, introduced seven years before, which ensured the noose was correctly positioned around the prisoner's neck and that they were given a drop of 6 to 10 feet, meant that Kate's death was instantaneous due to her neck being broken, and not drawn out by strangulation. No spectators or newspaper reporters were permitted to attend the execution, as a decision had been made to keep the proceedings strictly private. The crowd that had been waiting quietly outside the prison walls cheered when, a few minutes after 9.00, a black flag was raised on the flagstaff, indicating that Kate Webster was dead.

The next day, a sale of Mrs Thomas's furniture and effects was held at the Assembly Rooms in Richmond. The sale attracted a large number of spectators and buyers, including John Church, who appeared to be very jovial, as he informed everyone that he had attended the auction just to show them that despite the high expenses incurred by the trial, he was not bankrupt. There were cheers as Church, who was the main purchaser, bought numerous items including Mrs Thomas's gold watch and chain, the carving knife allegedly used by Kate to dismember her victim's body, the piano, and music stool.

In February the following year, a woman named Sarah Nelly Essam came forward and made a statement to the police at Uxbridge regarding the Richmond murder. She claimed that until recently she had been living with a man in Ealing, who was the father of Kate Webster's child. A fortnight before, they were having dinner, when he 'suddenly jumped up and went into another room in a great state of agitation'. Sarah followed him and asked him what was wrong, and he replied, 'For God's sake, Nell, don't ask me. I shall go mad, I know I shall.' When Sarah begged him to tell her, he began to cry and said that if she repeated to anyone what he was about to tell her, she 'was a dead woman'. He then confessed to having been present when Kate had murdered Mrs Thomas and had helped her cut up and dispose of the body. He had also been on the bridge when the box containing the remains of Mrs Thomas was thrown into the river.[9]

Shortly after, the editor of the *Standard* newspaper received the following letter from Kate Webster's solicitor, Fitzgerald O'Brien:

Sir, – My attention has been called to an article in your last evening's issue upon the Richmond Murder case, which one would have thought by this time had passed away from the public mind; but as the real truth of the matter must be revealed sooner or later, perhaps the statement of Sarah Nelly Essam is an introduction to the true solution of the mystery.

From the first moment that I received a telegram from Ireland to defend Mrs. Webster, I knew from my instructions that the mutilation of the body of Mrs. Thomas was the act of a man who was in the house, Vine Cottage, at the time, and who was afterwards seen on the bridge, and I called particular attention to the fact in my observations to the Bench of Magistrates at

Richmond at the close of the case. It was admitted in evidence that the man was seen on the bridge on the night of the 4th March, when the box was said to have been deposited in the river; and Miss. Ives, the landlady, swore that there had been great noise in the house, and persons walking about, and that a cab drove up to the door with two women and two or three men in it, and in addition there was ample evidence to show that Mrs. Webster was not alone in the house. The cutting up of the body of the lady suggested to have been murdered, was not the act of Kate Webster, who paid the penalty. It is true that she had had an altercation with Mrs. Thomas on the Sunday night, but the chopping up of the body was the act of a man, and not of my unfortunate client. I shall not be surprised to hear the full confession of the man in question one day, and as far as I am able to learn at present, a statement of the whole transaction will shortly appear.

There were numberless difficulties in the way of the prosecution, and but for the public prejudice against her, the unfortunate woman might have been saved from a penalty which in common justice, should have been paid by somebody else. Kate Webster, I affirm without hesitation – and I think you will admit that I ought to know and do know – did not commit the murder. I was with her in her last moments, when a telegram from the Home Office reached me, when she was on the brink of eternity. I well knew the actual state of her mind, and so far as the actual commission of the crime was concerned, Kate Webster was innocent, however, much to blame she may otherwise have been. Public prejudice, and the heinous nature of the crime, sent Kate Webster into eternity, and the real perpetrators remain at large.

Following his mother's arrest, poor John Webster was admitted into the workhouse, as the following extract taken from the minute books of the Poor Law Guardians in Wexford confirms:

> A child named John Webster aged about 6 years was admitted here on March 29th. His mother was charged with the murder of a woman named 'Thomas.' The boy was sent to the Workhouse with an order from W Ryan R.M. to have him admitted pending inquiry being made as to his reception into an Industrial School.[10]

Despite a thorough search covering the area around Richmond Bridge, the police never did find the black bag which contained crucial evidence to the 'Richmond Murder'. But many years later, in October 2010, workmen excavating the garden of renowned naturalist and broadcaster, Sir David Attenborough, in Park Road, Richmond, unearthed a human skull. Following carbon dating tests at the University of Edinburgh, an inquest was held on 5 July 2011, where the coroner, Alison Thompson, formally identified the skull as belonging to Julia Martha Thomas and recorded a verdict of unlawful killing. The cause of death was given as asphyxiation and a head injury. After 131 years, the crime that had originally been dubbed by the press the 'Barnes Mystery' had finally been solved.

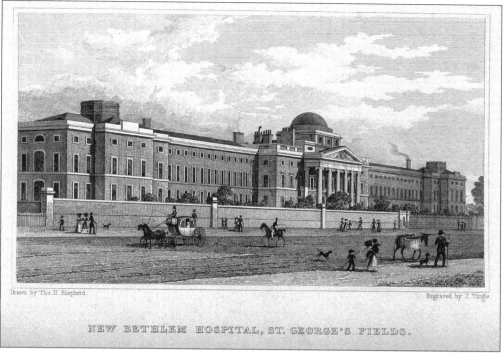

Bethlem Hospital. (Wellcome Collection)

Female workroom, Bethlem Hospital. (Wellcome Collection)

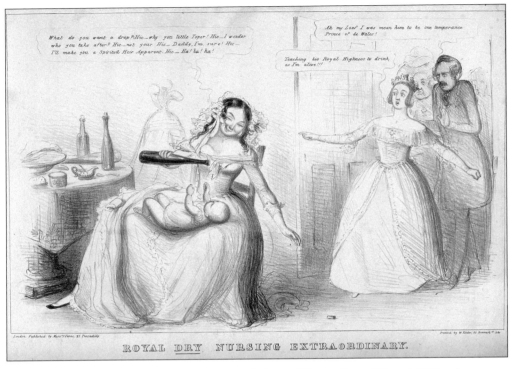

A drunken wet-nurse about to give the Prince of Wales (later Edward VII) a drop of alcohol as a horrified Queen Victoria and Prince Albert burst in on the scene. (Wellcome Collection)

*Above*: Seaham Infirmary – Mary Ann Cotton. (www.maryanncotton.co.uk)

*Left*: Mary Ann Cotton. (www.maryanncotton.co.uk)

*Right*: Johnson Terrace, West Auckland, Mary Ann Cotton's first home. (www.maryanncotton. co.uk)

*Below*: The Benders. (*The Benders in Kansas*, John Towner James, Kan-Okla Publishing, 1913)

Lizzie Borden's House, 92 Second Street, Fall River.

*Above left*: Lizzie Borden.

*Above right and below*: Abby Borden – crime scene. (lizzie-borden.com)

*Above left*: Andrew Borden – crime scene. (lizzie-borden.com)

*Above right*: John Church. (*The Penny Illustrated Paper and Illustrated Times*, 2 August 1879)

Kate Webster (left), Julia Martha Thomas (right). (*Illustrated Police News*, 12 July 1879)

RESIDENCE OF MRS. THOMAS AT RICHMOND.

Vine Cottages, Richmond, residence of Mrs Thomas at Richmond. (*Penny Illustrated Paper and Illustrated Times*, 5 July 1879)

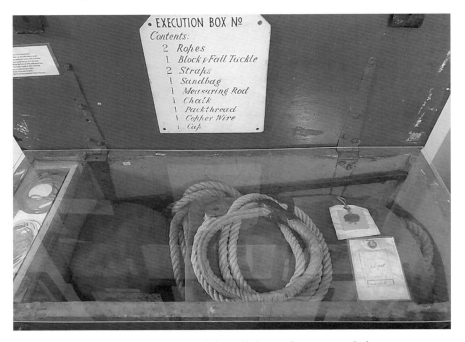

EXECUTION BOX Nº

Contents:
2 Ropes
1 Block & Fall Tackle
2 Straps
1 Sandbag
1 Measuring Rod
1 Chalk
1 Packthread
1 Copper Wire
1 Cap

British Execution Box, No. 8, containing all the equipment needed to carry out an execution. The boxes were held at Wandsworth and sent out to other prisons for each execution. (Wandsworth Prison Museum)

*Right*: Jane Toppan. (Bourne Archives)

*Left*: The Davis family pose in front of the Jachin Hotel around 1900. (Bourne Archives)

*Left*: The Davis family outside the Jachin Hotel. (Bourne Archives)

*Below*: Barnes Bridge, where the box containing the remains of Julia Martha Thomas was found. (*Illustrated London News*, 1 September 1849)

# Chapter 6

# Lizzie Borden's Secret
## Lizzie Borden, Fall River, 1892

On 8 August 1892, a gripping headline in the *Fall River Herald* newspaper read: 'SHOCKING CRIME: A Venerable Citizen and his Aged Wife HACKED TO PIECES IN THEIR HOME.'

The report told the residents of Fall River, Massachusetts, that on the morning of 4 August, 70-year-old wealthy businessman Andrew Jackson Borden and his 64-year-old wife Abby were found brutally murdered in their home at 92 Second Street. Both had been bludgeoned to death with what was believed to have been an axe or a hatchet, brandished with such force that they were almost unidentifiable. Andrew, believed to have been taking a nap, was found lying back on the sofa in the sitting room, his legs sprawled out onto the floor. He had received eleven blows to his head, his face 'hacked almost beyond recognition'. Blood spots splattered the floor and up the wall at the back of the sofa. His clothes and the rest of his body were undisturbed.

Upstairs in the guest bedroom, lying in a pool of blood, were the butchered remains of Abby Borden, her head pummelled to a pulp by the nineteen blows she had received. The only other known occupants of the house at the time were 32-year-old Lizzie Borden, Andrew Borden's youngest daughter from his first marriage, and their Irish maid, Bridget Sullivan. Though an unlikely suspect, Lizzie Borden was arrested for both murders a week later. The entire country was both shocked and fascinated by the murders and the trial, which took place the following year in June, would become one of the most famous and notorious murder cases in nineteenth-century America.

Lizzie Andrew Borden was the youngest of three daughters, born on 19 July 1860 to Andrew J. Borden and his first wife Sarah Anthony Morse, at Fall River, a mill town in Massachusetts. Lizzie's middle sister, Alice, had died in early childhood, and when Lizzie was just two years old, her mother also died. Two years later, Andrew married Abby Durfee Gray, a spinster who came from a respectable family. Many speculated at the time that the marriage was for convenience, rather than love, as Andrew wanted a housekeeper and mother to his two daughters, while Abby wanted a husband.

Although Lizzie referred to Abby as 'Mother', she never really accepted her and turned to her eldest sister, 14-year-old Emma, to be mothered. Emma returned her affection, having made a promise on her mother's deathbed to always look after 'baby Lizzie'. Neither of the girls seemed to have had a loving relationship with their stepmother; as Emma later said during the trial, 'We never felt that she was much interested in us.'[1]

The textile manufacturing city of Fall River was prosperous but divided in the late nineteenth century. The mill workers lived in tenement timber buildings down near the river close to the mills, while the wealthy mill owners lived in the grand houses in an elite neighbourhood known as 'the hill', where they enjoyed an opulent lifestyle of travel, extensive libraries, ballrooms, servants, and governesses for their children. Though the Borden family were one of several extremely wealthy and prominent families that regulated the town, not all members of the family inherited wealth and Andrew Borden was one of them. Unlike his relatives who lived up on the hill, he had made his own fortune through years of hard work, initially as an undertaker, then as a director of several mills. He owned substantial property and eventually became president of the Union Savings Bank, accumulating wealth of around $300,000.[2]

Andrew's wealth would have easily enabled him to reside in a fine house on 'the hill', but instead he chose to live in a modest house, in the middle-class, slightly shabby area of Second Street. The narrow two-and-a-half-storey timber house had originally been two identical tenement flats, one above the other, each with two larger rooms, two small rooms, and a kitchen. It had an unusual layout with no hallways, so each room led to another, which consequently offered very little privacy to the occupants. Andrew made some alterations to the house, by changing the upstairs kitchen into a bedroom and making the two rooms downstairs into a dining room.

Lizzie's and Emma's bedrooms were on the second floor, which was accessed by the front staircase. There was also a guest room on that floor and Andrew and Abby's bedroom and dressing room, with a door leading to it from Lizzie's bedroom, which was permanently locked, so their bedroom was accessed by the other staircase at the back of the house, which was reached by going back down the stairs and through the house. Although somewhat odd, this layout did enable Lizzie and Emma to have their own space on the second floor, where they would receive any visitors. Bridget Sullivan, often referred to as Maggie, slept in one of the two bedrooms in the attic. Outside there were several pear trees and a grape arbour, and at the side of the house was what the Bordens referred to as 'the barn', which was a small stable, with a disused privy behind it.

Andrew Borden lived a very frugal lifestyle, economising on basic living utilities in the home, such as water and lighting. He refused to update the house and unlike other middle-class homes of the late nineteenth century, which had running water and electricity, the Bordens' water (which was cold) came from a water pump in the sink-room. During the alterations to the house, Andrew had removed the water tank in the attic that provided water to the upper floor kitchen, considering it an extravagance to have running water on both floors of the house. Instead of electricity or gaslight, he lit the house using dated kerosene lamps, often sitting in the dark to save the kerosene. He kept old newspapers in the privy in the cellar for sanitary purposes and accounted for every dime spent in the household. It was later said that 'a leg of lamb first cooked on the Saturday before the murder was on the table in disguised form five days later.'[3] A man of his wealth could have easily fed his family on luxuries, but instead he insisted they ate mutton most days of the week.

Author Victoria Lincoln, who grew up in Fall River, recalled the extent of Andrew Borden's thriftiness: 'When he was an undertaker, people used to enjoy saying that he cut the feet off the corpses so that he could cram them into undersized coffins that he got cheap.' He was a ruthless landlord, evicting tenants with little notice, and would raise the rent if he 'suspected that a tenant was prospering', and 'was never known to give a penny to charity'. She describes him as being 'six feet two, and gaunt; his eyes were small, dull, and black, his voice and his skin were dry, and his lipless mouth turned down at the corners.' He always wore 'a black string tie and a knee-length, double-breasted Prince Albert (coat)', which he wore 'in the record heat on the August morning of his death'.[4] Andrew owned a farmhouse in Swansea, where he kept poultry and would occasionally be seen in the town, 'carrying a little wicker basket of eggs, solemn in his long black Prince Albert, peddling them to his business associates'.

As she grew older, Lizzie longed to join the social activities enjoyed by other young girls of their class, who wore elegant dresses and attended elaborate balls. Her father, however, having little time for the high life, dismissed such activities as tawdriness, so instead he restricted their social activities to the church. Lizzie joined the Central Congregational Church and taught Sunday school at the Mission Chapel. She was Secretary-Treasurer of the Christian Endeavour Society, was involved in the Women's Christian Temperance Union (WCTU), the Ladies Fruit and Flower Mission, and later joined the board of the Good Samaritan Charity Hospital.

But Lizzie yearned to live on 'the hill' and live the glamorous lifestyle enjoyed by her cousins and other relatives. She was 'by nature a spender, caring vastly for prestige and display',[5] and, unlike her father, longed to be more frivolous with money, but her paltry allowance restricted her spending. As there were few opportunities for unmarried women of her class, and a strict code of etiquette prevented her from leaving home and becoming independent, there was very little she could do to change the situation. She was known locally to be a shoplifter, and she had stolen from a department store in the city, but she was never prosecuted as the staff would make a note of the goods that she stole and send her father the bill, which he always paid.

Despite his strictness and penny-pinching ways, Andrew loved Lizzie and there are clear indications to suggest that his feelings were reciprocated. Lizzie had given him a ring, a token of her affection when she graduated from high school, which he was wearing on his little finger when he died, and several witnesses at the trial recounted conversations with Lizzie in which she expressed her affection for her father. However, it appears that she did not have the same feelings for her stepmother and at times their relationship was strained. It was an event that took place five years before the murder which would increase the tension between the two women, and leave Lizzie feeling pure contempt towards her stepmother.

Andrew had purchased a house for Abby, for her sister to live in, as the house she shared with her mother was being sold and they would be evicted. Neither Emma nor Lizzie knew about the transaction and were furious, especially as they found out about it through local gossip. They became more enraged when they found out that their uncle John Morse, brother of their mother Sarah, had known about the house purchase. As Andrew Borden had not made a will, the sisters felt that there was a risk of losing their inheritance if he was to die, as everything would go to Abby and, upon her death, it would then go to her sister.

Both women made it clear that they resented Andrew's favour to Abby's family and the atmosphere in the household became very tense. To pacify his daughters, Andrew gave them the old family home which he still owned at Ferry Street in Fall River, with full access to the money made from the rents at the property to spend as they wished.

Lizzie seemed to forgive her father, as she thought he had been coerced by John Morse and Abby, whom she blamed constantly for plotting behind her and Emma's back. Thereafter, she refused to call Abby 'Mother', addressing and referring to her as Mrs Borden, and she and Emma avoided eating with their father and stepmother at mealtimes.

Lizzie had also made her deep hatred towards Abby Borden known outside the family home, so the growing discord amongst the Bordens became common knowledge around the town. Later, at the trial, Mrs Gifford, who owned a small business in Fall River, recalled Lizzie's curt response after she referred to Abby as her 'Mother': 'Don't call her that to me. She is a mean, good-for-nothing old thing!' Lizzie then told Mrs Gifford that she avoided Abby, preferring to stay in her room.

After the incident of the house purchase for his wife, Andrew continued to be more generous to his daughters. Lizzie's allowance increased, enabling her to buy lavish clothes, and Andrew even allowed her to join her wealthy relatives on the Grand Tour of Europe. During the trip she shared a cabin with her cousin, Anna Borden, where she expressed her feelings of contempt towards her stepmother and her dread at returning to the Borden home. It seemed that neither Andrew's latest generosity nor the trip eased Lizzie's disdain towards Abby Borden.

Shortly after Lizzie returned home in the summer of 1891, the Bordens' house was burgled. Andrew and Abby Borden were away at their farmhouse in Swansea, leaving Lizzie, Emma, and Bridget the maid in the house. In addition to being occupied, the house was also very secure, with several bolts on all the doors and a six-foot fence topped with barbed wire outside. But despite the securities installed to prevent a robbery, the thief had somehow managed to enter the house in broad daylight, go straight to Abby Borden's room and steal her jewellery, her gold watch, some money, and a book of horsecar tickets, leaving the room in disarray. The rest of the house was left undisturbed.

Surprisingly, the thief's work was only discovered by Andrew and Abby when they returned, as none of the three women had seen anyone nor heard a sound. The police were notified, and an investigation ensued. Suspicion was aroused when an 'overexcited' Lizzie, talking 'incessantly', showed them the cellar door, which she had apparently found unbolted with a large nail stuck in the keyhole that she presumed had been used to pick the lock. Following Andrew Borden's request, the robbery was not reported to the newspapers and the investigation was dropped within a fortnight. Thereafter, every door in the house was kept locked and Andrew Borden always placed the key from his bedroom door on display on the mantelpiece in the sitting room, which was believed to have been a warning to the young women of the Borden household.

In July 1892, two weeks before the murders took place, Andrew Borden repurchased the house in Ferry Street from his daughters for $5,000, around $2,000 more than its market value, allowing Lizzie and Emma a gift of $1,000 each. Emma planned to visit friends at Fairhaven and Lizzie was to travel with her as far as New Bedford, where she would continue her journey on to Marion, where some friends were renting a cottage by the sea. However, when the two women parted ways, Lizzie didn't go to Marion; instead, she stayed in New Bedford, where she spent the next day and night in a boarding house. Later, evidence would confirm that while she was in New Bedford, Lizzie attempted but failed several times to purchase prussic acid.

On Tuesday, 2 August, Andrew and his wife became ill and were up all night vomiting. Bridget was also ill the next day, but Lizzie only mildly so. The next morning, Abby was so worried she hurried across the street to Dr Seabury W. Bowen. Andrew was livid and apparently shouted after her, 'Well, my money shan't pay for it!' At first, she claimed that they had been poisoned as her husband had supposedly received an anonymous threat, but when she mentioned that they had eaten fish that had been reheated from the previous day, the doctor laughed, but offered to go over the road and examine the rest of the family anyway. But Andrew, who was still fuming, met him at the door and was extremely rude, so the doctor hastily left.

Later that evening, Lizzie visited Alice Russell, her neighbour and family friend. She told her, 'I feel depressed. I feel as if something was hanging over me that I cannot throw off, and it comes over me at times, no matter where I am.' She told her about the family's sickness the day before, though she admitted that she herself hadn't vomited. At first, she blamed the baker's bread, then said that someone must have put poison in the milk can that was delivered in the mornings. 'I am afraid somebody will do something,' she exclaimed, 'I don't know what, but somebody will do something!' Lizzie thought her father had enemies who were trying to poison them. 'I am afraid sometimes that somebody will do something to him; he is so discourteous to people.' She told Alice about Dr Bowen's visit that morning and how 'mortified' she had been at her father's rudeness towards him, then she mentioned the robbery the previous year. 'I feel as if I wanted to sleep with my eyes half open – with one eye open half the time – for fear they will burn the house down over us.'

On the morning of 4 August 1892, John Morse, who had stayed in the guest bedroom overnight, having arrived the previous evening, sat down to breakfast with Andrew and Abby Borden. The transfer of ownership of the Swansea farmhouse was due to take place that morning at the National Union Bank and it was decided that John Morse would live in the farmhouse with his unmarried niece, who would be the housekeeper. Lizzie was not at breakfast and Emma was still away at her friends in Fairhaven. After breakfast, at around 8.45 am, John Morse left the house to visit relatives at Weybosset Street, about a mile away. As he went out, Andrew called after him, inviting him to come back for dinner. Shortly after, Andrew left the house to make his usual morning calls to his bank and other businesses. In the meantime, Abby instructed Bridget to wash the front windows inside and out on the first floor, while she went upstairs to make the bed in the guest bedroom. That was the last time she was seen alive.

Bridget, who was still feeling queasy, had been vomiting in the back yard and was in no hurry to start the windows, especially on an exceptionally hot August morning, so she stopped to chat over the fence to the maid employed by their neighbour, Dr Kelly. The time was just before 9.00 am. Only Lizzie and Abby were inside the house. Several witnesses said that they had noticed the wooden shutters of the window of the guest room were closed, which was unusual as they were never closed during the day.

Later that morning, Andrew Borden arrived back home earlier than usual, as he was still feeling unwell. He tried, as he usually did, to enter the house through the side door, but it was locked, so he went round to the front door, but his key would not open it. In her testimony, Briget said that she heard Andrew trying to unlock the door and went to let him in but found that instead of the usual spring lock used during the daytime, the night lock and bolt were also secured, making it more difficult to open. In her frustration she uttered an expletive, then heard Lizzie laugh from the top of the front stairs, and presumed she was laughing at her profanity.

When Andrew came in, he went straight into the dining room where Lizzie, who had come downstairs, joined him. She told her father that Abby Borden had received a note from a sick person that morning and had gone out. Andrew then went into the sitting room to relax on the sofa and take a nap, while Bridget continued washing the windows in the dining room. After she finished her chores, Bridget recalled seeing Lizzie in the kitchen before she went upstairs to her room in the attic, to lie on her bed. Shortly afterwards, she heard the nearby City Hall bell ring and saw by her clock on the bureau that it was 11.00. She estimated that between ten or fifteen minutes later, she heard Lizzie shriek, 'Maggie, come down quick. Father's dead, somebody came in and killed him!'

Bridget rushed downstairs to find Lizzie standing with her back to the screen door: 'I went to go right in the sitting room, and she [Lizzie] says, "Oh, Maggie, don't go in. I have to have a doctor quick. Go over. I have got to have a doctor." I went over to Dr Bowen's right away.'

Dr Bowen was not at home, but Bridget spoke to Mrs Bowen, and told her that Andrew Borden was dead. She hurried back to Lizzie, who told her to get Alice Russell, as she didn't want to be alone in the house. As she was going out the door, Bridget asked, 'Miss Lizzie, where was you? Didn't I leave the screen door hooked?' Lizzie replied that she was 'out in the back yard and heard a groan and came in and the screen door was wide open'.

By the time Bridget returned with Alice Russell, Dr Bowen had arrived, as had a neighbour, Adelaide Churchill. She had been walking along Second Street on her way back from the market and had seen Bridget crossing the street from Dr Bowen's to the Borden house:

> She was walking fast, she looked very white, and I thought someone was sick. I went into my house, put down my bundles and looked out my kitchen window. Miss Lizzie Borden was standing inside their screen door, at the side of their house. I opened the window and said, 'Lizzie what is the matter?' She replied, 'Oh, Mrs. Churchill, do come over. Someone has killed Father.'

Adelaide went straight over to the Bordens' house through the side gate and found Lizzie sitting on the bottom stair. She gently laid a hand on her arm and asked her quietly, 'Where is your father, Lizzie?' Lizzie told her he was in the sitting room. 'Where were you when it happened?' Adelaide asked. 'I went to the barn to get a piece of iron. Then I heard a distressing noise.' Just then, Dr Bowen, who had come through from seeing Andrew in the sitting room, exclaimed, 'Murdered! He has been murdered!'

Bridget was concerned for Abby Borden, and offered to go and find her, but Lizzie insisted that she had heard her return and asked Bridget to look upstairs. As Bridget was reluctant to go upstairs on her own, Adelaide Churchill offered to go with her, so Bridget nervously led the way up the staircase. But as she went up the stairs, Adelaide turned her head to the left, 'and when I got up so my eyes were level with the front hall, I could see across the floor of the spare room. At the far side, I saw something that looked like the form of a person. I turned and went back.' Downstairs, Alice Russell, having seen Adelaide's pale, stricken face, asked, 'Is there another?' Adelaide replied, 'Yes, she is up there.' As she entered the room, Bridget saw Abby Borden lying on the floor: 'I could see her body, her dress; and then I stood by the foot of the bed and looked at her,' she said, before she came back downstairs.

The police were summoned and, as the shocking news swiftly spread that a double murder had been committed in broad daylight, by the afternoon the street outside the house became blocked, as hundreds of people poured into Second Street. A reporter from the *Fall River Herald* gave an account of the horrific scene that met him when he arrived at the house:

> On the lounge in the cosy sitting room on the first floor of the building lay Andrew J. Borden, dead. His face presented a sickening sight. Over the left temple a wound six by four had been made as if the head had been pounded with the dull edge of an axe. The left eye had been dug out and a cut extended the length of the nose. The face was hacked to pieces and the blood had covered the man's shirt and soaked into his clothing. Everything about the room was in order, and there were no signs of a scuffle of any kind.

He then described the scene upstairs:

> On the floor between the bed and the dressing case lay Mrs. Borden, stretched full length, one arm extended and her face resting upon it. Over the left temple the skull was fractured and no less than seven wounds were found about the head. She had died evidently where she had been struck, for her life blood formed a ghastly clot on the carpet.

Dr William Dolan, the county medical examiner, arrived at the house just before noon. He performed autopsies on both bodies at the scene and collaborated with the police to try to establish the events of that morning. He found that the blood on Abby's head was 'matted and practically dry ... coagulated and of a dark colour', whereas the blood from Andrew Borden's wounds was bright red and still oozing, dripping onto the carpet. His hands were still warm, while Abby's were cold, which meant that he had died shortly before being discovered. These factors and the results of a more thorough autopsy a few days later, examining Abby Borden's stomach, deduced that she had died first, between 9.00 and 9.30 am, around 1½ to two hours before Andrew. It was a discovery that threw some confusion on the investigation.

Fall River photographer James A. Walsh took photographs of the crime scene and the victims' bodies, while the police searched the house. John Morse, who had returned for his midday meal, seemed to be unaware of the crowd that had gathered outside or what had happened inside the house, as he went round to the back yard, where he stood under the pear tree for some time, eating pears, before he entered the house through the kitchen door. 'Nothing attracted my attention at first,' he said.

Officer Medley went outside to the barn and climbed up the steep stairs into the loft, where Lizzie had said she had been when her father was murdered, but as there were unbroken cobwebs at the head of the stairs and no footprints imprinted on the thick dust on the floor, it was obvious that no one had been in there for some time.

Meanwhile, Dr Bowen suggested that Lizzie should lie down and rest in her room, so Alice Russell took her upstairs. She noted that when Lizzie came back downstairs a little later, she had changed out of her clothes into a pink and white striped dress. Upstairs, Deputy Marshal, John Fleet, asked Lizzie some questions, including if she had any idea who could have killed her father and mother, at which she promptly reminded him, 'She is not my mother sir, she is my stepmother! My mother died when I was a child.'[6]

Although she had remained surprisingly calm throughout her ordeal, the doctor gave Lizzie medication to steady her nerves. One investigating office remarked:

> I was surprised at the way Miss Lizzie carried herself and I must say that I admire her nerve. She did not appear to be in the least bit excited or worried. I have wondered why she did not faint upon her discovery of the dead body of her father. Most women would have done so, for a more horrible sight I never saw, and I walked over a battlefield where thousands lay mangled and dead.

By late afternoon, Second Street was blocked with thousands of people who had flocked to stand and gawp at the Bordens' house. The number of workers who had left their work at the mills was so great that they had to close. A telegram had been sent to Emma, who returned home in the evening, when the police had finally finished their investigation. That night, several police officers stood guard at the house, while Lizzie and Emma slept in their own rooms and Alice, who had offered to stay with them, slept in Mr and Mrs Borden's room. Bridget, who had been too scared to sleep in the house, slept with Dr Bowen's maid in her room at the doctor's house across the street.

The next day, the police returned to the house to resume their search, following a claim by Mr Eli Bence, a clerk at Smith's pharmacy in Fall River, that on the day before the murders, Lizzie had tried to purchase prussic acid from his store. Lizzie had said she wanted it to clean her sealskin cape to protect it from moths. When Mr Bence refused to sell her the poison without a prescription from a doctor, Lizzie protested, before leaving the shop. She was also recognised by two other people in the store at the time. While the investigation continued, Lizzie promptly sent for the family lawyer, Andrew J. Jennings. Also, later that day, the two sisters placed a prominent notice in the *Fall River*

*Herald* offering $5,000 reward for the arrest and conviction of the murderer. Perhaps it was a ploy to avert any arousing suspicion.

Despite the slaughter that had taken place, the house and its contents remained untouched. There were no signs of a robbery, the money in Andrew Borden's pockets had not been taken nor Abby Borden's jewellery, so it seemed unlikely that it had been a random attack from a stranger. Initially the police rendered the murders an attack of insanity and looked for suspects outside the Bordens' home, including members of the local immigrant population. Due to his reputation as a heartless landlord and miser, Andrew Borden had evidently gained many enemies in Fall River, and the general reaction to his death was that 'somebody did a good job'.[7]

So, it was possible that Andrew Borden's murder might have been an attack of revenge, but then the question arose: why had Abby Borden been killed first, and where had the murderer hidden during the time lapse between the two murders? The only evidence the police found that might have had any significance were three hatchets discovered in a box behind the chimney in the basement. One of the hatchets had a broken handle and the blade was covered in ash. On closer inspection with a magnifying glass at the city marshal's office the next day, Dr William Dolan found two hairs on the large hatchet and stains that he thought resembled blood. But after sending them to Professor Edward S. Wood, it was confirmed that the hairs were from an animal, possibly a cow, and tests carried out on the stains proved to be rust.

The police then started to look for suspects within the Bordens' home, the first being John Morse, but he had an airtight alibi. His relatives confirmed that he was with them at the time of the murders, and he gave names of the people that he had seen or met that morning, the number of the horsecar he had taken, and the number on the conductor's cap. Emma Borden was away in Fairhaven and Bridget Sullivan was eliminated from the enquiries, as it was thought she had no apparent motive and would not jeopardise her employment by committing such an act.

The only other person who had been in the house that morning was Lizzie, but during the nineteenth century, women of Lizzie's class were regarded as delicate, sensitive, and selfless beings, therefore it would have been unthinkable to suspect them of such a violent, horrendous crime. If murder was committed by a woman, it would most likely have been by poison. Lizzie was extremely respectable, had no criminal record, was a devout member of the church, and prominent in church work; however, the hatred she felt towards her stepmother was widely known, which prompted some suspicion.

On Saturday, 6 August, the funeral of Andrew and Abby Borden was held at Oak Grove cemetery in Fall River. During the service, just as the bodies were about to be lowered into the graves, a telegram arrived from Harvard Medical School requesting the skulls of the victims, so the coffins were promptly put back into the hearses. That evening, John Coughlin, the mayor of Fall River, visited Lizzie Borden to tell her that she was now the prime suspect.

A private inquest was held on Tuesday, 9 August at the Second District Court in Fall River, where Lizzie gave an ambiguous and inconsistent account of her actions on the morning of the murders. At first, she told District Attorney Hosea Knowlton that, shortly after her father had arrived home, she had gone to the barn to look for some lead to make a sinker for a forthcoming fishing trip; after further questioning, she then said that she wanted the lead to fix a broken screen, even though all the screens in the house were intact. She also said that she had spent around twenty minutes up in the loft of the barn, where in the stifling heat she stood looking out the closed window eating pears. She had full view of the back door but was adamant that she did not see anyone enter the house. There had indeed been lead in a box in the barn, but it was left untouched, and Officer Medley had already confirmed that there was no evidence of anyone having been in the barn recently.

Lizzie denied having gone to the drugstore to buy prussic acid and had no knowledge of the store's whereabouts, even though it was only a few minutes' walk from her house and had been there for over a decade. Throughout the inquest, Lizzie seemed to have difficulty remembering her whereabouts that morning. Hosea Knowlton, exasperated by her evasive answers and constant contradictions, implored, 'Miss Borden, I have been trying to get the story of that morning from yourself and Miss Sullivan and I have not succeeded. Do you desire to give me information or not?' He had heard that Lizzie had been ironing when her stepmother had been murdered, then she recalled that she had been reading a magazine in the kitchen, but had not heard a sound from upstairs, not even a cry or the thud of a rather plump (around 200 lbs) Abby Borden falling to the floor.

She had been downstairs in the kitchen when her father returned home, then she had been upstairs, then she wasn't sure, she could have been coming down the stairs. She said that her father took off his shoes and put on his slippers, but the photo taken after his death clearly shows that he was still wearing his boots when he died. When she came in from the barn, she found her father lying on the sofa in the sitting room, but she was 'so horrified and frightened' that she didn't notice he was dead. 'I don't know ... I have answered so many questions and am so confused that I don't know one thing from another,' she said. Not only did Lizzie's testimony differ from Bridget's account, but also those of the other witnesses.

Hosea Knowlton was convinced that Lizzie was guilty and, on Thursday, 11 August, she was arrested and charged with the murders of Andrew and Abby Borden. At her arraignment the next day, she pleaded not guilty to the charges. There were no facilities for women in the Fall River jail, so she was transported twenty miles away to Taunton jail, to stay until the preliminary hearing. Despite some initial doubt amongst the people of Fall River, Lizzie's spotless reputation ensured that most of the townsfolk decreed her innocent and came to her defence. She received support from the most significant citizens of the city, including her ministers, Rev. E. A. Buck and

Rev. W. W. Jubb, who declared in his sermons that Lizzie's 'acts and motives have always been pure and holy'.

Feminist groups, including the WCTU also declared her innocence in letters to the authorities, periodicals, and articles in their newspapers. Lucy Stone, the leading activist and founder of *Woman's Journal*, printed dynamic editorials proclaiming Lizzie's innocence and used her case to argue for the appointing of female jurors to give women a fairer trial. Mary Livermore, a journalist and advocate of women's rights, visited Lizzie in jail and wrote articles on her behalf. Nonetheless, negative reports still appeared in the press, namely *The Fall River Daily Globe*, which printed fictitious articles to convince its readers of her guilt.

The preliminary hearing began on Thursday, 25 August and lasted until 1 September, in which the counsel for the defence, Andrew Jennings, implored the judge 'not to put the stigma of guilt upon this woman, reared as she has been and with a past character beyond reproach. Don't let it go out in the world as the decision of a just judge that she is probably guilty.' But the judge did pronounce Lizzie 'probably guilty' and ordered her to face a grand jury. She was taken back to Taunton jail, where, unlike the other women, she was allowed certain privileges such as walks in the open air and meals from a local hotel. One newspaper journalist who visited her in jail reported that she was 'as well as ever, cheerful and contented ... she had a light in her cell, and there were flowers on the window ledge.'

The grand jury convened in November and, on 1 December, Alice Russell provided new evidence which would finalise the proceedings and destroy her friendship with the sisters forever. Alice recalled seeing Lizzie burn a blue dress in the kitchen fire three days after the murders, which had allegedly been stained with 'old paint'. Bridget Sullivan had previously stated in her testimony that Lizzie had been wearing a blue dress on the morning of the murders. The next day, on 2 December, the grand jury returned three indictments against Lizzie. The first charged her with the murder of Andrew Borden, the second with the murder of Abby Borden, and the third charged her jointly with both murders.

Lizzie remained in Taunton jail until her trial on 5 June 1893, held in the New Bedford Courthouse, Massachusetts, before a panel of three judges and a jury of twelve men. Her wealth bought her representation by two of the most eminent defence lawyers. In addition to Andrew Jennings, she was also represented by George Robinson, the former governor of Massachusetts, who allegedly charged $25,000 for his legal expertise.[8] There was no physical evidence connecting Lizzie to the murders, no blood was found on her clothes, there were no eyewitnesses, and no murder weapon had been found, so the prosecution, led by Hosea Knowlton and William Moody, built a case based on circumstantial evidence. They suspected that Lizzie's motive was either her bitter resentment towards her stepmother or her wish to procure her father's wealth.

Described by the press as 'the most sensational trial of the day', for the duration of two weeks, crowds of spectators and reporters surrounded the courthouse. Both local and national newspapers not only covered the legal proceedings, but also details of the flowers in the courtroom, the attire worn by Lizzie Borden, and the spectators who filled the court. Artists employed by some newspapers provided a visual display of the proceedings.

Following George Robinson's advice to go into mourning, for the first time since the murders, Lizzie entered the court on the arm of Rev. Buck, dressed in a black brocade dress, a black hat, and gloves. 'Her dress fitted her as perfectly as if she had been measured for it in Paris, but it was very old fashioned ... the front of the basque puffed with great fullness ... Her black straw hat was poked shaped, and of no existing fashion,' the *Boston Daily Globe* informed its readers. 'She is a very plain looking old maid ... likened to a typical school marm, plain and practical ... She has large, brown eyes, a fine high forehead, but her nose is a tilting one ... Her cheeks are very plump, and her jaws are strong and conspicuous.' Lizzie carried a fan which she used periodically to cover her face during a grisly testimony; sometimes a bunch of flowers were added, to accentuate her vulnerability and innocence.

On the second day, William Moody opened the case for the Commonwealth. In his opening statement, he affirmed that Lizzie was the only person with a motive and opportunity to commit the murders. The court heard of her resentment towards her stepmother, her ominous conversation with Alice Russell the night before the murders, her conflicting statements, and the burning of the dress she had worn on the morning of the murders, possibly destroying any evidence. Moody described the unusual layout of the Bordens' house and how it would be highly unlikely that an intruder could hide and remain undiscovered, to commit the second murder over an hour later. He argued that Lizzie, who had been in the house all morning, had the perfect opportunity to commit the murders, whilst Bridget was outside washing the windows. As there was no sign of a struggle, the killer must have been known to the victims.

As she sat listening to William Moody, Lizzie remained cold and detached, until he presented the previously examined head of the broken hatchet and stated that the length of its blade matched the wounds in the skulls of the murdered victims. To demonstrate this, the skulls, the flesh having been boiled off them, were brought into the courtroom, and the hatchet was inserted into the holes in the bones. Once Lizzie saw the skulls, she fell 'into a faint that lasted for several minutes, sending a thrill of excitement through awe-struck spectators'. Rev. Jubb and Andrew Jennings were immediately at her side with smelling salts and cold water. After a 'minute or two' she came round and regained her composure and continued with the same equanimity for the duration of the trial. However, the women in the court were not impressed by her cool indifference, as *The New York Tribune* noted:

> All the women hereabouts seem to have made up their
> minds that Lizzie Borden is guilty. They don't think she
> cries enough. One or two have softened a little since she

fainted in court the other day, and perhaps if she would faint regularly or sob and sigh at frequent intervals during the day … she might receive from some of her sex, some kindly glances.

On the third day of the trial, Dr Bowen testified that after the murders, he had prescribed a double dose of morphine for Lizzie, to alleviate 'mental distress and nervous excitement', which she continued to take 'up until the time of her arrest, the hearing and while she was in the station house'. In addition to pain relief, morphine was often prescribed to women during the Victorian era, to relieve symptoms associated with the menstrual cycle, such as menstrual cramps, depression, and mood swings. But given in double doses, it could affect the memory and trigger hallucinations, which could explain Lizzie's confusion during her testimony.

But by the time it came to the defence, the prosecution's case had somewhat weakened, as one newspaper commented: 'the prosecution was very weak. District Attorney Knowlton dwelt much on Andrew Borden's niggardliness, which had prevented him from even putting a stationary bathtub in his house.' The judges ruled out Lizzie's inquest testimony to be used as evidence for the prosecution as her attorney had been absent at the time of questioning. The testimony given by Mr Bence, the pharmacist, was also excluded, as his evidence was regarded as being irrelevant and too remote in time from the murders themselves to be of any significance, even though it happened only the day before. Emma Borden, a critical witness for the defence, confirmed that the dress that Lizzie had burned had been stained with paint and she had advised her to burn it. She denied that there had been any ill feeling within the family and Lizzie's relationship with her stepmother had been genial.

Governor Robinson decreed 'the defendant physically unable to commit the crime in the manner in which it was committed, and as for that, it was only possible for a maniac, a devil, to do it.' He then asked the jury to 'bring their homes, hearts and intellects into their decision in the case'. It was clear that there was no solid evidence to prove that Lizzie was guilty beyond reasonable doubt. Lizzie, who had been quiet throughout the trial, was now given an opportunity to speak. She said, 'I am innocent, but I will leave my case in your hands and with my counsel.'

On 20 June, the final day of the trial, so many people had rushed to the courthouse, hoping to obtain seats to hear the verdict, that extra policemen were appointed to man the gates. Judge Justin Dewey, who incidentally had been promoted to the bench a few years previously by Governor Robinson, delivered the charge to the jury that was very much in favour of the defence. It took the jury just an hour and a half to deliver the verdict of not guilty. 'Then all the dignity and decorum of the courtroom vanished. A cheer went up which might have been heard a mile away through the open windows and there was no attempt to check it … Miss Borden's head went down upon the rail in front of her and the tears came where they had refused to come for many a long day,' wrote *The Morning Call*.

An hour later, Lizzie was taken by carriage back to Fall River, where the crowd of people (around 2,000 according to one reporter) waiting outside the Bordens' home to congratulate Lizzie on her acquittal was so great that Lizzie and Emma stayed at a friend's house that night, where they enjoyed a celebratory party before returning to Second Street the next day.

However, despite the huge support shown for Lizzie, there were some people who still thought she was guilty. Many presumed she would move away, but within a few months she purchased a grand property in French Street on 'the hill' in Fall River. She had a housekeeper, a cook, and servants, and furnished her new home with the luxuries she had so long desired. Though it was not acceptable to name houses in Fall River, Lizzie named her house 'Maplecroft', which she had engraved in granite on the top front step. Neither was it acceptable for single women to change their name unless they married, but Lizzie changed hers to Lizbeth Borden, though not officially.

In the following years, Lizzie's friends gradually became very hostile towards her, and she was shunned by the people of Fall River. She was criticised for not wearing mourning for her parents and blatantly displaying her wealth that had come to her after the murder of her father. Even in church, she was ostracised and sat alone in the empty pew owned by her family.

Despite her wealth, it seemed that her days of shoplifting were not over, as in February 1897, both local and national newspapers reported an 'incident' regarding the theft of two porcelain paintings from the Tilden-Thurber store in Providence. Lizzie was suspected of having stolen them, and following an investigation, the police found the paintings hanging on the wall in her home. She insisted that she had bought them from the store, but Tilden-Thurber had no record of the purchase. A warrant for her arrest was issued, but was never served, and it was believed that Lizzie settled the matter out of court.

Twenty years after the trial, in 1913, a small piece of news in the *Fort Mill Times* read:

> Lizzie Borden still lives in Fall River, but as far as Fall River is concerned, Lizzie Borden is an outcast, an Ishmael, a social pariah. Her name is uttered with contempt, and her friends and relatives who comforted her during the months of her imprisonment and throughout the ordeal of her trial have long since ceased their visits. Today her nearest neighbours pass her without a nod or sign of recognition ... She has been punished and persecuted as no other innocent woman in history. She has lived to know the tragedy of a verdict of acquittal.

However, Lizzie frequently travelled to Boston, where she would go to the theatre in the evening, and soon formed a close friendship with the renowned actress Nance O'Neil. She held extravagant parties for Nance and her theatre company at Maplecroft, much to the disgust of the other residents in the neighbourhood, and her sister Emma, who unlike Lizzie wanted a quiet, sedate life. Gossip soon circulated that Lizzie and Nance were sexually intimate. By 1904, Emma had had enough and one night, during one of the parties, she left Maplecroft and went to live in Providence, then later settled in New Hampshire, and never returned. She told the *Boston Sunday Herald* in 1913, 'The happenings at the French Street house that caused me to leave I must refuse to talk about. I did not go until conditions became absolutely unbearable.'

On 1 June 1927, following complications of gall bladder surgery, Lizzie Borden died, aged 67. Nine days later, her sister Emma Borden died, aged 76. Both sisters were buried in the family plot in Oak Grove cemetery, Fall River. Lizzie, who had always been extremely fond of animals, left $30,000 in her will to the Animal Rescue League in Fall River, as she said, 'Their need is great and there are so few who care for them.' She left $500 to the city of Fall River for the care of her father's grave and substantial amounts of money to her friends and servants.

There have been many assumptions as to what really happened on 4 August 1892, but to this day there has not been a conviction and the murders remain unsolved, attracting thousands of people to Fall River each year, many staying at the house in Second Street, which now operates as a bed and breakfast. The famous ditty below, though exaggerated, has been sung by children as a skipping song for generations and can still be heard in playgrounds today:

Lizzie Borden took an axe,
And gave her mother forty whacks,
When she saw what she had done,
She gave her father forty-one.

# Chapter 7

# The Boston Borgia
## Jane Toppan, Massachusetts, 1901

Born Honora (Nora) Kelly in 1857, to poor Irish immigrants Peter Kelly and his wife Bridget (née Finn), who were living in Boston, Massachusetts, Jane Toppan had a troublesome and unstable childhood. Following her mother's death from tuberculosis while she was still an infant, Honora and her sisters were left in the care of her abusive, alcoholic father, whose violent outbursts earned him the name locally of 'Kelly the Crack' (short for crackpot).

In February 1863, Kelly took Honora, aged six, and her sister Delia, aged eight, to the Boston Female Asylum for Destitute Girls, an orphanage founded in 1800 by Hannah Stillman, wife of Reverend Samuel Stillman, whose mission was to 'receive, protect and instruct female orphans until the age of ten years old, when they are placed in respectable families'. Kelly pleaded with the managers to take his two youngest daughters; they could see by the girls' shabby dress and poor hygiene that they had been neglected. After a unanimous vote, the girls were approved by the Board of Managers, who noted in the official documents that they were 'rescued from a very miserable home'. By signing the 'Form of Obligation' and surrendering his daughters to the asylum, Peter Kelly was legally obliged not to interfere in the 'management' of the girls and relinquished 'all right and claim' to them until the age of 18. He would have been allowed to visit them in the presence of a Governess, but sadly the day the girls entered the asylum would be the last time they would ever see their father, who himself was eventually committed to an asylum when he allegedly tried to sew his own eyelids shut, whilst working in a tailor's shop.

The Boston Female Asylum accepted children from 3 to 10 years of age and provided regular schooling and instruction in knitting, sewing, and domestic skills. The children attended church every Sunday with the Governess, who read a chapter from the Bible and prayed with them every morning. She ensured that they also read from the Bible and other religious books and said grace before and after their meals to 'instil into their young, and tender minds, the principles of religion'. They were also taught to 'pay a sacred regard to truth, and to the performance of every moral duty'. At the age of 11, the girls were placed with a 'virtuous' family as a live-in house servant under an indentured contract until the age of 18 (unless they married within that time), when they would receive a payment of $50.[1]

However, for reasons that are unknown, Honora seems to have been an exception to the asylum's rules, as in November 1864, when she was just 7 years old, she was indentured to Mrs Ann C. Toppan, a 59-year-old widow, originally from Nova Scotia, Canada, living in Lowell, Massachusetts. The Board of Managers, who took the 'greatest care' in selecting places for those who were to be 'bound out', thought Mrs Toppan a 'very respectable woman', and were in no doubt that Honora would benefit from living in her home that 'appeared to possess many advantages'. Unfortunately, Honora's sister Delia was not so lucky, as four years later, when she was 12 years old, she was placed as an indentured servant to a family in New York, but later turned to prostitution and eventually died a destitute alcoholic in squalid conditions. Honora's older sister Nellie, like her father, also went insane and from her twenties onwards spent the rest of her life confined to various institutions.

During the mid-nineteenth century, hundreds of thousands of Irish immigrants arrived in the United States, fleeing from the horrendous and devastating conditions caused by the Great Irish Famine, with more than 29,000 settling in Boston in 1849 alone. Other than subsistence farming, many had few skills and were forced to take low-paying jobs such as labourers, domestic and unskilled factory work. Signs saying 'No Irish need apply' were often seen throughout the city and many had to resort to living in the developing slums such as the North End. America was still a predominantly Protestant nation and as most of the Irish immigrants were Catholic, they were viewed with hostility and suspicion and ostracised for their religious faith. In some cities, even Catholic churches were burned by anti-Irish mobs. Many also viewed them as violent drunks and the more affluent households who employed Irish servants referred to the men as 'Paddys' and the women as 'Bridgets'.

Ann Toppan or 'Aunty Jane' was a kind woman, instilling 'reasonable discipline' when needed, but due to the stigma associated with the Irish at the time, outside the home, she made it known that dark-eyed, dark-haired Honora, whose 'dusky skin looks as if it might betray a strain of Portuguese blood', was an orphan whose parents had died at sea of ship fever (epidemic typhus), during their journey to America. Even indoors, Honora was made to feel inferior and ashamed of her Irish roots and was told that though she 'could not help being Irish, she need not be a "paddy"'. Her name was changed to Jennie or Jane, and she was never called by her birth name, Honora. Before long, Jane started to lie about her Irish heritage and joined in with the bigotry, openly making disparaging remarks about the Irish. Although she would live with the Toppans until she was 28 but was never formally adopted by Ann, Jane took her surname and became known as Jane Toppan.

A few years after Jane was fostered, Ann's daughter Elizabeth returned home with her husband, Oramel A. Brigham. A 'well-built, broad shouldered' man, Oramel was a railroad conductor for the Boston & Maine Railroad, who later became deacon of the First Trinitarian Congregational Church in Lowell. Unlike her mother, Elizabeth, who was over twenty years Jane's senior, was much kinder to her. But, despite Elizabeth's kindness, as the years progressed, Jane grew envious of her older foster sister, who seemed to have the life she had been denied. She yearned to be loved and treated like a daughter, the same as Elizabeth.

Despite her traumatic childhood and her secret yearnings for a loving family, Jane had a lively, cheerful personality and was a popular child, gaining a reputation as a 'clever and amusing' storyteller. When she was in the asylum, she would tell the other girls wonderful stories of how her father had become a captain at sea, sailing the oceans of the world, and that her sister's beauty had captured the heart of an English lord. But as she grew into her teens, Jane's glamorous fabrications soon developed into compulsive, deceitful lies. At school, she became known as a snitch and a gossip; when hoping to gain favourable attention from her teachers, she would spread nasty rumours about her classmates to get them into trouble. But she was always devious enough not to get caught herself and gradually became the teacher's pet, which made her very unpopular with some of her peers. Nevertheless, her bubbly personality did win the favour of others, as one friend later recalled that whilst in Jane's company, 'it was not necessary to provide other entertainment'.

In 1874, when Jane reached the age of 18, she was released from her service with the Toppan family and received $50 as stipulated by the indenture agreement. However, she continued to live with the Toppans for another ten years as a servant, eventually moving out of their home in 1885. Jane's resentment towards Elizabeth had increased over the years, and the relationship between the two women, which had always been difficult, had become more and more strained. Nevertheless, they appeared to part on good terms, and as Jane left the family home which she had known for over two decades, Elizabeth assured her that she would always be welcome to return if she so wished. In the meantime, Jane secretly harboured feelings of hatred towards her foster sister that would just continue to grow.

At 28 years old, Jane was still single and, having gained quite a few extra pounds in weight over the years, was described by some people as 'plain' and 'portly' or, in the words of the *Boston Post*, she was 'rather inclined to stoutness'. Several newspapers later claimed that in her early twenties, Jane had courted a young man named Charles May and soon afterwards they became engaged. However, the engagement was short-lived, as Charles accepted a position in Holyoke that had better prospects, where shortly afterwards he fell hopelessly in love with his landlady's daughter, whom he married. The engagement ring he had given Jane had been engraved in the image of a bird, and Jane was said to have been so upset that she forever possessed a hatred of birds, 'whether alive, dead or represented by printing, engraving or carving on the art of a jeweller'. Thereafter, it seemed that Jane was destined to remain a spinster for the rest of her life.

After leaving her foster home of twenty-one years, Jane lived with friends for a while, then in 1887, perhaps wanting to be more independent, she decided she wanted to train as a nurse and enrolled at the nursing school attached to Cambridge Hospital in Boston, joining the vast number of Irish women who had decided to pursue a nursing career in the United States during the late nineteenth century. In Boston alone, the majority of students who enrolled at the Boston Lying-In Hospital and Infirmary for Women and Children's course were either born in Ireland or were first-generation Irish Americans and, in the hospitals, almost the entire nursing staff had Irish surnames.

Professional nursing education was relatively new to the United States, the first formal training course for nurses having been developed in 1862, at the New England Hospital for Women and Children, which later expanded into the first general training school for nurses in America in 1872. In 1873, three more nursing schools modelled after Florence Nightingale's training school in Great Britain were founded in Massachusetts General Hospital in Boston, New Haven Hospital in Connecticut, and Bellevue Hospital in New York. By the 1880s, there were fifteen nurse training schools in America, all of which were adjoined to hospitals. Prior to the 1870s, a small number of physicians had set up courses for those interested in pursuing a career in nursing, but it was during the Civil War that experimental training programmes for nursing started to emerge, greatly improving the nursing standards in hospitals, where previously much of the nursing care had been provided by incompetent drunkards, former convicts, and prostitutes, who had been allowed parole providing they served a certain length of time as nurses.

In the early schools, the length of training for nurses was initially one year, but by 1880, it had been extended to three years. At the start of their training, the student nurses or Probationers (or 'Probies' as they were often called) were responsible for the cooking, laundering, and heavy cleaning, before they gradually progressed to caring for the patients. The training period was extremely tough and ruthless; student nurses were expected to work seventy to ninety hours a week, seven days a week, under the strict supervision of the superintendents, who continued to keep a watchful eye on them even when they were off duty. They were also required to attend lectures conducted by physicians on nursing theory that were usually held late in the evening between their shifts at the hospital. The demanding schedule often took its toll both mentally and physically on the students and many dropped out before the end of the three-year training period.

Having worked most of her life as a full-time servant, Jane would have been well prepared for the physical and gruelling work that lay ahead at nursing school. From the onset, she threw herself into a professional career that was both challenging and interesting, carrying out her duties willingly and without complaint. Described as 'a large, kindly-faced woman of jovial disposition', she proved to be very popular amongst the patients and medical staff at Cambridge Hospital, and soon became known as 'Jolly Jane', a nickname that would stick with her throughout her life. Her fellow students, however, were not so taken in by her charm and some grew to detest her. Just as she had previously done at school, Jane would spread malicious rumours about anyone she disliked, and took it even further by going directly to a member of the senior medical staff, which, to her delight, resulted in students being dismissed from the nursing school on several occasions.

To the doctors and senior staff, Jane appeared to be a passionate and conscientious nurse, her vibrant personality lit up the wards, and she was thought to be an asset to the profession, so there was never any question that she was the one at fault. She continued to lie quite unashamedly about herself and her background, on one occasion inventing a ludicrous story of how she had been picked out by the Tsar of Russia to join his personal nursing staff, and was also suspected of stealing small items from the nursing staff and some medical supplies, though it was never actually proven.

Although most of the other trainee nurses disliked Jane, her patients loved her bubbly personality, and she soon became their favourite nurse on the wards. Jane became quite fond of some of her patients too; in fact, so much so that she would deliberately alter their medical charts by adding false symptoms or administer a small dose of medication in order to make them sicker, so that they would remain in hospital for a little longer. Yet she looked upon the vulnerable, elderly patients with contempt, and would often say with a smile on her face that there was 'no use in keeping them alive'. A remark that at the time was taken as a joke, but little did anyone know that Jane could not have been more serious.

As the training progressed, Jane became increasingly fascinated with autopsies, and during lectures would bombard the doctors with a barrage of questions, rigorously taking notes on the subject. At first, they were a little concerned and thought it odd that one of their students should have such a morbid obsession with death, but soon dismissed it as their star pupil just having a curious mind and an eagerness to learn.

Jane began conducting what she later referred to as her 'science experiments', where she would secretly administer her patients with doses of morphine, then stand by their bed to examine the effect it had on them. She soon realised that watching their pupils constrict and their feverish bodies twitch gave her enormous pleasure to such an extent that she would increase the dose so that they would lose consciousness and slip into a coma. The ultimate feeling of satisfaction was when the patient died, especially if the body convulsed near the time of death.

Years later, Jane calmly told a group of physicians that the desire to see a person die due to her own methods was so strong it overpowered her. 'Soon the mania became an uncontrollable passion,' she said. 'No voice has as much melody in it as the one crying for life; no eyes as bright as those about to become fixed and glassy; no face so beautiful as the one pulseless and cold.' Recalling the first patient she had killed, a young man who had almost recovered from his illness, she admitted that as she leant over his cold, motionless body, she felt 'voluptuous delight'[2] as she kissed him.

It is not known how many patients died in Jane's care during her training at Cambridge Hospital; even Jane, who later claimed she suffered from memory lapses, was unsure of the exact number, estimating that there may have been dozens. 'They were just hospital patients,' she said, indifferently, 'and I experimented on them to learn just what could be done with poisons. I can't recall the names of those patients, because I did not know them – they just went by numbers in the ward ... I killed people because I wanted to get them out of the way, and poisoning is the easiest way to do it.'

Jane had only just started a killing spree that would continue unnoticed until the start of the next century. She painstakingly researched the properties of various poisons, asked numerous questions, read books, and gathered as much information as possible on the subject. Her meticulous scheming and cheery demeanour ensured that no one ever suspected that 'Jolly Jane' could ever be capable of such heinous crimes.

It wasn't long before Jane wanted to take her killings to the next level, to experience what she considered to be the ultimate thrill: she wanted to control exactly when her victims died. She discovered that if she combined morphine with the drug atropine, not only were the effects on her victims much more dramatic, but she also found that her crimes could be more easily concealed. 'I used morphine and atropine because those are vegetable poisons and can hardly be detected, even before death,' she said. 'After death, it is difficult, you know, to find either drug.' By intricately timing various doses of the two drugs, Jane developed a mixture of symptoms so baffling that the doctors were unable to determine a true diagnosis, and often attributed the patient's death to several causes such as heart failure, chronic diabetes, and apoplexy (stroke).

Jane loved the animated effects of the atropine. She toyed with her victims as she watched them suffer, first injecting them with a high enough dose of morphine to induce a coma, excitedly watching as their breathing slowed and their pupils contracted, then she would give them the atropine to wake them up, before sending them back into unconsciousness with more morphine. Sometimes she would give them injections or doses of morphine and atropine tablets in a glass of mineral water or in a dilution of whisky, but if the patient had lapsed into unconsciousness, she would turn them on their side and administer it rectally in the form of an enema, allowing it to flow directly into their bowels. Smiling, she watched her victims endure their torturous journey back and forth near to death, revelling in the pain and suffering she had inflicted on them, until she finally decided it was time for them to die.

As her victims lay unconscious, Jane would climb into the bed and hold them intimately, whilst gently caressing and kissing their face. Then, when death was imminent, she would fondle them and stare into their eyes, 'as if to see the inner workings of the soul'. She later declared that she felt 'exquisite delight' as she held the bodies of her victims, 'feeling the breath grow faint and the pulse flicker lower and lower until all warmth had departed'. Her 'greatest joy' was when they took their last breath. 'When the climax of the mania passed, I realized what I had done,' she said.

> I have known that my patients were dying. Then my greatest thought was to resuscitate them. I have then worked over them, trying to bring them back to consciousness. I have

sent for doctors and other nurses and tried my best to save them ... Sometimes I have been successful, but many times the poison was too much. They were beyond recovery, and they died.

On these occasions, Jane would bask in the praise she received from the doctors for trying to bring her patients back from the brink of death.

One patient who survived her horrendous ordeal and lived to tell the tale was 36-year-old Amelia Phinney, who told her story years later. She had been admitted to Cambridge Hospital in 1887 suffering from a uterine ulcer, the treatment of which involved surgery, a procedure where they cut off the bottom of the stomach and reconnected the intestine. Amelia claimed that as she lay in her bed recovering from the surgery, feeling increasingly uncomfortable with the pain, she repeatedly asked Jane to fetch the doctor. But Jane assured her that there was no need for the doctor as she had something that would make her feel much better. She then slid her arm under Amelia's shoulders, and gently raised her forward, telling her to drink from the cup she pressed to her lips. As Amelia sipped the bitter-tasting liquid, she felt her throat go dry, her eyelids grow heavy, and her body began to feel numb, as she started to slip into a state of semi-consciousness. She felt the bedclothes being gently pulled back and the mattress sag as she realised to her horror that Jane had got into bed beside her.

As she cuddled up to Amelia, Jane gently stroked her hair and kissed her tenderly all over her face, before intimately caressing and fondling her, whilst peering into her eyes, watching the reaction of her pupils. Jane tried to give Amelia another drink, forcing the cup against her lips, but Amelia resisted, pressing her lips tightly together, turning her head away. At that critical point, Amelia was aware of Jane suddenly jumping up off the bed and hastily leaving the room, presumably after being disturbed by voices in the corridor. After being discharged from hospital, Amelia thought the incident so bizarre that it must have been a dream and kept the story to herself for fourteen years, until she finally revealed it during her testimony in court.

In 1888, armed with glowing references from several prominent physicians, Jane left Cambridge Hospital to further her training at the prestigious Massachusetts General Hospital, whose nursing school was renowned nationally for its high standards. Initially, the superintendent of the nursing school, who considered Jane of 'low origin' and did not think 'that class of persons equal to such important work', rejected her admission, but after reading such high recommendations from the doctors at Cambridge Hospital, she decided to give Jane a trial. Despite the superintendent's misgivings, Jane proved to be a competent and proficient nurse and passed her probation with ease. She impressed her superiors so much that when a head nurse took temporary leave, the superintendent chose Jane to take her place until she returned.

Jane may have again gained the favour of the senior staff, but her colleagues soon grew to dislike and mistrust her. Outside of work, she was full of fun, but just as before, on duty back in the hospital, she would constantly belittle her colleagues and criticise their work, to gain recognition for herself. Rumours soon started to circulate amongst the other nurses that Jane had been altering the patients' medical records and giving them incorrect doses of medication. They also suspected her of stealing small amounts of money, other small items, and a diamond ring from a private patient, though according to Charles Follen Folsom, a doctor working in the hospital at the time, theft was quite common in the training schools; he knew of at least three other nurses in Jane's class who were caught stealing several substantial items. As was the case at Cambridge Hospital, the physicians held Jane in such high esteem that they believed her lies, so her crimes continued undetected, as did the merciless killing of her patients.

During this time, Jane suffered from 'severe headaches' and was under the care of Dr Folsom. On one occasion, she spent almost a week in a private hospital and the doctor, fearing that the underlying cause might be cerebral tumours, regularly examined her and kept a close eye on her condition. During these bouts of illness, Jane would shut herself in her room and go to bed. Charles Folsom later suspected that she may have used opiates to relieve her headaches, which may have led to her developing a 'morphine habit'.[3]

Towards the end of her training at Massachusetts Hospital, Jane had become extremely unpopular, not just with the other student nurses, but also with the senior staff. Two head nurses who strongly believed that Jane had falsified their records on more than one occasion considered her a 'slippery' character, 'not to be trusted'. In the summer of 1890, Jane broke one cardinal rule of the hospital: she left the building without permission. Her supervisor was quickly informed of her absence and, when she returned, Jane was instantly dismissed. She had taken and passed her final exams, and was about to receive her diploma, but left the nursing school without her licence.

After working as a private nurse for a while, Jane returned to Cambridge Hospital in the autumn of that year, hoping to get her licence, but within a few months, she was dismissed for administering opiates recklessly. A drug derived from opium, opiates are routinely used for numbing pain and can produce additional side effects such as slowed breathing, confusion, and drowsiness. Jane was undoubtedly experimenting with opiates to study the effects on her victims.

Undeterred and confident that she 'could make more money and have an easier time by hiring myself out', in the summer of 1891, Jane decided to become a full-time private nurse. Although a private nurse could earn more money caring for patients in their own homes, employment could be sporadic and uncertain, so if there was a long lapse in work, the extra wage would not be as beneficial. A private nurse was rarely off duty and was expected to care for her patient throughout the day and night, as Miss Marion Smith, head nurse at the Philadelphia Hospital, told *The Philadelphia Times*:

> I have a letter here from one of our girls, who tells me she has been on duty with a private patient 230 hours out

of 240 without sleep, practically for ten days. That is an example of a nurse's duties. And in all that time, except, perhaps, ten or fifteen minutes in the day, the nurse is in complete charge of her patient – his life is in her hands.

Miss Smith then continued to emphasise the dedication, hard work, and responsibility of a private nurse:

> Ordinary persons can hardly appreciate the seriousness of the work of the women who follow this profession. Do they know that she is on duty always? Do they realize that upon her falls the responsibility for the slightest change in her patient's condition – that she must battle with this change, that she must not falter nor fall in critical moments? It is an accepted fact that among medical experts that the average working life of a nurse, because of the nervous strain and the responsibility, is but eight years.

Contacts made during their training were crucial to their freelance nursing career. Often, nurses would make themselves known at the physicians' office in the hope that they would send them some of their patients:

> And then, a nurse is obliged to keep up to her standard of ability. Almost all of them are sent out from clubs or associations in which they are registered. If the doctors who employ them send back unfavourable reports, they cannot find further employment. As a result, they are as fine a class of women, morally and physically, as there is in the world.

Despite her previous misconduct, Jane seemed to have no trouble finding regular work, as once again she came highly recommended by some of the most prominent physicians in the hospital. She was considered by one surgeon to be the 'best nurse he had ever known to assist in severe operations'; another eminent doctor thought that she 'excelled in nursing fevers'. Jane soon gained the reputation of being the best private nurse in Cambridge, becoming highly sought after and very much in demand, working for some of the most respected families in the city. Her patients and their families grew very fond of her and were eternally grateful to receive care from such a highly regarded nurse. Even when she stole $100 from one of her patients, the family refused to testify against her, because they felt that they owed her so much.

Working as a private nurse gave Jane the perfect opportunity to carry out her murders undisturbed, especially late at night when the other members of the household were asleep in bed. Despite Miss Smith's predictions, Jane's career as a private nurse was to last for the next ten years, during which time she would claim the lives of countless more victims, many of whom could not be identified due to her memory lapses. 'I have great difficulty in remembering things. My memory,' she claimed, 'is very good at times, but on other occasions I cannot recall what I have said or done.'

In between her live-in nursing positions, Jane lodged on and off for three years with Israel P. Dunham and his wife Lovey, an elderly couple in their eighties, who lived at 19 Wendell Street, Cambridge. In 1895, Jane decided that Israel was growing 'feeble and fussy', so she slowly poisoned him, nursing him when he became ill, whilst administering her usual combination of morphine and atropine, until he eventually died on 26 May. The doctor recorded the cause of death as a 'strangulated hernis'. Jane was on hand to comfort Israel's devastated wife, Lovey, and stayed on as a lodger to keep her company. But by the late summer of 1897, she had grown tired of her 87-year-old landlady, whom she later claimed had become 'old and cranky', so using the same method she had used previously on her husband, Jane slowly poisoned Lovey Dunham as well, nursing her until she died on 19 September.

Jane had spent the last four summers in a rented cottage in the pretty village of Cataumet, along the shores of Buzzard Bay on Cape Cod. Owned by local prominent landlords, Alden and Mary 'Mattie' Davis, Jachin Cottage was adjacent to their hotel, the Jachin House. The elderly couple and their family had become very fond of 'Jolly Jane', who was always cordial and willing to offer medical help and advice when any of them were ill. 'Aunt Jane', who adored children, would often be seen walking hand in hand down the road with the Davises' grandchildren. In return, by way of appreciation, the Davises let Jane rent the cottage at a reduced rate. However, Jane often took advantage of the couple's generosity, and at the end of every summer vacated the cottage owing them money, until eventually she had run up a debt of around $500.

Despite her embittered resentment towards her foster sister Elizabeth Brigham, Jane had kept in touch with her and her husband Oramel over the years and had visited them on several occasions. Jane had always kept any ill feelings towards Elizabeth well-hidden and the couple were always happy to see her and welcomed her back into their home with open arms. In August 1899, Elizabeth received a letter from Jane inviting her to spend some time with her at the cottage in Cataumet. As Elizabeth had been suffering from melancholia (depression), her husband Oramel, thinking that some time spent by the sea would do her good, urged his wife to go, so Elizabeth wrote back to Jane, accepting her invitation.

Jane's hidden feelings of hatred towards her foster sister escalated when she found out that her foster mother, Ann Toppan, who had died in 1891, had excluded Jane from her will. The grudge that Jane had harboured all those years had now come to a head, and she started planning Elizabeth's murder. 'I felt rather bitter against Mrs. (Elizabeth) Brigham after Mother Toppan's death, because I always thought she destroyed the will that left me some of the old lady's property,' she later confessed. 'Mrs. (Elizabeth) Brigham came down to visit me at Cataumet on Buzzards Bay, where I was spending the summer of 1899 in one of the Davis cottages. That gave me a good chance to have my revenge on her.'

The day after Elizabeth arrived at the cottage, the two women took a picnic down to the beach, where they spent an enjoyable afternoon, happily chatting and eating the corned beef, taffy (candy), and mineral water that Jane had packed for them. Later that evening, Elizabeth began to feel unwell and retired to bed early. As the night progressed, she deteriorated and the following morning, when she did not come down for breakfast, Jane went next door to the home of her landlords, and asked Alden Davis to summon a doctor, as 'her sister had taken sick'. Jane then sent a telegram to Oramel in Lowell, informing him that Elizabeth was gravely ill. Alarmed, Oramel left Lowell immediately and boarded the next available train to Cape Cod, but when he arrived the next morning, his wife was already in a coma and died the next day on Tuesday, 29 August.

The local doctor believed that 69-year-old Elizabeth had died of apoplexy and certified the death accordingly. Jane, who later admitted that she had wanted to marry Oramel Brigham, claimed that 'Elizabeth was really the first of my victims that I actually hated and poisoned with a vindictive purpose'. She wanted Elizabeth to suffer a slow and agonising death, 'So I let her die slowly, with griping torture … I fixed mineral water so it would do that, and then added morphia to it.' As Elizabeth lay dying, Jane held her in her arms and 'watched with delight as she gasped her life out'.

Shortly after her death, Oramel was slowly collecting his wife's belongings, before making the journey back to Lowell, when he noticed that there was only $5 in her pocketbook. He was surprised as he was sure she had taken $50 with her on her trip to Cape Cod. When he asked Jane if she knew what might have happened to the remaining money, she looked at him innocently, and said that as far as she knew, that was the amount Elizabeth had on her when she arrived. Taking Jane at her word, Oramel turned back to his wife's belongings, and as he collected the last few items, she gently rested her hand on his arm and told him that before Elizabeth had slipped into a coma, her final wish was for Jane to have her gold watch and chain as a keepsake. As it was typical of his dear wife to make such a thoughtful gesture, Oramel willingly handed them to Jane. In the years that followed, as he had never seen Jane with the pocket watch, Oramel presumed she had valued it so much that she did not want to risk wearing it and had kept it somewhere safe. However, when Jane was later arrested, the police found pawn tickets amongst her possessions that showed she had pawned both the watch and chain the following day.

In late December that year, Dr Walter Wesselhoeft called upon Jane to care for Mary McNear, a 70-year-old wealthy widow, who had fallen ill while she was staying at her daughter's house over the Christmas period. Apart from a cough and slight congestion on her lungs, the doctor didn't think there was any need for concern and advised Mary to drink hot tea and rest. Her family, who thought differently, insisted that she have a trained nurse to care for her, and hired nurse Jane Toppan, who came highly recommended by Dr Wesselhoeft.

When Mary McNear's granddaughter visited her a few days after Christmas on 28 December, she found her grandmother to be in a cheerful mood, 'laughing and chatting' and making plans for family celebrations for the New Year. But later that day, after taking her usual dose of medicine, Mary McNear slipped into unconsciousness. Jane assured Mary's relatives that there was no need to be alarmed, as she 'would do everything that was necessary', but Mary died early the next morning, with her family at her bedside. According to Dr Wesselhoeft, Mary McNear had 'suffered a stroke of apoplexy'.

As with all her other victims, no one ever suspected that the kind and pleasant nurse, who attended to her patient so attentively during her final hours, and who now stood calmly by her deathbed, could possibly be the person responsible for her demise. Even when it was discovered shortly afterwards that some of Mary McNear's clothes were missing, after a hint of suspicion towards Jane, Dr Wesselhoeft immediately sprang to her defence and would not hear of anything said against 'one of the finest women and best nurses he knew'. Mary McNear was unusual in that she was the first and only known victim that Jane had murdered less than twenty-four hours after meeting her, as all her other victims had either been her patients or people that she had known.

Less than a month later, during one of her regular visits to Lowell, Jane, who still had designs on Oramel Brigham and wanted to eliminate any competition she might have in that direction, poisoned his middle-aged housekeeper, Florence Calkins, on 15 January 1900. 'I was jealous of her,' she admitted. 'I knew she wanted to become Mr. Brigham's wife.'

A week later, Jane reconnected with an old friend, Myra Connors, who was employed as a matron in the refectory at the Episcopal Theological School, in Cambridge, a position that came with its own apartment and a private maid. Jane, who had grown tired of nursing, had wanted Myra's job for a long time, and was determined to have it. Forty-year-old Myra had been suffering from 'localised peritonitis', but after taking the prescription provided by her physician, Dr Herbert McIntire, her condition began to improve. When Jane heard that Myra was unwell, she wasted no time in offering her services, and promptly arrived on 7 February to care for her. But shortly after Jane's arrival, Myra went rapidly downhill, and after suffering convulsions so severe that her arm became twisted and contorted, she died a few days later, on 11 February. According to Dr McIntire, who was puzzled by Myra's symptoms, the cause of death was caused by a 'complication of diseases'. However, he did admit later that the symptoms imitated the effects of strychnine poisoning, though at the time he had no reason to suspect foul play.

Myra's brother, B. T. Saulisbury, who had taken an instant dislike to Jane, had asked his sister to find someone else to nurse her, but Myra refused, saying that Jane was her friend and was taking good care of her. Just before she died, Myra had told her brother that Jane had borrowed $200 from her and had not paid it back. She had been saving up for a vacation and told him where there was $160 of gold she had put away for that purpose and that if she died, he was to have it. Saulisbury looked for the money after his sister's death but could find no trace of it. He had no doubt that Jane had taken it, as she was the only other person who knew where it was hidden.

Myra's funeral was barely over when Jane approached Dr Hodges, the dean of the Theological School, and informed him that before she had fallen ill, Myra had been planning a sabbatical and had instructed Jane in the 'duties of her position' so that she could temporarily replace her. Dr Hodges believed Jane's lies and appointed her to fill the vacancy, at least until the end of term. But due to her incompetence through lack of experience and 'business training', she was dismissed after eight months, in November that year. Immediately after her dismissal, Jane went back to her apartment, where she 'took to her bed' and sobbed 'like a child'.

By January 1901, having lost her apartment shortly after her dismissal, Jane was back lodging at 31 Wendell Street, just a few doors down from the house where she had previously murdered her former landlords, Israel and Lovey Dunham. Jane's new landlords, Melvin Beedle, a former city councilman, and his wife Eliza, employed a housekeeper, Mary Sullivan, who also had some experience in nursing. As Jane's intention was to worm her way in and take Mary's place, she wanted her out of the way as soon as possible. When Jane arrived, Eliza Beedle was already confined to her room, convalescing from pneumonia, so all she needed to do was to restrict Melvin's movements as well, then her plan could go ahead, only this time, uncharacteristically, it did not involve murder. Soon enough, having drunk the mineral water Jane gave him, Melvin was also laid up in bed suffering from 'violent gastro-intestinal irritation', the result of what his physician diagnosed as ptomaine poisoning (food poisoning).

Jane needed to convince the Beedles that Mary Sullivan was neglecting her duties. So, she slipped enough morphine in Mary's drink to make her appear intoxicated, then told Eliza Beedle that their housekeeper had been secretly drinking the family's whisky for three days and now she was slumped on her bed, drunk. Jane then took her landlady to Mary's room to show her. Subsequently, Mary was instantly dismissed and replaced by Jane, who, much to Eliza Beedle's relief, took control of the household.

That summer, towards the end of June, Mattie Davis decided that she had waited long enough for the money owed on her holiday let and decided to travel to Cambridge to pay Jane a visit. The country was in the second week of a prolonged heat wave, dubbed by the press as the 'Deadly Hot Wave'. By the beginning of July, the temperatures had soared as high as 102°F in Philadelphia, exceeding previous records and claiming thousands of lives nationwide. Despite the scorching heat, Mattie was determined to recover the outstanding debt and planned to take the first train due to leave at 6.48 am the following morning, to reach the city before the heat of the day.

Early in the morning of 25 June, the temperatures had already reached 70° when Mattie set out to the train station, about 300 feet from Jachin House. A diabetic and in poor health, 60-year-old Mattie, who was already feeling the effects of the heat, was feeling tired and weak, and was also running a few minutes late. She was still coming down the long flight of steps at Jachin House when the train pulled into the station. As she scurried towards the depot, she tripped and fell to the ground. Alden, who had hurried ahead to ask the conductor to hold the train for his wife, turned to see her sprawled on the ground and dashed back to help her. But, before he reached her, Mattie was already back on her feet and limping towards the platform. Badly shaken and covered in dust and dirt, she flushed a little with embarrassment as Alden and Charles Hammond the conductor helped her to her seat in the last carriage of the train. After reassuring her husband that she was feeling fine, Alden left the carriage and the train started to pull away.

Several witnesses who believed that Mattie had been badly injured by her fall were surprised her husband allowed her to board the train.

As there were no smoking carriages on the train that morning, the last carriage, which catered for both passengers and baggage, was full of men standing around smoking. According to one of the men, George Hall, 'Mrs. Davis appeared on the point of collapse, we all watched her as the conductor escorted her to a seat in the middle of the carriage, fearing that she would not be able to reach the seat before breaking down. When the conductor had helped Mrs Davis to a seat, she almost fell into it, so weak was she.' George remarked to a fellow passenger standing next to him that he believed that the fall would be her 'death blow'.

Willard Hill, an acquaintance of the Davis family, who had witnessed Mattie's fall, was very concerned and as he sat down in the seat opposite her, he asked how she was feeling. 'Nothing hurt but my dignity,' she replied. While the train chugged along, Mattie seemed much calmer and relaxed, as she chatted to Willard for the rest of the journey. When the train reached Boston, Willard's destination, he stayed with Mattie and made sure that she boarded the train to Cambridge safely.

Mattie had intended to retrieve her money and return home the same day, but when she arrived at the Beedles' house in Wendell Street, they were all about to have dinner and Jane, who guessed the reason for Mattie's visit, persuaded her to join them, to distract her and delay a trip to the bank. Mattie ate her meal heartily and drank the Hunyadi water Jane had given her, unaware that she had laced it with morphine. When she finished, she began to feel extremely drowsy and by late afternoon, she was so unstable she could barely stand, so Jane helped her into the spare bedroom and onto the bed. As Mattie lay on the bed groaning, Jane topped up the dose of morphine using a hypodermic syringe to quieten her.

That evening, Jane telegraphed Mattie's husband Alden and their daughter, Genevieve Gordon, to inform them that Mattie had fallen ill. When Genevieve arrived from Chicago the following day, she insisted they send for a doctor immediately. Jane tried to convince her that she was quite capable of looking after Mattie herself, but Genevieve ignored her and summoned the doctor. When Dr John Nichols arrived, Jane informed him that Mattie was a diabetic who had overindulged on the wrong food earlier that day and promptly handed him a urine sample she had collected earlier. As the sample did indeed contain a high amount of sugar, Dr Nichols, never suspecting anything untoward from such a diligent nurse, was convinced that Mattie had slipped into a diabetic coma.

So as not to arouse suspicions within the household, Jane used a combination of morphine and atropine, administered at various doses and intervals during the day and night, to simulate a diabetic coma. For a whole week, Jane toyed with Mattie as she lay helpless in her bed, bringing her in and out of consciousness, sometimes lowering the dose to bring her round to give her family false hope that she might recover, then torment her before letting her slip back into a coma. Until finally on the eighth day, 4 July, she gave her the final dose of morphine that killed her.

Not only had Mattie Davis suffered a cruel and lingering death in the hands of Nurse Toppan, but it had taken place while Genevieve, Dr Nichols, and the Beedles had been present in the house. 'I always had my own way in every case that I had as a nurse,' boasted Jane. 'I would not allow either doctors or members of the family to dictate to me. As I was always jolly, they didn't mind my dictating to them.' The Davis family, who never doubted Jane's nursing skills for one moment, confirmed, 'We certainly could not get anybody that mother would like better.'

Many friends and relatives of the Davis family travelled down from Cambridge to Cataumet to attend Mattie's funeral. Jane stood amongst the mourners at the graveside, and smiled inwardly as she thought, 'You had better wait, and in a little while I will have another funeral for you. If you wait, it will save you going back and forth.' After the funeral, Jane was on hand to comfort Mattie's husband, Alden, who was so utterly grief-stricken that he agreed to let Jane move into his home and care for him until he was more able to cope. Genevieve and her older sister, Minnie Gibbs, who lived close to her parents' home with her husband, Captain Irving F. Gibbs and her 10-year-old son, Jesse, were also staying with their father, and were only too glad to have help at such a difficult time. Little did they know that the person they trusted the most and were about to let into their home was already planning to eradicate the rest of the family. Only, this time, Jane decided to use a different method of murder: she intended to set fire to the Davises' house and burn it to the ground with the family still inside.

Within a few days of moving in with the Davis family, Jane started what would be the first of three arson attempts. 'I had borrowed money from Alden Davis,' she said, 'and the thought occurred to me, if I should burn the house, all those papers would be destroyed.' The family were asleep in bed upstairs when Jane started a small fire in the closet by the fireplace, 'so it might appear the chimney had caught fire'. Fortunately, Alden happened to be awake and smelled the smoke; he rushed out of his bedroom and managed to put out the flames in time. Jane, who was in her own room, 'danced with delight', before running out to help, then 'to avoid suspicion' threw water on the fire, all the while hoping 'that the house would burn down'.

One evening, a few days later, Jane started another fire in the pantry, then sauntered round to her neighbour's house, knocked on the door, and casually struck up a conversation with him. Her intention was to divert suspicion in case she had been seen in the vicinity. The neighbour, a businessman from Boston who was staying in the house for the summer, was surprised to see Jane as she was not in the habit of calling round. While they chatted, he noticed smoke coming from the Davises' house. Jane feigned surprise and they both rushed to get help. Again, the fire was put out before any serious damage was done. After her third and final attempt to burn the house, which was also unsuccessful, Jane decided to go back to her old ways and use poison. But not before she informed Alden that, shortly before the outbreak of the fire, she had noticed a strange man lurking around outside the house.

Having thrown Alden off the scent, Jane moved on to her next victim, Genevieve Gordon. 'I thought if I could get her out of the way, I could be a mother to her child and get her husband to marry me,' she said. But apart from some heart trouble, 38-year-old Genevieve appeared to be a strong, healthy woman, showing no signs of illness, so her murder would require a little more planning than the previous victims, so as not to arouse suspicion. Mattie's death had left all the family completely bereft, but Jane noted that Genevieve, despite trying to appear strong for her father, seemed to be struggling the most. She had spent an extremely fraught and despairing week by her mother's bedside, and was anxious and concerned for her elderly father, who suffered from melancholia, and was immensely fragile following his wife's death. She was also missing her husband terribly, who had stayed at home in Chicago with their son. The last few weeks had taken its toll on Genevieve, who was feeling anxious, lonely, and depressed.

Jane made sure that Alden was out of earshot, then discreetly took Minnie to one side and expressed her concern about her younger sister's worrying behaviour. She told her she had seen Genevieve in the garden shed, examining a small box of Paris Green, a highly toxic insecticide. She had looked uneasy and agitated and Jane feared she might have taken some of the poison, had she not interrupted her. Jane was afraid Genevieve had sunk so low that she might be contemplating suicide. Minnie was shocked to hear that her sister might be feeling suicidal; she was also familiar with her father's suicidal impulses during his attacks of melancholia, and thereafter she vowed to keep a closer eye on Genevieve.

A few days later, on the morning of 31 July, Jane, who had been caring for Genevieve during the night after a bout of severe vomiting, woke Minnie to tell her that her sister had died. Though the physician certified the cause of death to be 'heart disease', friends and neighbours believed that it was a combination of exhaustion and grief that had killed broken-hearted Genevieve. Shortly afterwards, Jane told Minnie's father-in-law, Captain Paul Gibbs, that she was sure that Genevieve had injected herself with the insecticide from the garden shed, as she had found an empty syringe lying next to her body. Not wanting to cause Alden and Minnie any more anguish, she immediately threw it away. Alden was inconsolable as he buried another member of his family in just a matter of weeks. Later, Jane gloated, 'I went to the funeral and felt as jolly as could be ... and nobody suspected me in the least.'

Whilst making the arrangements for his daughter's funeral, Alden had become involved in a heated argument with the undertaker, over what he considered to be an exorbitant bill. A week later, he travelled to Boston to arrange for an article to be printed on the alleged extortion practised by coffin manufacturers. The blistering eastern heatwave of 1901 had lingered into August, and Alden returned home after his trip, hot and exhausted. As he wearily slumped into the chair, he gladly accepted the drink of mineral water Jane offered him. By the next morning, he was dead.

Alden's death came as no surprise to the residents of Cataumet. The emotional trauma of losing both his beloved wife and daughter within just a few weeks, combined with his recurrent attacks of melancholia, plus the stress of the fires and the dispute with the undertaker, then finally his trip to Boston, was thought to have been too much for the 65-year-old's heart. 'I made it lively for the undertakers and gravediggers. Three graves in a little over three weeks in one lot in the cemetery,' Jane remembered with a smile. 'Then I turned my attention to the last surviving member of the Davis family, Mrs Minnie Gibbs.'

Once the funeral was over, Captain Paul Gibbs tried to persuade Minnie to bring her two sons back to his home in Pocasset, to stay with him until her husband Irving returned home from sea. Minnie politely declined his offer as she felt she should stay and deal with her deceased parents' estate. She convinced the captain that he need not worry as Jane had agreed to stay a little longer, her cousin Beulah Jacobs would be arriving from Cambridge in the next day or two, and Harry Gordon, Genevieve's widowed husband, was also staying for a few more days, so she had plenty of help and support. The captain, satisfied that Minnie was in safe hands, returned to Pocasset with his eldest grandson, Paul, leaving his younger brother, Jesse, with his mother. 'It was a very sorrowful occasion,' Beulah later recalled.

> Everyone was low spirited. Miss Toppan seemed anxious to cheer us up as much as possible. It was very hard to feel gay, but Miss Toppan did her best to make us forget what had happened. She told stories and joked, laughed, and tried to keep Mrs Gibbs in good humour. Her purpose appeared to be to take her mind off the affliction she had suffered.

A few days later, on 12 August, Jane suggested that Minnie might benefit from some fresh air, so that morning they all took a carriage to Falmouth, returning home just after lunch. Though she was obviously heartbroken, Minnie seemed to be bearing up quite well as she ate her supper with the others that evening and, apart from suffering from an 'old complaint' for which she had been prescribed regular medicine, she appeared perfectly healthy. After supper, Jane asked Minnie if she would like some Hunyadi water. She then went downstairs, where she poured the water into three glasses, lacing one with morphine. Back upstairs, she gave one to Minnie, one to Harry Gordon, and the third she drank herself. Jane watched as Minnie finished her glass.

Shortly after, Minnie complained of feeling extremely tired and wanted to go to bed, but when she tried to get up from the chair, she was seized by a sudden numbness and could hardly move. She felt so ill she was unable to climb the stairs to bed and slumped onto the sofa. When Beulah remarked that Minnie had been 'awfully sick' since drinking the mineral water, Jane handed her a glass of cocoa wine with some ice to give to Minnie, but she refused to drink it, saying that she wanted water. However, later that evening she relented, and after accepting the wine from Jane, she rapidly went downhill. Beulah recalled seeing Minnie at around 9.00 pm. 'Mr Gordon was in the room with her. She was very sick; her eyes were closed, and she could not recognise me.' When the rest of the household retired to bed, Harry Gordon carried Minnie upstairs to her bedroom. He wanted to send for Dr Latter, the family physician, but Jane objected, insisting that she would stay up and care for her.

Throughout the night, Jane tended to Minnie the same way she had done with all her other victims, insisting she drink her usual concoction of morphine and atropine, disguised in mineral water, boosting the dose with a syringe as she lay semi-conscious, until she eventually slipped into a deep coma. Early the next morning, Beulah was alarmed to see that Minnie had deteriorated so quickly during the night and immediately summoned Dr Latter. After he examined Minnie, the doctor asked Jane what she thought might be wrong with her old friend, to which Jane replied she believed she was 'all tired out' after her trip to Falmouth the previous day. Baffled by Minnie's symptoms, the doctor advised that she must be 'kept perfectly quiet', then he left, promising to return shortly.

Minnie lay comatose and motionless throughout the day, except for twitching on the left side of her mouth and her left leg. As she lay dying, Jane, who had slept in the same room as Minnie, did something even more perverse this time. Instead of climbing into the bed and holding her victim as she had done so many times in the past, she brought Minnie's ten-year-old son Jesse into bed, and cuddled him as his mother lay dying in the bed next to them. As Jane was known to be very caring towards children and had in the past often comforted and looked after the children of her murdered victims while the rest of the family grieved, this apparent act of compassion was not thought to be unusual.

Dr Latter returned a few hours later to find that Minnie had drastically deteriorated. By now she was so weak that he was unable to administer any medicine, so he gave her an injection, but when that failed to rouse her back to consciousness, he called Dr Frank Hudnut of Brookline, who was visiting a patient nearby in North Falmouth. Dr Hudnut arrived at 2.00 pm and was immediately ushered into the room where Minnie was laying. 'She appeared to be in a profound state of a coma,' he later testified. 'Her skin was pale and dried. I examined her eyes. Both pupils were slightly dilated, one pupil being slightly larger than the other, but there was no twitching of the eye. I examined her body carefully but found no evidence of any accident.' The doctor administered various medications by injection, but none were successful in rousing Minnie from her coma.

Later that afternoon, after hearing the terrible news that Minnie was dying, Captain Paul Gibbs, Minnie's father-in-law, arrived. Standing by her bedside with Jane and Dr Latter, he took Minnie's hand and asked, 'What's the matter with her, doctor?' to which the doctor replied, 'I don't know. It looks funny to me.' Minutes later, at around 4.00 pm, 39-year-old Minnie Gibbs died. Dr Latter certified the cause of death as 'exhaustion'. Captain Gibbs, however, was not convinced and thought that an autopsy should be performed. 'There is no need of an autopsy. There were no suspicious circumstances,' Jane said, indignantly. Shortly afterwards, she calmly walked hand in hand with Jesse down the road to the post office, as she so often did.

In just six weeks, Jane had managed to wipe out the entire Davis family without arousing any suspicion. She had made it known that she was very fond of the Davises, particularly Minnie Gibbs, whom she regarded as one of her closest friends. All the family trusted her completely, as Beulah, who thought Jane a 'very bright, jolly, good-natured woman', confirmed: 'We all had great confidence in Miss Toppan's judgement, as she had known the Davis family for five or six years, and we left everything to her. There was no one that questioned her wisdom, and what she advised was done … We thought so well of her that we considered her quite as capable in ordinary sickness as a doctor.'

Some residents in Cataumet believed that the Davises' house was cursed, while others thought there was nothing suspicious about the tragic events, only that the poor family had suffered a run of bad luck and had all perished through grief. Some even thought that there might have been 'something wrong with the drains'. No one suspected foul play as Minnie was laid to rest beside her parents, Alden and Mattie Davis, and her older sister, Genevieve. No one, that is, apart from Captain Paul Gibbs. He had a great deal of confidence in Dr Latter and had always thought Jane a very capable nurse, but the more he mulled things over in his mind, the more he became convinced that something was not quite right. Four deaths in the same family within such a short space of time was too much to accept as a coincidence.

Though incredibly grief-stricken, Minnie had been in good health on the Monday, the day before she died. Harry Gordon had told the captain that she had been 'lively and in the best of spirits' when they had returned home from Falmouth, as did her cousin Beulah, who said she had found Minnie 'to be as well as usual'. Harry had also said he believed that Minnie had been afraid of Jane, as he noticed that when she was ill, she 'shrank away from her every time she came into the room', and one time he had walked in to find Jane administering a syringe in Minnie's arm as she lay motionless in bed, at which point he was quickly ushered from the room. Both he and Captain Gibbs agreed that before Minnie had lost consciousness, she might have suspected that something was wrong.

According to Beulah, Jane had been with Minnie the whole time she was ill, as she had with the other members of the Davis family. The housekeeper worked in the kitchen most of the time and kept away when anyone was ill, so no one else would have had the chance to give them anything unless Jane knew about it. Jane had not only cared for the family while they were ill, but she had also prepared the bodies for the undertaker after they had died.

The captain knew that Jane had previously been urging Minnie to sign a paper releasing her from the debt she still owed the Davis family, but Minnie would not sign it. Then there was the mystery of the disappearing money. Harry had told the captain that when Minnie had returned from Falmouth, she had shown both him and Jane her pocketbook, which contained $57.50, but after her death it was discovered that she only had $7.50. The missing $50 had never been found. All these facts were niggling at the captain and though he could not ignore his suspicions, he decided to keep them to himself, for the time being, anyway.

Minnie's husband, Captain Irving Gibbs, the commander of the schooner, *Golden Ball*, built by his father Captain Paul Gibbs, had been away at sea and had not received the tragic news that his wife was in a coma until his ship had docked at Norfolk, Virginia. He rushed back to Cataumet to find that his wife had already died. He was inconsolable, but as usual, Jane showed concern and offered to move into his home to help look after his two young sons. If Jane had planned to take Minnie's place, she must have been disappointed, as Irving declined her offer, so Jane left Cataumet and headed back to Lowell. Before she left, she told her friends that she doubted if she would ever return to Cataumet again, as it held too many sad memories for her.

Since Elizabeth's death, two years previously, Jane had on several occasions visited Oramel Brigham and, thinking that he was now finally on his own with no females to block her marriage prospects, she arrived on her next visit to Lowell full of optimism. But, to her disappointment, she found another female visitor staying in the house, Oramel's older sister Edna Bannister, who had turned up a few days earlier, having decided to stop off and visit her brother on her way to the Pan-American Exposition, the new world fair held in Buffalo, New York.

During the afternoon of 26 August, Edna, who suffered from heart trouble, complained of dizziness, and went to lie down in her room. Later that afternoon, when Edna started to feel better, Jane brought her a glass of mineral water to drink. Shortly after she drank the water, she deteriorated and, during the night, under Jane's watchful eye, she slipped into a coma and died the following morning. As Edna had suffered from heart trouble, the doctor attributed her death to heart disease. 'Mrs Bannister was a poor old woman and was better off out of the way anyhow,' Jane later wrote.

In the meantime, while Jane was happily consoling Oramel Brigham, an investigation into the unexpected and mysterious deaths of the Davis family was underway. Dr Ira B. Cushing, a physician from Brookline, had been vacationing in Cataumet every summer for many years, and had become well acquainted with all the local and summer residents there. He knew that Mattie Davis had suffered from diabetes and had been in poor health, so when he received news of her death that summer, he thought no more of it. However, he was shocked to hear that Alden Davis had died suddenly during the night, as he had only seen him the day before at the train station, where he appeared to be in good health. When Dr Cushing asked what had caused his death, he was told that it was probably apoplexy. 'I thought his death looked strange,' he told the *Boston Post*. 'Soon I learned of the other deaths, and then I took steps to have the matter investigated.'

Dr Cushing knew he had a hard task ahead, trying to convince the residents of Cataumet that all the Davis family had been poisoned. He spoke to several people, but none of them wanted to get involved in an investigation, except for Captain Paul Gibbs, who already had his suspicions, but had kept them to himself. As Dr Cushing didn't know Captain Gibbs well enough to approach him, he first spoke to his friend and fellow seaman, Captain 'Ed' Robinson, whom he knew would converse with Captain Gibbs, and told him of his suspicions that the Davis family had been poisoned. The news that Dr Cushing also shared his suspicions gave Captain Gibbs the final push he needed to go to the police.

District Attorney Holmes ordered that the bodies of Genevieve Gordon and Minnie Gibbs be exhumed from Cataumet cemetery, and on 28 August, Josephus Whitney, the detective assigned to the case, visited Jane in Lowell. Jane seemed surprised to see Whitney and appeared to be unaware that she was under suspicion for murder. Apparently, she chatted 'freely' and discussed 'at great length' the circumstances surrounding the deaths of each member of the Davis family, also offering her own opinion. When Detective Whitney informed Jane that the bodies of Minnie Gibbs and Genevieve Gordon were to be exhumed in the next day or two, she made the following statement in which she insinuated that Harry Gordon, Minnie's brother-in-law, was responsible for Minnie's death:

Mrs. Gibbs was very much distressed at the death of her mother, father and sister, and especially after her father died. She was suffering from the shock and was in no condition to attend to the affairs of her father's estate. Mr. Gordon insisted upon Mrs. Gibbs joining him in an inspection of Alden P. Davis' papers. He kept her at work on the papers with him all day Sunday and during Sunday night, until she was almost prostrated from the nervous strain and the fatigue.

Monday she was tired out, although she went to Falmouth. That evening Mr. Gordon wanted her to continue the work, but she was so weak that she could not. The idea of having to go over these papers again revived her grief over her father's death, and she was taken sick. Mrs. Gibbs then lay on the lounge and I attempted to prescribe for her and to make her comfortable. Mr. Gordon ordered me out of the room and said, 'Mrs. Gibbs prefers to be with her relatives. She does not want you here.'

Mrs. Jacobs was with Mr. Gordon and Mrs. Gibbs, and I left. I think I could have helped Mrs. Gibbs, as I could perhaps have made her comfortable, but Mr. Gordon would not allow me to do anything for her or even stay beside her. He prevented me acting as a nurse. I did not have charge of Mrs. Gibbs until Dr. Latter came the next morning and told me what to do.

I feel very sure that Mrs. Gibbs' death was hastened by the nervous and physical strain to which she was subjected by her work upon her father's papers with Mr. Gordon.

Jane added that there had been a heated discussion between Minnie Gibbs and Harry Gordon regarding the appointment of an administrator for the estate of Alden Davis, as Harry Gordon wanted Minnie, as the only immediate heir, to allow him to take charge of the property, to which Minnie objected.

Later that day, Jane visited a friend of Harry Gordon. She appeared 'excited' and 'greatly worked up' as she told him that the bodies of Minnie Gibbs and Genevieve Gordon were to be exhumed.

I suppose that I shall be asked to go down when the autopsies are held, as they usually have a nurse to help the doctors at the autopsy. Gen Whitney, the state detective, has been to Lowell to see me, and I felt obliged to tell him all I knew about it … I told Mr. Whitney that Mr. Gordon would not let me do what I ought to have done as a nurse, and I said that I thought that he was responsible for Minnie's death in making her work so hard when she was not able to stand it … It seems to me that Mr. Gordon is in a very serious situation.

After hearing Jane's statement, Detective Whitney went straight to Beulah Jacobs in Somerville, to record her version of events. Beulah confirmed that from the moment Minnie Gibbs had fallen ill, Jane had taken full charge of the nursing. She and Harry Gordon had gone to bed, leaving Minnie in the hands of Nurse Toppan, and she was quite sure that Mr Gordon did not see Mrs Gibbs from the evening until early the next morning, when she was unconscious.

On Friday, 30 August, Dr Faunce of Sandwich performed the autopsies on the bodies of Minnie Gibbs and Genevieve Gordon and sent the stomachs of the deceased women to Professor Edward S. Wood of Harvard University, for analysis and examination at his laboratory at Cambridge. In the meantime, as there was not sufficient evidence to arrest Jane, she was put under surveillance and thereafter her movements were closely monitored by Detectives Josephus Whitney and John Patterson.

While the detectives kept track of her movements outside the house, inside the walls of Oramel Brigham's home at 182 Third Street, Jane was desperately attempting to secure her marriage to the 60-year-old widower. She had talked about marriage on several occasions, but when her proposals fell on deaf ears, she endeavoured to coerce Oramel into taking the step. She took over the duties of his housekeeper, devotedly tending to his every need, but when her efforts failed to impress the deacon, who had no desire to make Jane his wife nor his housekeeper, she tried another approach. She laced his tea with morphine, though she had no intention of killing him, only to make him ill so that she could nurse him back to health and win his affections. But this ploy also failed.

Meanwhile, rumours were circulating of a blossoming romance between the deacon and Miss Martha M. Cook, a woman a few years younger than him and a member of the same church. When the news of a possible rival reached Jane, she flew into a rage and threatened to ruin Oramel's reputation by spreading gossip that he was the father of her unborn child. She even wrote a letter to the Rev. George Kengott, pastor of the church to which Oramel belonged, requesting that he take the matter further. Fortunately, Deacon Brigham's reputation was not to be tarnished and Jane's lies were ignored. This was a step too far for Oramel and on Saturday, 29 September, he ordered Jane to leave his house.

Later that day, Oramel's housekeeper found Jane slumped on her bed upstairs in a stupor. Oramel immediately summoned his physician, Dr William H. Lathrop, who arrived to find Jane in an 'extremely drowsy state, as if she had taken some form of opium'. He injected her with an emetic, which made her vomit profusely. 'Why didn't you let me die?' Jane said to the doctor when she recovered. 'I am tired of life, no one cares for me. People talk so about me that I am sick of living.' Although Oramel Brigham thought 'it was probably done to work on my sympathies', and Dr Lathrop believed that the amount of poison Jane had taken would not have been fatal, Ann Tyler, a private nurse, was called in and remained by Jane's bedside throughout the night, 'keeping an eye upon her every minute for fear that she would make a second attempt at suicide'. She asked Jane what poison she had taken, but Jane refused to say. Though it was doubtful that Jane had taken arsenic, as the *Boston Post* pointed out, 'As a nurse, Miss Toppan must have been familiar with the agony that follows arsenic poisoning, and it is likely that she tried to bring about her own death in a less painful manner.'

Jane slept soundly all night and the next morning awoke in such 'fine spirits' that Nurse Tyler decided that it would be safe to leave her and go downstairs to get some breakfast. When she returned, she was surprised to find that during her absence Jane had attempted suicide a second time and was in a critical condition. 'Her face was slightly black, and the muscles of her body were rigid,' Nurse Tyler recalled. 'Her teeth were tightly clenched making impossible the introduction of an emetic through the mouth … I began rubbing the patient and giving the usual external treatment recommended in cases where medicine cannot be introduced.' At that moment, Dr Lathrop, who had just arrived for his morning visit to check on Jane's progress, promptly injected apomorphine into both of her arms; almost immediately she vomited, expelling the poison from her stomach. It was clear to Dr Lathrop that Jane had consumed more poison than the day before and that this time she had 'most certainly wanted to die'.

According to Nurse Tyler, her patient recovered quickly, but Jane still insisted that she should go to the hospital. Arrangements were made for the doctor to call the next morning with a carriage at 7.00 am. But, according to Oramel Brigham, 'she would not wait for him and went off at 5 in the morning'. Jane spent the next two weeks in Lowell General Hospital under the care of Dr F. W. Chadbourne. The doctor, having been informed that Jane had attempted suicide twice and was under surveillance for her alleged connection with the sudden deaths of the Davis family, was expecting to find evidence of insanity in his patient, but after close observation, he concluded that Jane's mind was 'unaffected' and that she was suffering from nervousness. He advised her not to 'worry' and 'tried in every way to induce a spirit of cheerfulness'. He also asked Jane what poison she had taken in her attempts at suicide, but again Jane refused to say. As he thought it possible that Jane might attempt suicide during her stay in hospital, all medicines were kept hidden, and she was closely watched by the nurses.

While Jane was recuperating and under observation in one ward, Detective Patterson was closely watching her from another ward a short distance away in the lower part of the hospital. Dr Chadbourne was aware that the detective was working undercover, and treated him with 'prescribed harmless medicines', which the nurses, who believed Patterson to be a genuine patient, administered 'at regular intervals through the day', just as they would any other patient. As Patterson was a healthy man, who also had a healthy appetite to match, he was admitted to hospital supposedly suffering from a mental disease, and entered on the hospital books as a hypochondriac, which meant that he was suffering from a condition which caused him to imagine that he was sick. The nurses were told to give him 'all the food that he asked for, irrespective of its character', and he was told to take plenty of outdoor exercise. This enabled him to carry out his work undetected and without the restrictions of an ordinary patient.

Back in the house at 31 Wendell Street, the detectives, who hoped to find a substantial amount of money hidden away to show that Jane had a motive for the alleged poisonings, searched her room, and examined her clothes and belongings for evidence of any financial transactions. Throughout her nursing career, Jane had been constantly employed with a good salary, yet she was completely skint and in debt. After making enquiries about Jane's spending habits, her friends confirmed that though she was known to be 'liberal' she was not a 'spendthrift', and despite her income, she did occasionally resort to borrowing money.

Two weeks later, on 14 October, Jane was discharged from Lowell General Hospital. She travelled to Amherst, New Hampshire, to stay with Sarah Nichols, an old friend, who lived with her brother George in a grand yellow farmhouse, situated on the main road just under a mile from the village. She later wrote, 'I had a fine time out there. I don't think I ever enjoyed myself as much as I did that fall. There was a jolly lot of people there, and I had the kind of time I like to have.'[4] But Jane's time of fun and merriment was to be short-lived, as unbeknown to her, Detective Patterson, who had followed her from Lowell, was staying in a boarding house just across the road.

Every day, Jane would walk to an old unoccupied farmhouse about half a mile down the road from the Nicholses' house, where she would sit alone for hours. Watching from a safe distance, but just within earshot, Detective Patterson could hear Jane talking to herself, her speech often rambling. According to Patterson, 'She seemed to be arguing with herself as to whether she could do this or that thing; when she had an umbrella, she would stand poking the point to the rotten boards of the flooring.'

Jane was followed on her frequent trips out to the village and the neighbouring town of Milford, where her mail was examined at the post office, but the detective could not find the evidence needed to warrant an arrest. Finally, on 29 October, two months from the start of the investigation, Detective Whitney received the evidence he needed to secure a warrant for the arrest of nurse Jane Toppan. During his analysis, Professor Wood had found large quantities of poison in the viscera of both Minnie Gibbs and Genevieve Gordon, which was enough, according to the *Boston Globe*, 'to have depopulated the summer colony at Cataumet', so Whitney, accompanied by two other officers, Inspector Thomas Flood and Deputy Marshall Wheeler, made their way to Amherst to inform Detective Patterson. All four officers went straight to George Nichols's house, where they arrested Jane for the murder of Minnie Gibbs.

The police finally had their suspect, but they still had the difficult task of proving that it was Jane who had committed the murders. As there was no proof that Jane had given poison to any of the Davis family, they knew it could take weeks to gather enough evidence for a trial, and even then they might only have circumstantial evidence. There had been other people in the house when Minnie's sister, Genevieve Gordon, died, so Jane could not be charged for her murder, but as she was alone with Minnie Gibbs during her illness and at the time of her death, and there was poison found in her stomach, the police would try to prove that Minnie could not have received it from anyone else other than Jane. There was evidence to prove that Jane owed the Davises money for the holiday cottage, but was unable to pay it, so she may have decided to kill them as a means of wiping out the debt. Another theory, which the police thought to be the most feasible, was that she was 'mentally deranged' and that her 'mania' was to cause death by poison.

District Attorney Holmes had been relying on a testimony from Dr Latter, who had attended the Davis family before their deaths, but unfortunately he had died ten days before and had not made an ante-mortem statement, which could have been used as evidence. But, shortly before his death, the doctor had made his suspicions known to the authorities, that his patients had been poisoned, and had provided information that would help them in constructing a case against Jane Toppan.

George and Sarah Nichols were utterly shocked at Jane's arrest. 'We did not have the slightest suspicion that she was believed to be guilty of the crime now charged against her,' George told a reporter from the *Boston Globe*.

> She appeared to be very nervous, and I soon discovered that she was addicted to the morphine habit. Still, we had always known her as a woman of good character and do not see how she can be guilty of the terrible crimes alleged against her. If she is guilty, it must be because of her being addicted to the morphine habit.

Jane on the other hand, appeared surprised, but calm and composed as she gathered her belongings and went with Detective Whitney to the police station at Nashua, where she would spend the night. She told Whitney that she was 'willing to do anything she could to assist in clearing up the mystery surrounding the deaths of which she is suspected'. In the police court the following morning, Jane entered a plea of 'not guilty' to the charge of murder, before Detective Whitney escorted her back to Boston.

Often described as an 'exemplary' or 'very fine woman', whose nursing skills were known to be second to none, the news of Jane's arrest was met with shock and disbelief by those who knew her. Hon F. H. Raymond, treasurer of the Cambridge electric light company and head of one of the many distinguished families Jane had worked for during her freelance nursing career, told the *Boston Globe* that the news had come to him 'like lightning out of a clear sky'. Dr Walter Wesselhoeft, whom Jane had accompanied on several important cases, was adamant that the nurse who had been arrested and charged with murder was not Jane Toppan. 'Why, that isn't the same woman at all,' he insisted. Even Melvin Beedle, whom Jane had drugged earlier that year, said,

> Miss Toppan appeared to me to be a big, jolly woman, whenever I saw her ... I know absolutely nothing of her

antecedents. She came to us from another family in the vicinity, and as we generally let one room to a student and the student had vacated his room, we thought it would be less trouble to have her than a man about the house. I never heard anything detrimental to her character, or against her honesty in any respect. Certainly, we never had occasion to suspect her in that respect.

The following afternoon, escorted by officer Simon F. Letteney, Jane was taken by train to Barnstable jail, all the while staunchly maintaining her innocence. 'I am innocent of all they suspect me of and charge me with,' she told Letteney. 'Those people all died natural deaths, excepting old man Davis. He was crazy and I think he poisoned himself.' According to Letteney, Jane was cheerful and relaxed, chatting pleasantly throughout the journey. She 'laughed and joked about the stories of her arrest and alleged crime', which she read in newspapers on the train. 'I had nothing to do with all this,' she said, 'they are accusing me wrongfully.' Several times she mentioned the death of Alden Davis, 'There was something funny about it,' she said. 'He disappeared from Cataumet for two days and went to Boston. Either then or when he came home, I think he took something which caused his death.' A newspaper reporter who was also at the station that afternoon noted that Letteney had 'his face buried in the afternoon papers. He looked careworn and worried.' While Jane 'watched the passing crowd through the car window with an ever-changing smile, her little half-shut eyes sparkling with amusement.'

It had been barely a month since Jane, the popular and highly respected nurse, had waved goodbye to her friends at the railroad station at Bourne; now she returned to the same station a criminal in the custody of a detective, accused of one murder and suspected of having caused the death of the entire family. Crowds of people, who had once 'scoffed' at the very idea that murder had been committed in their quiet town, least of all by 'Jolly Jane' Toppan, their favourite nurse, now gathered outside the rail station, where it 'seemed as if everyone who possibly could get to the station was there to see the once popular trained nurse return a prisoner of the law', said the *Boston Post*. 'It is probable that many expected to witness a hysterical, sobbing woman, shackled to a burly officer. But if so, they were disappointed. Miss Toppan appeared but little concerned over her serious predicament,' as she 'alighted from the train smiling and unconcerned. Those in the crowd whom she knew she greeted cheerily, and with no evidence of emotion.'

The following morning, on Thursday, 31 October, Jane was arraigned in the district court at Barnstable before Judge Swift. She looked nervous as she 'tottered' into the little courtroom and sat on the small wooden bench against the wall near the door, which served as the prisoner's dock of the district court. Jane's attorney, James Stuart Murphy, who was also an old friend of the family, had not yet arrived from Lowell, so Jane had no legal representation. When the clerk called her name, she arose, holding onto the back of the bench to brace herself. She trembled as she stood clinging to the wooden rail in front of her, looking wearily at the clerk as he read out the complaint.

'What do you say to this complaint?' asked the clerk when he had finished.

'Not guilty,' Jane replied in a quivering voice, then sat back down.

The case was continued for nine days, until 8 November, when Jane was to be remanded in custody, during which time an inquest was expected to be held over the body of Minnie Gibbs. Jane arose, stepped halfway through the doorway, and then quickly gripped the door frame, as if she required support. After a moment's pause, she walked unsteadily along the narrow hallway to the stone steps that led outside, and, escorted by Detective Letteney, walked slowly to the jail, to her cell on the second floor in the women's wing, where she took off her hat and jacket and sank onto her bed.

The newspaper reporters who had gathered outside the court sent a message to Jane through Letteney, saying that they 'would be very glad to publish anything she cared to say in her defence, or would see any friends who might tell anything that would be a pleasure to her to have printed in connection to the case.' But Jane politely replied, 'Thank you very much but I think I shall keep my own counsel until I have an opportunity to talk with my attorney … I am very sorry that I am obliged to endure this wide publicity, and the only wish I could offer would be that my name does not appear in the papers anymore.' Unfortunately for Jane, her wish for anonymity was not to be granted, as the newspapers would continue to follow her for years to come.

Later that evening, in contrast to her appearance earlier in court, where she seemed 'almost on the verge of collapse', Jane was back to being the usual cool and collected woman she had always been, probably due in part to James Murphy having arrived earlier on the afternoon train. After a long consultation with Jane, Murphy emerged outside the jail and addressed the reporters:

> Miss Toppan is an innocent woman, and I am satisfied that she is the unfortunate victim of a series of suspicious circumstances. She tells me that she is innocent, and she is confident that when the truth is known she will be vindicated. I suppose that there was sufficient suspicions to warrant the government in proceeding against her. But when it comes to proving those suspicions it is a very different matter. Miss Toppan regrets the unfortunate death of Dr. Latter. She is sure that if he had lived, this charge never would have been brought against her. He knew how devoted she was to the patients and he could have declared her innocence. Merely the finding of poison in the body of Mrs. Gibbs is no evidence that Miss Toppan administered it. The finding of arsenic has a long way from proving that she had anything to do with its administration.

To quash the rumours surrounding Jane's stay at the Nicholses' farm, Murphy added,

> I should like to correct any statement or intimation that Miss Toppan went to New Hampshire for concealment. Gen Whitney knew she was in Amherst and her friends knew it also. She was in poor health and she went there for a rest. She has been there on other occasions when she had become tired and sick from overwork. So, I think in justice to her, it should not be said that she had any intention of concealing herself when she went to New Hampshire.
>
> It is a very serious charge that they bring against a woman of Miss Toppan's reputation. She is an intellectual woman and a nurse of great experience. She has attended cases for leading physicians, and they have indorsed her work. She has always shown skill and fidelity to duty. In all the cases she has had, the attending physicians have been most satisfied with what she has done in carrying out their orders and caring for the patients. This I think should be something in refutation of the probability of the truth of this charge against her.

Murphy then read out the following statement made by Jane:

> I know nothing about the poisoning either of Mrs. Gibbs or any members of the Davis family. I supposed they all died from natural causes. I am willing to tell you all about these cases. I have nothing to conceal. I am sorry that Dr. Latter is dead. Were he alive I would not have the slightest difficulty in clearing my name. The officers knew where I was all the time. I was not hiding and could have been found at an hour's notice. Such talk as my hiding from arrest is absurd.

In order to build a case against their suspect, the government needed to produce evidence that would show that Jane had either purchased or possessed arsenic prior to the death of Minnie Gibbs. This would prove to be more difficult than they first thought. The detectives scoured the pharmacies, hoping 'to locate any druggist who remembers having sold the deadly compound to Miss Toppan', but with no success. Meanwhile, the local undertaker, W. C. Davis, revealed that the embalming fluid he used to prepare the bodies of Genevieve Gordon and Minnie Gibbs for burial contained arsenic. The government now needed to prove that the arsenic found in Minnie Gibbs's body had been administered through the mouth and could not have been any residue of the embalming fluid. But, as one newspaper suggested, Jane could have obtained some embalming fluid while she was assisting the undertakers. 'This would provide her with a deadly poison which would never be traced to her. She could easily have secured in this way enough to have killed a regiment. As the locating of the purchase of arsenic by her, seems to be less likely, this theory is gaining ground.'

As Jane had never used arsenic to kill any of her victims, when one police officer suggested that she might have given them poison in Hunyadi water, she responded, 'How foolish, as if anyone would give poison in Hunyadi water!' There was circumstantial evidence to point the finger at Jane, but not enough solid evidence to build a case against her. The prosecution's proof merely depended upon the fact that Jane would have had the perfect opportunity to poison Minnie Gibbs while she had been nursing her.

One person who disputed the fact that Minnie Gibbs had been poisoned with arsenic was her father-in-law, Captain Paul Gibbs. Knowing that it was Captain Gibbs's suspicions that had instigated the investigation at the beginning, newspaper reporters were keen to speak to him. When one reporter spoke to the captain and told him that large amounts of arsenic had been found in the viscera of both his daughter-in-law and Genevieve Gordon, he appeared surprised and said, 'I didn't think Jeannie Toppan would use anything as easily detected as arsenic.'

Incarcerated in her cell on the upper floor in the southeast corner of Barnstable jail, Jane remained calm and collected and never complained about the conditions. She was not permitted any visitors and was only allowed to walk about in the corridor for an hour a day. Mrs Cash, the jailer's wife, who brought Jane her meals, also supplied her with magazines, periodicals, and newspapers, which she carefully read each day to see what was being said about her.

On the morning of 8 November, as the town clock struck 9.00, a small crowd gathered outside the jail to see Jane come out of the door, her eyes cast down, and walk with faltering steps, arm in arm with her lawyer, James Murphy, towards the Court House, less than 25 feet away. She was to appear before Judge Smith K. Hopkins, accused of the murder of Minnie Gibbs. Inside the cramped court room, Jane sat near the door, her head bent forward, her counsel sitting beside her. She wore the same dress of black cheviot she had worn on the day of her arrest, but this time, according to a reporter from the *Boston Post*, 'neatness was lacking'. She looked 'almost unkempt' as her 'black hair, tinged with grey, strayed out from beneath her black bonnet. A carelessly tied large white lawn ribbon encircled a wide front collar.' Unlike her appearance on the day of her arrest ten days before, when she was 'bright and cheery', Jane looked like 'a hunted animal at bay', as she sat 'pale cheeked, hollow eyed, ill at ease, and trembling with emotion', while she 'faced her accusers'.

During the proceedings, Jane sat nervously entwining her gloves around her fingers; her face was drawn, and her lips trembled. She kept her eyes down, but several times briefly looked up at the crowded court room. At the end of the short hearing, Judge Hopkins ordered that the accused be held without bail until 15 November. As Jane rose to her feet, she shuddered, and it was thought that she might collapse. Then, as she turned to leave the court room, she faltered and grabbed James Murphy's arm for support. Closely followed by Detective

Letteney and jailer Cash, Jane 'could hardly keep her balance' as she walked back along the corridor to the door that led outside and back to the jail. However, after spending half an hour in the jailer's office with her counsel, she had 'quite recovered her composure', and returned to her cell.

At 10.30 that morning, the inquest into the deaths of Minnie Gibbs and Genevieve Gordon had begun before Judge Frederick C. Swift, at Buzzards Bay. Conducted under strict conditions in utmost secrecy, no one 'except the officials and witnesses under examination, was permitted to hear any of the proceedings'. Only one witness was allowed at a time into the court room, and each one 'strictly enjoined to maintain secrecy as to the nature of the evidence enclosed'. Captain Paul Gibbs, Oramel Brigham, Beulah Jacobs, Professor Wood, and medical examiner Dr R. H. Faunce, who performed the autopsies, were among the witnesses called for the prosecution. After four hours, at 2.35 pm, the inquest was adjourned.

Later that day, the press revealed that the detectives had finally found the druggists where Jane had purchased the drug or poison. Back in July (while she was attending the Davis family), Jane had telephoned Mr Benjamin Waters, proprietor of the drug store in Wareham, stating that she was a trained nurse and 'competent to use poisons', and ordered a bottle of 'the strongest possible' morphine tablets, which were to be enclosed in paper wrapper and delivered to her address at Cataumet. The druggist, who said that 'the bottle contained enough poison to kill a score of persons', confirmed that it was 'delivered to Miss Toppan and paid for by her'.

The following month, Jane telephoned Benjamin Waters a second time and ordered more morphine tablets, this time by express COD. The delivery man was again able to prove that Jane purchased the morphine by her signature and date in his delivery book. There was also evidence to show that on another occasion during the summer, Jane purchased morphine from another drug store in Falmouth. The proprietors of both the drug stores said that, as Jane stated she was a professional nurse, they sold her the drug without question. In one of her statements, Jane had said that any medication she had given her patients had been under Dr Latter's orders. But, when Detective Whitney had asked the doctor if he had ever prescribed morphine for Minnie Gibbs, Genevieve Gordon, and Alden Davis, he had replied, 'No, I have never given any morphine to any member of that family. I did not dare to, for I knew that their constitutions were so weak that they could not stand it.'

Shortly after 8.00 am on the morning of 15 November, James Murphy arrived at Barnstable jail, bearing a large bunch of chrysanthemums and a basket of fruit for Jane, who was as 'happy as a schoolgirl when he presented them to her'.[5] Murphy, who had visited Jane the night before, had assured her that he would be able to convince the court she was innocent. As she left the jail, accompanied by Murphy, State Detective Letteney and jailer Cash, Jane was 'wreathed in smiles' and 'chatted merrily' with her counsel, while she walked briskly ahead towards the courthouse. When she realised the others were behind, she stopped and waited, remarking cheerfully that she was 'rather a fast walker'. A crowd of newspaper reporters holding cameras were waiting outside the big stone courthouse to get a photo of the prisoner. Unperturbed, Jane turned to Murphy and said, 'Oh, look at the cameras. They are trying to get a snapshot of me.'[6]

In contrast to her last appearance, Jane appeared 'neatly dressed' in a black suit, with matching hat, and calmly sat 'with head erect and eyes bright', next to her counsel, in the same seat she had occupied the previous week. The proceedings lasted less than five minutes, during which time James Murphy was granted his request to have the hearing continued until 11 December. When Judge Swift asked the prisoner to rise, Jane, her hands by her sides, looked him squarely in the face, while he committed her to back to jail without bail, until the following month. According to the *Boston Globe*, Jane, who was convinced that it would 'no longer be difficult to prove her innocence', was chatting and 'laughing merrily' as she was escorted back to her cell. Murphy remained with his client until it was time for him to catch the 10.25 train back to Boston. As he walked to the depot, Jane could be seen watching him from the barred window of her cell, 'casting longing glances after the one in whom she has confided all, and upon whom she relies to secure her freedom.'

On the morning of 20 November, the bodies of Alden and Mattie Davies were exhumed by undertaker Davis, who had buried the couple a few months before. That afternoon, Medical Examiner Dr R. H. Faunce performed the autopsies in the carriage shed adjoining the Methodist church, where according to one report, it was found that both bodies were 'in a remarkable state of preservation', despite having been in the ground for three months. After the viscera was removed, it was given to Professor Wood for chemical analysis, who expected to make his report within the next ten days, in time for Jane's hearing on 11 December, by which time it was hoped that the government would be in possession of all the facts relating to the causes of the deaths of all the members of the Davis family and strengthen their case for the prosecution. Whereas Jane, who looked forward to the hearing with the 'utmost eagerness', where she expected to be able to speak on her own behalf, was convinced she would be released on bail.

However, a few days later, on 23 November, it was revealed that the prosecution had found new evidence that established the cause of the deaths of Genevieve Gordon and Alden Davis, which was sufficient to charge Jane with murder. While Professor Wood had been trying to ascertain if the arsenic found in the bodies of Genevieve Gordon and Minnie Gibbs was residue of the embalming fluid or had been administered through the mouth, he had discovered the presence of another poison. After performing the appropriate tests, he had found a substantial amount of morphine present in their viscera.

The detectives were also investigating the deaths of the other patients which had occurred under Jane's care, including Oramel Brigham's wife, Elizabeth, his sister, Edna Bannister, and his housekeeper, Florence Calkins, and they had found several medicine bottles containing the medicine prescribed by Dr Latter, hidden between the mattresses of Genevieve Gordon's bed, which showed that it had not been administered.

Captain Paul Gibbs had told the police that a few days after Minnie's funeral:

> I asked Dr. Latter what caused the death of Mrs. Gibbs, and he told me frankly he did not know. He insinuated that there was something about the deaths that needed explanation and within a few days after that conversation, he told me that he had been reading some medical books and had come to the conclusion that some of the Davis family might have died from poison.

It had also transpired that the members of the Davis family were all supposed to have had money at the time of their deaths. The money had disappeared and had not been found since.

> Miss Toppan was the one person in the world who had every opportunity to get this money. She was with the Davis family all the time they were ill, she washed and dressed their bodies when they died and there was not a section of the house to which she did not have perfect knowledge. I am positive that Mr. Davis had $500 a day or two before he died.
>
> I am sure that no one in the house but Miss Toppan took it, as often before she went to the house, he had three times that amount in his pockets. It was thought after this that he might have deposited the money, but we soon found that he did not.

After a brief pause, the captain continued: 'It was the same with the money the others had just before they died. We know it was in their possession when they became ill; we know that Miss Toppan was alone with them a good deal of the time they were sick.'

The regular session of the Barnstable grand jury was not usually held until April, but a week before the preliminary hearing, District Attorney Holmes made the surprising and unexpected decision to summon a special session, to be held on Friday 6 December. In doing so, he was avoiding a preliminary hearing in the district court, where he would have had to reveal the evidence of the prosecution, and Jane would not be able to make a statement as planned.

Although this was disappointing news for Jane's counsel, Murphy appeared both unsurprised and unperturbed as he told a reporter from the *Boston Globe*,

> I thought that is what they would do … When the inquest was adjourned, I was satisfied that it would not be resumed, but that the grand jury would hear the case as soon as possible. Of course, the government can do this. It simply brings the exoneration of Miss Toppan nearer by hastening things as Mr. Holmes has done.

Murphy, who had recently requested that 'for her own peace of mind' Jane would not have access to the daily newspapers, had yet to break the news to his client. Jailer Cash, who had read the morning paper, decided that he would not be the one to tell his prisoner the bad news, so Jane had no idea of what had been written about her.

In the meantime, unaware of the sudden change of events, Jane was still confident of a release, and remained calm and complacent. As she eagerly waited for the day of the hearing in the district court, she whiled away the long hours in Barnstable jail, sewing, reading magazines, illustrated weekly papers, and comic publications, supplied by her friends and counsel and books from the prison library. 'I am having a good rest here, anyway,' she told the jailer's wife, Mrs Cash. She also enjoyed regular visits from jailer Cash's two-year-old granddaughter,

Lucy, who 'toddles up to the cell door, grasps the bars with her tiny fingers, and stands for an hour at a time talking with the nurse.' Jane grew so fond of little Lucy that she wrote to James Murphy, requesting that he send her old picture books, which were stored in the garret of Oramel Brigham's house, so that she could cut out the pictures for the little girl. She was so sure that she would be able to clear her name at the hearing and be released to spend Christmas at home with her friends that she even promised Lucy she would buy her a present.

On a dull, grey morning, 6 December, the grand jury, consisting of twenty-three men from various towns across Cape Cod, assembled in the little stone courthouse opposite the jail, to hear the evidence against Jane Toppan. At 9.00 am, the 'slow clanging of a harsh-toned bell' in the tower of the courthouse and the 'brisk, cold northeast wind which blew down the bay, sent the sounds of its funeral-like rolling reverberating through the sand dunes,' as though emphasising the prospect of impending doom. After hearing the testimonies of six witnesses, the grand jurors, who had heard all they needed to, decided that the seventh witness, Benjamin Waters, the druggist who had sold the morphine to Jane and who had been 'walking up and down the stone paved corridor all afternoon' waiting to be called, would not be needed to testify.

At 5.00 pm, accompanied by her counsel and two deputy sheriffs, Jane left the jail and started to walk briskly towards the courthouse. Beulah Jacobs and Oramel Brigham were standing near the rear entrance to the building and, when Jane saw them, she hesitated and 'staggered as if she was attempting to make a detour to take her farther away from them'. She faltered, and James Murphy caught her arm and directed her towards the side entrance of the building. Looking straight ahead, Jane walked steadily into the courtroom, taking the seat placed for her in front of the row of the jury. Her face was very pale, as 'white as the chiffon ribbon' that she wore around her neck, and her eyes were wide as she focused on Chief Justice Albert Mason. District Attorney Holmes addressed the court, 'Your honour, the grand jury have returned three indictments against Jane Toppan for murder. I ask that she now be arraigned.' After a slight nod of the head from the judge, the clerk, Smith K. Hopkins, ordered Jane to stand.

In the fading twilight, Jane rose slowly from her seat, her steady gaze now fixed on the elderly clerk, as he started to read out the three indictments one by one. She stood for ten minutes, tightly gripping the rail in front of her, while in the dim light, the clerk squinted and stumbled through the first indictment charging her with the murder of Mary 'Minnie' Gibbs. A kerosene lamp was brought in to assist him, but it seemed to make so little difference that by the second indictment, to spare her 'further agony', Jane's counsel stood up and waived the reading of the remaining two indictments, the deaths of Alden Davis and Genevieve Gordon, caused by the administration of morphine and atropine. Chief Justice Mason agreed, and Hopkins asked Jane three times if she were guilty or not guilty of the charges brought against her, to which she replied each time in a low, husky voice, 'Not guilty.'

As Jane had no money, James Murphy, who had not charged a fee to represent her, rose from his seat and requested that the court appoint counsel for his client, who had 'no funds' and would not be able to employ a counsel for her defence. Judge Mason replied that he 'would take the matter under advisement'. He then dismissed the jury, and Jane was escorted back to her cell to await her trial the following spring.

Several reports claimed that Jane had been 'considerably worked up' and 'under severe mental strain' when she returned from the court room; however, by the following week, she seemed to be less anxious and was 'bearing up well'. Despite being kept in an isolated cell, with no visitors allowed except her counsel, jailer Cash said that Jane was cheerful, 'enjoying perfect health', and had a good appetite, eating the prison food with 'relish'. On Christmas Day, she was permitted to join jailer Cash and his family for an hour in his apartment to eat Christmas dinner with them. Afterwards, she went back to her cell 'loaded down with gifts of various kinds and it took her most of the afternoon to examine them all'.

James Murphy's request to Chief Justice Mason was granted and at the beginning of January, Judge Fred M. Bixby, Justice of Brockton police court, was appointed Jane's senior counsel and James Murphy was to be her junior counsel. Jane seemed to have great confidence in her new counsel and firmly believed that she would be acquitted after the trial, which, due to the defence requesting more time to prepare their case, had been delayed until June. But by now, her sanity was being questioned, and Judge Bixby, along with Attorney Holmes, approached Attorney General Parker proposing they appoint a commission of physicians to determine whether Jane was mentally responsible for her actions at the time of the murders. If the court judged Jane to be insane, there would be no trial and she would be placed in an asylum.

At the beginning of March, three prominent physicians – Dr Hosea M. Quimby, superintendent of the Worcester Insane Asylum, Dr Henry R. Stedman of Brookline Sanitorium, and Dr George F. Kelly of Boston – were assigned to conduct an examination to assess Jane's mental state of mind. Jane now not only had the charge of the deaths of the entire Davis family hanging over her, but was also suspected of being implicated in the deaths of Edna Bannister, Florence Calkins, Myra Connors, and Mrs McNear.

On Thursday, 20 March, all three alienists visited Jane at Barnstable jail, where they found her in a 'defiant mood'. When she was told that the commission was going to visit her, she exclaimed, 'Why, how absurd. Me insane? Of course I am not. I'll show them that I am not insane.' She was determined that the alienists would leave with a 'positive impression that she was mentally sound'. During the interview, Jane appeared calm and relaxed, as she laughed and joked with the physicians. Still steadfastly maintaining her innocence, she talked freely about the deaths of Minnie Gibbs, Genevieve Gordon, and Alden Davis, until the doctors finished their interview later that afternoon, and caught the train back to Boston. After comparing their observations, they all agreed that they would need to conduct several more interviews before they made a final decision.

A week later, despite the alienists having not yet submitted their formal report, information was leaked to the press, confirming that they believed Jane to be insane. 'She will never be brought to trial for the 11 deaths alleged against her,' declared the *Boston Post*, 'but will live her life out in an asylum.'

Aside from being an avid reader, Jane was also a prolific letter writer, and during her time in prison had penned countless letters to her counsel and friends. According to the report, the piles of correspondence, nearly all of which appeared to be fabrication of the truth, had been influential in the doctors' decision:

> In some instances, Miss Toppan has written letters on two consecutive days to the same person, exactly contradictory of each other. The stories which she has told in these missives all border on the marvellous and seem to have been written with an absolute disregard for the truth. Some tell of fabulous wealth left her; another of a marriage soon to take place with some prominent man; while a third speaks of a trip around the world on a private yacht to be presented to the writer by some young man whom she had infatuated.
>
> These fancies seem to have been written with no object in view. There was nothing for her to gain by the deception, and the doctors are of the opinion that the letters could have been the product of a disordered mind alone.

During that week, Jane received another blow when a small piece of news in *The Journal* revealed:

> While Jane Toppan waits in Barnstable Jail for that day when she will be buried from the world within the walls of an insane asylum, the man whom she wished to marry

and to gain whose love she is supposed to have committed many crimes, is planning to wed the woman whom Miss Toppan hated.

Deacon O. A. Brigham, with whom Miss Toppan lived, it is expected, will soon marry Miss Martha M. Cook, a woman a few years younger than the deacon, and a member of the same church.

On 23 April, the *North Adams Transcript* reported that during a conference attended by District Attorney Holmes, Attorney General Parker, and Fred Bixby, it was agreed that Jane Toppan was suffering from a 'form of uncurable insanity, having defective control of an irresistible impulse and will be taken into court at Barnstable and evidence given about the crimes with which she is charged and about her moral and mental condition.' The proceedings were expected to be brief, after which it was believed that Jane would be committed to Taunton Insane Hospital. When the physicians told Jane that they believed her to be insane and that she ought to be confined, she said:

> I know I am not a safe person to be at large. It would be better if I were locked up where I could do no one any harm. No one can tell when I am liable to have another paroxysm. I do not know myself until it comes. I have never been so happy in my life as since I have been in jail. I know I am safe. I have been treated considerably. Everyone has done all that could be done to make me comfortable.

Afterwards, Jane's counsel recommended she change her plea to guilty.

It was during the last interview with the alienists that Jane finally confessed to having caused the deaths of Minnie Gibbs, Alden Davis, and Genevieve Gordon. Believing that 'it was knowledge due to them as physicians', with brutal frankness, she calmly described to them how she poisoned Minnie Gibbs by giving her morphine and atropine, administered in the form of pellets. She admitted that the night before Minnie died, she gave her two large doses of tablets, of which there were so many she couldn't remember the exact number, claiming that she 'could not restrain herself from doing so'. Then, as Minnie lay unconscious, she administered an injection of the poison. Jane also described how she had poisoned ten other people by the same method, knowing that the atropine would counteract the effect of the morphine and render detection impossible. After hearing her confession, James Murphy suggested that she must be insane to carry out such heinous crimes, but Jane was adamant:

> Insane! How can I be insane? When I killed those people, I knew that I was doing wrong. I was perfectly conscious that I was not doing right. I never at any time failed to realize what I was doing. Now, how can a person be insane who realizes what she is doing and who is conscious of the fact that she isn't doing right? Insanity is complete lack of any feeling of responsibility, isn't it?

'Yes, but have you no remorse?' Murphy asked.

> No, I have absolutely no remorse. I have never felt sorry for what I have done. Even when I poisoned my dearest friends, as the Davises were, I did not feel any regret afterward. I do not feel any remorse now. I have thought it all over, and I cannot detect the slightest bit of sorrow over what I have done.

Jane stopped and paused for a moment before she went on:

> There is one thing that makes me think my mind is not right. I have great difficulty in remembering things.

My memory is good at times, but on other occasions
I cannot recall what I have said and done.

On Monday, 23 June, the day before the trial, villagers living as far
as a mile from the courthouse rented out any spare rooms or available
space they had to accommodate the scores of people flocking to
Barnstable, hoping to witness the long-awaited and much anticipated
trial of nurse Jane Toppan. 'Farmers are sleeping in their kitchens and
letting their bed chambers, and still rooms are wanted,' reported the
*Boston Post.* Many people, including the newspaper reporters, were
forced to find accommodation in Hyannis, five miles away. The little
stone courtroom seated 200 people, but ten times that number were
expected to turn up at the trial, hoping to gain entry. Several groups
of women intended to arrive early the next morning at dawn with
lunch baskets and camp on the courthouse lawn, so they were there
for when the doors of the courthouse opened.

Meanwhile, despite having spent nearly eight months in jail,
according to jailer Cash, Jane was still upbeat and cheerful and had
for the past several months been writing a book, believed to be a
sentimental novel. During that afternoon, Jane's counsel, Fred Bixby
and James Murphy, visited her to discuss the trial. They entered her
cell to find her 'smiling in a half-perplexed manner over several sheets
of manuscript' that she was holding in her hand. When the two men
tried to talk to her about her appearance in court the next day, Jane
was more interested in discussing the title for her new book. She told
them that she was so confident that the book would be a success and
that 'thousands of copies' would be sold that she would be able to pay
them out of its profits. Murphy, who was starting to lose his patience,
tried to divert Jane's attention to her trial:

'You know you go into court tomorrow, Jane,' he said.

'Oh, yes,' replied Jane, 'but tell me, Mr. Murphy, do you think that
"Sweet Blue Eyes" would be a good title for my book? I want it to be a
good one, you know, because so much depends upon its being catchy.

I have thought of "Maude's Misery," and "Fair, Fettered Florence," also, but I think that I like "Sweet Blue Eyes," best, don't you?'

Murphy started to say that 'all of the titles would do well enough…'

'Well enough,' Jane interrupted. 'Well enough! Don't you know that this book is going to make you a rich man? You ought to be interested I should think.' Murphy tried again to remind Jane about her court appearance the next day, but she continued to ignore him, wanting only to talk about her book, until eventually her lawyers gave up and left, hoping that by the morning their client would be focused on the more important matters at hand.

The morning of the trial dawned warm and bright with a clear blue sky. At 7.00 am, while Jane was enjoying her breakfast, a crowd had already started to congregate outside the jail, hoping to catch a glimpse of Barnstable's most notorious prisoner, now dubbed by the press the 'modern Lucrezia Borgia'. In between mouthfuls of food, Jane chatted about the day ahead to Theodosia Cash, the jailer's daughter. 'But it was not to ask of the possible chances of her acquittal, not to proclaim her innocence, nor express hatred for those who had caused her arrest,' claimed the *Boston Post*. Instead, Jane spent the 'brief half hour asking advice as to what she would wear'. After breakfast, she began to get ready for the trial, where 'every waist, every skirt was put on and taken off at least a dozen times, and still she was not pleased with the effect.' When Judge Bixby arrived, 'she was still undecided as to which combination best suited her'.

At 9.00, the iron doors of the rear courtroom swung open, and the crowd swarmed into the building. Within ten minutes the gallery was 'packed to the dome'. At 10.00, Judge Braley and Judge Bell entered the courtroom, then Jane, accompanied by Deputy Sheriff Hutchins, walked slowly to her seat in the prisoner's dock. Dressed in black with a large black hat, trimmed with forget-me-nots and a veil, and a white ribbon around her throat, Jane had grown much stouter since her last court appearance in December, due to her healthy appetite combined with limited exercise during her incarceration.

After waiting all those months to have her say in court, when Judge Braley finally gave Jane the opportunity to 'address the jury in her own behalf', she declined. While the jury was out, Jane 'chatted, laughed and was exceedingly jolly'. After twenty-seven minutes, the jury returned a verdict of 'not guilty of murder by reason of insanity', and Jane was committed to spend the remainder of her natural life at Taunton Insane Hospital. Afterwards, Jane left the courtroom 'with a contented smile', and told her counsel, 'I realise that I am not fit to free, and I think you have done the best for me.'

Nonetheless, there were many who did not believe that Jane was 'morally insane', and thought that she should have received the rightful punishment of the electric chair. As Oramel Brigham told a reporter from the *Boston Globe*:

> Jane Toppan appeared as saucy as ever when I saw her in the courtroom. She bowed to me, but I did not return it. I think she is sane and believe she should suffer the punishment of people convicted of murder. She poisoned my wife, our housekeeper and Mrs Bannister, and I believe attempted to poison me. I told the judge I believed she was sane.

The following day, Jane, who according to one report 'looked as happy as if she were bound on a shopping tour', left Barnstable jail, and, accompanied by James Murphy, travelled by train to Taunton Asylum. Built in a neo-classical style in 1854, the State Lunatic Hospital at Taunton (as it was originally called) was set in over 100 acres of grounds that offered its patients plenty of sunlight and fresh air. After her arrival, Jane was assigned to a small room on Ward 6, which faced southeast, overlooking the front campus of the building, having full benefit of the rising sun every morning and pleasant, uninterrupted views across the lawn that sloped down to a little lake. The next day, Jane joined her fellow patients on what would become a regular walk through the meadow and woodland adjoining the asylum.

A few days later, the newspapers were awash with reports that Jane had confessed to killing at least thirty-one people. Judge Bixby had compiled a list of the victims as Jane repeated their names whilst checking off the number on her fingertips. During her confession to the alienists, Jane openly discussed the murders as if she were a 'student in medicine or surgery at a clinic' and implied that it was to 'gratify an abnormal passion that she put patients to death'. Yet despite admitting to having an 'uncontrollable passion' which could only be satisfied by taking a human life, Jane laughed when she was told that she would spend the rest of her life in an institution, as she believed that, after a few years, she would no longer have the irresistible urge to kill and would be granted her freedom, as she would not be a danger to society.

Shortly after the trial, William Randolph Hearst published as a supplement in the *New York Journal* what he claimed was Jane's full confession, where she admitted that she had wanted the panel of alienists to find her insane. She knew that a person who really was insane would always deny it, so she repeatedly insisted that she was not insane to trick the physicians into thinking that she was.

Initially, Jane seemed to adjust quickly to her life in the institution and happily entertained the other patients and attendants with her elaborate fictitious stories, which according to some reports 'eclipsed all her previous efforts'. One morning, shortly after her arrival, a nurse found her groaning, lying on her bed, and looking 'very ill'. After telling the nurse that she had taken some poison which she had brought into the hospital sewn in her skirt, a doctor was summoned, who, having experienced similar situations many times before in the asylum, doubted that Jane's performance was genuine. His diagnosis was confirmed when, after a course of treatment, she quickly recovered. On another occasion, one of the attendants in the asylum overheard Jane boasting to a group of her fellow patients that she had killed eighty-four people. 'There was just eighty-four,' she told them. 'I was going to make it just a hundred then stop.'

At first, there was little change in Jane's personality and according to the attendant physician, during her first year in the hospital, she remained 'sociable, quiet, cheerful, amiable and helpful', and spent much of her time reading. Her favourite authors were Kipling, Scott, Dickens, Marie Corelli, and Mrs Radcliffe. But by February 1904, her mental and physical health had deteriorated. The hospital staff noted that Jane had been 'showing no pity or sorrow for others in trouble and distress, displaying on such occasions a great deal of glee. Trouble and anguish in her fellow patients seemed to excite in her general merriment and joy, instead of sorrow and compassion.'

She began to invent the most outrageous lies about the nurses, the hospital attendants, and the other patients, accusing them of 'vices undiscoverable in the annals of the most corrupt civilizations'. She was convinced that the staff at the hospital were trying to poison her and became so paranoid that she refused to eat her food, for fear it would be poisoned. At first, she would hide the food at mealtimes, before eventually refusing it altogether. As a result, she had lost over 80 lbs in weight, or half her body weight, and had to be force-fed through a tube, after which she would eat just enough food for a while, to avoid being fed again. Oddly enough, Jane was fully aware that her mind was 'weakening', which added to her anxiety.

Jane wrote numerous letters in which she stressed her fear of being poisoned. In correspondence with one of her friends, she wrote, 'Do you know, the supervisor put some poison in my tea. A patient saw her and told me, and I didn't touch it. The lady heard the supervisor say she had fixed Jane Toppan this time.' In a letter to James Murphy dated 15 March, Jane wrote:

I am the victim of nerve paralysis, the result of food. I have to eat or I am fed with a tube with nerve paralyzing food that I choose from the tray. Oh, I think that you and

Mr. Bixby were criminals to put me through this. It was an awful thing to do to any human being, and I have my opinion of everybody who takes a hand in it. I think as the nerves of my body get more benumbed, my brain becomes clearer to the outrageous course that has been taken with me. I suppose the next thing, something will be given to put me out of the way altogether. That would be a mercy to this.

Dr Stedman, who had been visiting and corresponding with Jane since her arrest, received several letters from her on the subject, including the following in July:

I wish to inform you that I am alive in spite of the deleterious which has been served to me. Many efforts have been made to poison me in this institution, of that I am very sure. I am thin and very hungry all the time. Every nerve is calling for food. Why can't I have help? I ate a pint of ice cream and four oranges Saturday and Sunday. That was all.

During one of his visits, Jane complained to the doctor that everything was 'rotten', that the meat was 'embalmed' beef, and the vegetables were 'rank poison'. Everything was 'filthy', she told him, even the brick walls which must be 'saturated with the filth of years'. Even the water supply, which came from an artesian well, was 'polluted with sewage'. She spoke anxiously about a 'general feeling of numbness' and asked the doctor what caused it. 'She was entirely inaccessible to explanation, argument or even positive proof as to the impossibility of her statements,' observed Dr Stedman. 'Occasionally she would burst out unexpectedly with peculiar and piercing shrieks of laughter which would seem impossible to one in her weak condition.'

Although the alienists declared Jane to be 'morally insane', opinions had always been divided regarding her sanity, as to whether she really was insane. As Jane herself wrote in a letter to Dr Stedman, when she was first admitted to the asylum, 'I don't appear like these other patients. I can read a book intelligently, I don't have bad thoughts, so I don't see where moral degeneracy comes in.' But now, just over two years after her committal, Dr Stedman had no doubt in his mind that Jane was, and had been for more than a quarter of a century, insane. Though, as one report noted, her 'malady is of such a peculiar and heretofore unheard of order, that it left her intellectual faculties absolutely unimpaired until a very short time ago'.

By the end of the year, Jane, who had entered the asylum a 'plump, good looking, happy woman', and who had gloated in 'fooling the doctors' into thinking she was insane, had now, according to the reports, become a 'mere skeleton' and a 'raving maniac'. She had become violent and abusive towards the other patients and hospital staff and had been moved to a secluded cell in the north wing of the hospital. She had again attempted suicide, wherein she had knotted her bed clothes, fastening one end to the high head of her bedstead, and had almost been successful, had the nurses not discovered her just in time. From then on, four of the hospital's largest female nurses were assigned to watch Jane both night and day and were under strict orders to have at least two in attendance at all times. Even though Jane was still very weak, it was considered much safer than having a single nurse on duty. The staff had also replaced the high bedstead Jane normally slept on with a lower platform secured to the floor, where a nurse sat either side.

According to some reports, Jane would often talk about the people she had poisoned, muttering their names and gloating as she recalled how they suffered, often laughing and clapping her hands as she did so. 'Do you see her now?' she would cry to the nurse, 'See how she suffers. Isn't it worth watching? But she will soon be dead, and I will have to kill someone else.' One evening, she allegedly said to a nurse,

'Get me some morphine and take me out among the sick people and you and I will enjoy watching one of them die.'

At other times, Jane was convinced that her dead victims had risen from their graves and were trying to poison *her*, as she anxiously told the nurse one morning:

> I saw them all last night ... all the people I have killed. They all came and gathered round my bed in the night. There were the Davises, and Mr. and Mrs. Dunham, and Myra Connors, and Mrs. Brigham, Mrs. Bannister, Mrs. Gibbs and Mrs. Harry Gordon – Oh, I'm sorry I killed her, she is so pretty ...

Jane's voice trailed off, before she burst into tears. After she composed herself, she continued: 'But they're all after me now – thirty-one of them – some want to poison me, and some come at me with their skeleton hands, as if they would choke me. See, they're coming for me now – help, murder!'

On another occasion, after hearing cries from Jane's ward, a nurse rushed into her room to find her 'fighting off some imaginary assailants'. Convinced that Minnie Gibbs had 'put morphia' into her arm, Jane pulled up her sleeve to her shoulder to reveal blood dripping from where she had 'scratched it with her own fingernails in her wild desire to dig out the imaginary poison'. She had become paranoid that people were trying to burn her alive and often at night would cry out that someone was setting fire to her bed while she was asleep. 'It is as though she were experiencing the combined torture of all those whom she had made suffer,' wrote one newspaper.

When James Murphy (who was now Jane's guardian) visited Jane just before Christmas, she did not recognise him and refused to speak to him, as she believed he was one of her enemies who was out to poison her. Murphy said that Jane was 'greatly emaciated under her self-enforced fast, having eaten little for several months', and that the attendants used 'artificial nourishment' to keep her alive. According to the institution accounts, her speech was 'incoherent and rambling, coupled with the threats of what she would do if again free'. Jane's health had deteriorated so rapidly that the doctors did not expect her to live much longer than a few months.

But, despite the numerous reports predicting Jane's impending death, 'America's Lucrezia Borgia' went on to live for another thirty-four years. Her fears of being poisoned gradually dispersed, so that she accepted food and gained weight. She continued to have periods of violence, where at times 'it was necessary to keep her in a straight-jacket', but gradually the outbursts dwindled and in her remaining years, Jane became a 'quiet old lady', who was 'just another patient who caused no trouble'. In the summer of 1938, Jane fell ill with broncho-pneumonia and died two weeks later, on 17 August, at the age of 81.

The number of people who met their premature death in the hands of 'Jolly Jane' Toppan is still unknown; even Jane herself could not be sure of the final total. After her death, several newspapers reported that while she was in Barnstable jail, she had casually said to one journalist:

> I have given the alienists and Herbert Parker the names of 31 persons I killed, but, as a matter of fact, I killed many more whose names I cannot recall. I think it would be safe to say that I killed at least 100 from the time I became a nurse at a Boston Hospital, where I killed the first one, until I ended the lives of the Davis family.

# Notes

## Chapter 1

1. The killing of a young child under the age of twelve months.
2. Marland, Hilary, *Dangerous Motherhood: Insanity and Childbirth in Victorian Britain*, Palgrave MacMillan, 2004, p. 168.
3. Another name for a white witch.
4. He was registered at birth as Louis Tavern Drake, though some accounts give his name as Lewis.
5. Beeton, Isabella, *The Book of Household Management*, S. O. Beeton, 1861, p. 84.
6. W. Hamish Fraser, *The Coming of the Mass Market*, 1850–1914, The Macmillan Press, 1981, p. 21.
7. Jack Whicher was a distinguished member of the original team of eight Scotland Yard detectives formed seven years before in 1842.
8. *The Standard*, 8 December 1849.
9. *Trewman's Exeter Flying Post*, 27 December 1849.
10. *The Observer*, 13 January 1850.
11. The killing of one's own child.

## Chapter 2

1. A. C. Benson, *Reginald Brett, Viscount Esher, The Letters of Queen Victoria, Vol 1: 1837–1843*, Cambridge University Press, 1907, p. 14.
2. Jane Ridley, *Bertie: A Life of Edward VII*, Chatto & Windus, 2012, p. 15.
3. George Earle Buckle, *The Letters of Queen Victoria, Vol 5: 1870–1878*, Cambridge University Press, 1926, p. 410.
4. G. Barnett Smith, *Life of Her Majesty Queen Victoria*, George Routledge & Sons, 1887, p. 167.
5. *A Diary of Royal Movements and of Personal Events and Incidents in the Life and Reign of Her Most Gracious Majesty Queen Victoria*, Elliot Stock, 1883, p. 165.

6. *The Morning Post*, 18 November 1841.
7. Ibid.
8. *The Bradford Observer*, 22 June 1854.


# Chapter 3

1. Arthur Appleton, *Mary Ann Cotton: Her Story and Trial*, Michael Joseph, 1973, p. 48.
2. From Mary Ann Cotton's letters written during her imprisonment, which appear in Arthur Appleton, *Mary Ann Cotton: Her Story and Trial*, Michael Joseph, 1973.
3. Arthur Appleton, *Mary Ann Cotton: Her Story and Trial*, p. 53.
4. Due to the flourishing industry of life insurance and the simultaneous sales of arsenic, from 1850, the lives of children under three years old could not be insured for more than £3.
5. *The Leeds Mercury*, 15 October 1872.
6. Ibid.
7. *The Times*, 16 October 1872.
8. *The Northern Echo*, 22 February 1873.
9. *Shields Gazette and Daily Telegraph*, 21 March 1873.
10. *The Dundee Courier*, 31 March 1873.


# Chapter 4

1. John T. James, *The Benders in Kansas*, The Kan-Okla Publishing Co., 1913, p. 14.
2. Ibid.
3. Ibid., p. 36.
4. Ibid., p. 37.
5. Ibid., p. 42.


# Chapter 5

1. Walter Wood, *Survivors Tales of Famous Crimes*, Cassell & Co, 1916, p. 84.
2. Elliot O'Donnell, *Trial of Kate Webster*, William Hodge & Co, 1925, p. 22.

3. *Daily News*, 9 April 1879.
4. The Slate Club was a burial club where a monthly payment could be made to cover the cost of funeral expenses.
5. *Manchester Weekly Times and Examiner*, 12 July 1879.
6. Major Arthur Griffiths, *The Chronicles of Newgate*, London, 1884, p. 552. Griffiths refers to Kate Webster as a 'fierce and brutal female savage', who was 'one of the worst prisoners ever remembered in Newgate'.
7. *The Illustrated Police News*, 2 August 1879.
8. Elliot O'Donnell, *Trial of Kate Webster*, p. 72.
9. *The Bury and Norwich Post*, 2 March 1880.
10. Kindly provided by Susie Douglas at www.bordersancestry.com.

## Chapter 6

1. Victoria Lincoln, *A Private Disgrace: Lizzie Borden by Daylight*, Seraphim Press, 1967, p. 21.
2. Ibid., p. 17.
3. Arthur Sherman Phillips, *The Phillips History of Fall River*, Dover Press, 1946, p. 99.
4. Victoria Lincoln, *A Private Disgrace*, pp. 19–20.
5. Ibid., p. 19.
6. *The Fall River Daily Herald*, 19 June 1893.
7. Victoria Lincoln, *A Private Disgrace*, p. 20.
8. Janice Schuetz, *The Logic of Women on Trial: Case Studies of Popular American Trials*, Southern Illinois University Press, 1994, p. 62.

## Chapter 7

1. *An Account of the Boston Female Asylum*, Boston, 1833.
2. A nineteenth-century term for sexual thrill.
3. Charles Follen Folsom, *Studies of Criminal Responsibility and Limited Responsibility*, privately printed, 1909, pp. 110–111.
4. Dr Henry R. Stedman, 'A Case of Moral Insanity with Repeated Homicides and Incendiarism and Late Development of Delusions', *Boston Medical and Surgical Journal*, 1904, p. 5.
5. *The Boston Globe*, 16 November 1901.
6. Ibid.

# Bibliography

## Books

Appleton, Arthur, *Mary Ann Cotton: Her Story and Trial* (Michael Joseph, 1973)

Bartley, Paula, *Queen Victoria* (Routledge, 2016)

Buckle, George Earle, *The Letters of Queen Victoria, Volume 5: 1870–1878* (Cambridge University Press, 2014)

Case, Nelson, *History of Labette County, Kansas, and Representative Citizens* (Biographical Publishing Company, 1901)

Coles, Prophecy, *The Shadow of the Second Mother: Nurses and Nannies in Theories of Infant Development* (Routledge, 2015)

Diner, Hasia R., *Erin's Daughters in America* (Johns Hopkins University Press, 1983)

Flanders, Judith, *The Invention of Murder* (Harper Press, 2011)

Folsom, Charles Follen, *Studies of Criminal Responsibility and Limited Responsibility* (Privately Printed, 1909)

Hall, Valerie G., *Women at Work, 1860–1939: How Different Industries Shaped Women's Experiences* (The Boydell Press, 2013)

Hardy, Allison, *Kate Bender, The Kansas Murderess: The Horrible History of an Arch Killer* (Hademan-Julius, 1944)

James, John T., *The Benders in Kansas: The Complete Story* (Kan-Okla Publishing Co., 1913)

Judd, Deborah, Sitzman, Kathleen, and Davis, G. M., *A History of American Nursing: Trends and Eras* (Jones and Bartlett Publishers, 2010)

Kilday, Anne-Marie, and Nash, David, *Law, Crime and Deviance Since 1700: Micro-Studies in the History of Crime* (Bloomsbury Academic, 2017)

Lincoln, Victoria, *A Private Disgrace: Lizzie Borden by Daylight* (Seraphim Press, 2012)

Mangham, Andrew, '"Murdered at the Breast": Maternal Violence and the Self-Made Man in Popular Victorian Culture'. *Critical Survey*, 16/1, 2004

O'Donnell, Elliot, *Trial of Kate Webster* (William Hodge & Company, 1925)

Parsons, Sara E., *History of the Massachusetts General Hospital Training School for Nurses* (Whitcomb & Barrows, 1922)

Phillips, Arthur Sherman, *The Phillips History of Fall River* (Dover Press, 1941)

Porter, Edwin H., *The Fall River Tragedy: A History of the Borden Murders* (George R. H. Buffinton, 1893)

Ridley, Jane, *Bertie: A Life of Edward VII* (Chatto & Windus, 2012)

Ryan, Dennis P., *Beyond the Ballot Box: A Social History of the Boston Irish, 1845–1917* (University of Massachusetts Amherst, 1979)

Schechter, Harold, *Fatal: The Poisonous Life of a Female Serial Killer* (Pocket Books, 2012)

Schuetz, Janice, *The Logic of Women on Trial: Case Studies of Popular American Trials* (Southern Illinois University Press, 1994)

Scull, Andrew, *Madhouses, Mad-Doctors and Madmen: The Social History of Psychiatry in the Victorian Era* (University of Pennsylvania Press, 1981)

Ward, Margaret, *Female Occupations: Women's Employment 1850–1950* (Countryside Books, 2008)

Whorton, James C., *The Arsenic Century: How Victorian Britain was Poisoned at Home, Work and Play* (Oxford University Press, 2010)

Wood, Walter, *Survivors' Tales of Famous Crimes* (Cassell and Company, 1916)

## Newspapers and Periodicals

*An Account of the Boston Female Asylum, Boston, 1833*
*Annual Register of World Events: A Review of the Year*
*Boston Globe*
*Boston Post*
*Boston Sunday Herald*
*Bucks Herald*
*Daily News*
*Fall River Daily*
*Fall River Herald*
*Household Narrative of Current Events (ed. Charles Dickens)*
*Huddersfield Chronicle & West Yorkshire Advertiser*
*Illustrated Police News*
*Kansas City Times*
*Leeds Mercury*
*Liverpool Mercury*
*Lloyds Weekly*
*Manchester Weekly Times*
*Morning Chronicle*
*Morning Post*
*Newcastle Daily Chronicle*
*Newcastle Weekly Courant*
*New York Tribune*
*North Adams Transcript*
*Reynold's Newspaper*
*Royal Cornwall Gazette*
*Sheffield & Rotherham Independent*
*The Guardian*
*The Standard*
*The Times*
*Topeka State Journal*
*Weekly Kansas Chief*

*Wichita City Eagle*
*Yorkshire Herald*

## Websites

www.oldbaileyonline.org
www.findmypast.com
www.ancestry.com
www.maryanncotton.co.uk
www.newspapers.com
www.britishnewspaperarchive.co.uk

# Index